JOHN DEWEY'S PHILOSOPHY OF EDUCATION

JOHN DEWEY'S PHILOSOPHY OF EDUCATION

AN INTRODUCTION AND RECONTEXTUALIZATION FOR OUR TIMES

Jim Garrison, Stefan Neubert, and Kersten Reich

palgrave
macmillan

KH

JOHN DEWEY'S PHILOSOPHY OF EDUCATION
Copyright © Jim Garrison, Stefan Neubert, and Kersten Reich, 2012.

First published in 2012 by
PALGRAVE MACMILLAN®
in the United States—a division of St. Martin's Press LLC,
175 Fifth Avenue, New York, NY 10010.

Where this book is distributed in the UK, Europe and the rest of the world,
this is by Palgrave Macmillan, a division of Macmillan Publishers Limited,
registered in England, company number 785998, of Houndmills,
Basingstoke, Hampshire RG21 6XS.

Palgrave Macmillan is the global academic imprint of the above companies
and has companies and representatives throughout the world.

Palgrave® and Macmillan® are registered trademarks in the United States,
the United Kingdom, Europe and other countries.

ISBN: 978–1–137–02617–0

Library of Congress Cataloging-in-Publication Data

Garrison, James W., 1949–
    John Dewey's philosophy of education : an introduction and
    recontextualization for our times / Jim Garrison, Stefan Neubert, and
    Kersten Reich.
        p. cm.
    ISBN 978–1–137–02617–0 (hardback)
        1. Dewey, John, 1859–1952—Criticism and interpretation.
    2. Education—Philosophy. 3. Education—Social aspects.
    I. Neubert, Stefan. II. Reich, Kersten. III. Title.

LB875.D5.G37 2012
370.1—dc23   2012011139

A catalogue record of the book is available from the British Library.

Design by Newgen Imaging Systems (P) Ltd., Chennai, India.

First edition: September 2012

10 9 8 7 6 5 4 3 2 1

Printed in the United States of America.

11/10/13

CONTENTS

FIGURES

INTRODUCTION

John Dewey is considered not only as one of the founders of pragmatism, but also as an educational classic whose approaches to education and learning still exercise great influence on educational discourses and practices internationally. In his day, Dewey had a global reputation. His ability to organically unify such powerful and distinct forces of modernity as science, democracy, and the individual was enormously appealing to members of many different cultural traditions. Among many other places he visited, taught, and lectured were Turkey in the Middle East and China in the Far East (reawakened today after decades of communist censorship). His influence can still be felt in these countries in our day as well as many other nations in Europe, South America, and Africa. Indeed, Dewey probably exercised more international influence on education than any other figure in the first half of the twentieth century.

However, in the decades since his death in 1952, his influence waned in both philosophy and education because of the dominance of analytic philosophy (especially in the United States) and the turn in psychology and education first to narrow behavioristic and then to more cognitive approaches both of which underestimated the significance of experience and culture for education. Far too many educational theorists and practitioners neglected the importance of having a well thought out philosophy of education. However, since the late 1980s there has been a renaissance of his thought in philosophy and education on a global scale. Among other things, the publication of his *Collected Works* has helped to improve the conditions for studying and further developing his approach. Many think that the end of the Cold War also helped because his ideas about science, democracy, and the individual were so different than those that prevail in the West and were accentuated by the conflict. Indeed, these prevailing themes remain, although they are now received with much more hospitality in our current period. The increased interest in Dewey has not only influenced debates in pragmatism like the turn to so-called neopragmatism or pragmatic postmodernism in Richard Rorty and others but also contemporary debates about a philosophy of education that is comprehensive enough to understand education in diverse contexts of an increasingly global and multicultural world. We can see how researchers in the fields of teaching and learning have reconnected to Dewey in such things as their approaches to problem-based learning and learner-centered teaching, which draw on Deweyan ideas. Others are once again inspired to approach collaborative and small group learning from a Deweyan orientation. Especially, the recent social constructivist turn in educational theories and practices has many affinities with Deweyan education and continues lines and perspectives of pragmatism.

We seek to recontextualize Dewey for a new generation who has come of age in a very different world than that in which Dewey lived and wrote. To do so in an exemplary way by connecting his philosophy with six recent and influential discourses is the intention of the fourth part of our book. However, we first provide an innovative introduction that seeks to understand the *philosophical* thinking that offered the background for his pedagogical proposals. We have two reasons for providing our novel introduction before proceeding to our recontextualization. First, we largely concentrate on texts most educators only rarely read yet should if they are to deeply comprehend Dewey's pedagogical thinking. Sometimes these are texts educators may read, but cannot understand fully if they do not properly appreciate their larger philosophical background. Second, Dewey is a holistic philosopher, which presents readers with a hermeneutic challenge. They must grasp all of him to properly understand the parts, and yet must grasp the parts to comprehend the whole. Where are they to begin? Educators too often confine themselves to reading only a limited number of explicitly educational texts from Dewey. We here include these readings but address the depth of his approach by providing a larger, more philosophical, context. Our book attempts to provide easier access to some of his more difficult ideas.

Educators often misinterpret Dewey because they have not addressed the hermeneutic problem posed by such a large and organic philosopher. Too often, they merely plunder fragments of his writing to apply to their own narrow projects. In the field of education, there is a tendency to think one can get by with a little theory and perhaps no philosophy of education at all. However, we all have a tacit theory of teaching and learning as well as a philosophy of education, whether or not we ever articulate it to others or ourselves. Similarly, we all have a tacit theory of what it is to be an individual human being, the make up of science, and the meaning of the word democracy, even if we never think about them. Frequently, educators will turn to Dewey for insight or inspiration, but they will misread him as conceiving science, individuality, and democracy much as they do themselves; that is, according to the dominant Western paradigm. As in his time, this often leads to terrible misunderstandings. For instance, Dewey was already aware, and most contemporary philosophers of science would agree, that all inquiry is theory-laden (or concept-laden) as well as value-laden. These concepts and values constitute the presuppositions of the scientific questions we ask of physical and human nature (see part 2). Dewey understood the mind and self as a contingent social construction that emerges from a biological matrix (see part 1 and part 2). He thought of democracy primarily as the best way to construct the mind and self of not only individuals but also groups, communities, and classrooms (see part 3). Beginning by thinking that all the big questions are already answered, and often assuming very poor, even dangerous, answers at that, today's educational researchers and practitioners attempt to reduce pedagogy to rules, regulations, and empty rituals, which seek to maximize PISA (Programme for International Student Assessment) scores as if the human mind and self was merely an array of numbers. Dewey's emergent empirical naturalism was meant to save us from such catastrophic reductionism and inhumanity. If they read Dewey's philosophy of education at all, they do so in ways that reduce his thinking to fit into small, preconceived containers. Our introduction will help the reader overcome such reductionism not only in their reading of Dewey, or even their theory and practice of education, but also their very lives.

In the introduction that precedes our recontextualization, we try to help the reader by exposing certain critical target texts using other more difficult, or often misunderstood, texts that appear deceptively simple. This way we may develop the structure and content of Dewey's thought with far more scope than most educators usually encounter, thereby alleviating the hermeneutic problem. Finally, we provide references to the specific target texts exposited, which we urge the reader to examine and interpret on their own.

This book is a coauthored text with four parts. Part 1 has been written mainly by Kersten Reich, part 2 by Jim Garrison, and part 3 by Stefan Neubert. In part 4, all three authors have contributed from the background of their current research. We have collaborated together on many different projects over the years and are confident that what follows is not a fragmented collection but rather a coherent project in which all parts have been discussed and worked out in their final form together. The result is a unity in diversity since each of us has a somewhat different interpretation of Dewey within our broad and substantial agreement. The book is an open-ended text that we believe readers will find inviting since we often leave it to them to decide issues for themselves. This will become especially evident in part 4, in which each section concludes with open-ended discussion questions for the readers' further reflection.

Part 1 develops important aspects of what we call the cultural turn in Dewey. For him, culture is essential for education. It must be reflected explicitly in order to understand educational processes in a properly critical way. We speak of a turn because in educational traditions before Dewey's time, the role of culture was not sufficiently thematized as a systematic part in education. The discussion proceeds in six steps:

1. First, we will focus on the relation of nature and culture as a core question of education. We will see that Dewey here argues from a double perspective. On the one hand, he takes a Darwinist position that recognizes the import of nature for human culture and action. On the other hand, he clearly understands that the developments of human culture and action also influence and change nature. Nature and culture are seen as the tensional relationship in which human living and its potentials take place.
2. In this tensional relationship, culture and experience are results of human development and growth as well as crucial preconditions for further development and growth.
3. In this connection, education can be seen as a necessary function of social life.
4. The distinction between formal and informal education helps to clarify the complex relations of individual and social growth.
5. The basic process that links culture and education, according to Dewey, can be found in communication. It involves interaction or transaction, core concepts that have to be discussed for a thoroughgoing understanding of Dewey's approach.
6. Closing part 1, we provide a brief commentary of selected target texts from Dewey's works to which readers may turn to deepen their understanding.

Having become familiar with Dewey's empirical naturalism in part 1, part 2 looks more closely at his theory of inquiry and the reconstruction of experience. We here speak of a constructive turn in Dewey because he emphasizes the role of construction in education and learning in ways that exceed educational and psychological approaches before his time. We will see that for him the relations connecting aspects within the flux of experience are themselves drawn from experience. Hence, rationality itself emerges out of experience rather than existing apart from it. For Dewey, rationality itself is constantly subject to reconstruction along with all the rest of experience.

Part 2 involves eight steps:

1. As a Darwinian, Dewey appreciated that experience emerges from a biological matrix. Indeed, he even titles chapter 2 of his *Logic: The Theory of Inquiry* "The Existential Matrix of Inquiry: Biological" (LW 12: 30). The two basic principles of an educational experience, interaction and continuity, characteristic of all living creatures interacting with their environment arise from this matrix. The living creature is a complex function comprised of many intricate subfunctions. "But every function tends to maintain itself," Dewey states, "that is the most obvious fact about life" (MW 13: 378). Many educators overlook the extraordinarily obvious fact that all living creatures (which certainly includes all our students) must constantly maintain a dynamic equilibrium with their environment (what the biologist call homeostasis). The biological basis of learning for Dewey was the ability to form habits (second nature). Embodied habits are implicitly logical in that they are generalized responses to a class of stimuli. If we can reconstruct our habits, we can reconstruct our experience.

2. This brings us to an exposition of the social matrix of experience, the dimension of linguistic experience that yields meaning, value, and the self. Hence, if we can reconstruct our meanings and values we can reconstruct our experience. Further, since the self is social, if we can reconstruct our web of social relations, we can reconstruct our experience, including our experience of our selves.

3. For Dewey, the aim of education is growth through the reconstruction of experience. However, by "growth," he does not primarily mean just becoming a bigger version of the present self, he means functional development in the ability to discriminate our environment and respond more intelligently to it thereby transforming the world as we transform ourselves. Such transformation requires the potential to change. Rather than something passive, Dewey thought of potentiality as a "capacity, an ability, a power" (MW 9: 46). What students do not know is not weakness; it is their potential, the power, to learn.

4. Dewey was president of the American Psychological Association before he was president of the American Philosophical Association. His famous 1896 "Reflex Arc" paper is often perceived as the first clear statement of what became functionalist psychology, which continues to dominate psychology on many continents. Commonly disregarded, by educators, it remains perhaps the most important single paper ever published in the history of American psychology. The critical idea is the constant functional coordination (i.e., reconstruction) of experience in which the "the 'response' is necessary to constitute the stimulus" (EW 5: 102). This is exactly the opposite of the notion, still often encountered today that the stimulus controls the response of the organism when really, it is a functional circle in which stimulus and response emerge together as the organism strives to functionally coordinate its actions. The implications for the educational concept of motivation are extensive.

5. As a living creature begins to make backward-forward connections between what it does and what occurs as a consequence, habits of action begin to emerge. Dewey goes so far as to claim that the functional coordination of our actions constitutes the biological basis of the mind and self. Forming intelligent habits allows us to control impulses not by suppressing them, but by properly organizing and structuring them. Intelligently reflecting on our habits and reconstructing them is how we learn to control ourselves. For Dewey, "Intelligence is the key to freedom in act" (MW 14: 210). Dewey writes, "Reason, the rational attitude, is the resulting disposition, not a ready-made antecedent that can be invoked at will and set into movement. The man who would intelligently cultivate intelligence will widen, not narrow, his life of strong impulses while aiming at their happy coincidence in operation" (ibid., 136–137).

6. Dewey's notion of intelligence is robust and embodied; it involves hot imagination, impulse, and emotion, not just cold cognition. This is important to remember when we consider Dewey's theory of inquiry and reflective learning. The theory of inquiry, according to Dewey includes five steps that we discuss extensively with regard to their educational implications.

7. This leads to an elaboration of more abstractly theoretical or philosophical issues that are developed today by using the discursive themes of "construction," "reconstruction," and "deconstruction."

8. Again, we close the chapter by giving an overview of selected target texts in Dewey.

Part 3 develops central aspects of what we call the communicative turn in Dewey, that is, it discusses the importance of communication for education. We speak of a turn in the sense that this importance was relatively underestimated in educational thought before Dewey's time. There are six steps contained in this part:

1. We point out Dewey's core concept of communication and discuss its complexity and its necessary relation to education.
2. This relation is made more specific and concrete by discussing Dewey's emphasis on joint activities as an essential starting point of learning.
3. Dewey believes that democracy and education are mutually connected. He understands democracy as a participative way of life that realizes the potentials of communication in a modern society. We exposit the democratic vision that he developed in the context of his time and show some important implications for our times.
4. Participation and diversity are core claims and central components of democratic thought and practices in this connection.
5. Dewey responds to the challenges that are implied in these and other democratic developments by offering a theory of social intelligence that sums up core threads in his theories of communication, education, learning, and democracy.
6. We close this part, too, with a description and brief commentaries on selected target texts for further reading.

In part 4, we shift the perspective from which we write about Dewey and his educational philosophy. We no longer give an introduction in the proper sense but rather focus on what we think can be fruitful ways of recontextualizing his tradition in and for our times. Dewey himself was an active scholar for over 70 years from the early 1880s until the early 1950s. The world changed rapidly around him in those years and, as the good evolutionary Darwinist philosopher he was, Dewey strived to adapt his philosophy to his times. Known as the philosopher of reconstruction, Dewey reconstructed himself many times in his career in dialogue with the people and events around him. Times have changed, events have continued to evolve, and new voices have come upon the stage of life. What would Dewey have said to such thinkers as Zygmunt Bauman, Michel Foucault, Pierre Bourdieu, Jacques Derrida, Emmanuel Levinas, or even his great admirer, the neopragmatist Richard Rorty? We do not attempt to give any final answer to this question. Rather, what we intend is putting Dewey into a critical and creative tension with some selected prominent late twentieth- and early twenty-first-century scholars. We reconstruct Dewey for our times by placing him in an open-ended dialogue with these thinkers, and eventually, you, the reader. Of course, our selection of dialogue partners is limited and to a certain degree arbitrary. We could indeed have chosen other important partners, and we sincerely invite the reader to imagine other dialogues for themselves. For us, the chosen authors are important because they help us to understand and critically reflect central challenges of reconstructing Dewey in our time. We think they are especially productive in this connection because they show crucial affinities as well as differences to the pragmatic tradition. This at least delimits the arbitrariness of selection in a certain way. We indicate points of similarity and dissimilarity before challenging the readers to decide for themselves what they think. After all, you, the readers, are the ones that will not only reconstruct Dewey, but also Bauman, Foucault, Bourdieu, Derrida, Levinas, Rorty, and many others for your times.

We approach the task of recontextualizing and reconstructing Dewey from the stance of Köln (Cologne) interactive constructivism. Founded by one of the present authors (Kersten Reich), Köln constructivism has been critically and creatively reconstructing Dewey for their needs, purposes, and principles.[1] Located at Universität zu Köln, Germany, the Cologne Dewey-Center (http://www.hf.uni-koeln.de/dewey/) is one of eight such centers internationally. The center and the scholars that write from the perspective of Köln interactive constructivism along with other colleagues at the University that also find Dewey valuable have approached Dewey from a global outlook derived from the international programs they have long been involved with. For over a decade, the Köln constructivists Kersten Reich and Stefan Neubert have written papers elucidating Dewey for a new generation, especially in Europe, but also globally.[2] They have published essays rethinking Deweyan pragmatism from the perspective of Köln constructivism. They have also encountered other scholars in similar ways. The school of Köln interactive constructivism appreciates, appropriates, but does not merely attempt to copy, Dewey from a contemporary international perspective that allows us to rethink him for our time. Most importantly for our present purpose, they have written papers that craft dialogues between Dewey and such thinkers as Bauman, Foucault, and Bourdieu. Indeed, our recontextualization draws, in part, on this work. The North American (US) educational philosopher Jim Garrison writes from a more traditional pragmatist perspective from which he has developed a pragmatist version of social constructivism. He, too, has written essays that venture to connect

Dewey's work with more recent developments in cultural psychology as well as in philosophy such as we find with Derrida and Levinas. Those from other national, regional, or simply intellectual perspectives are sure to read Dewey in somewhat different ways from all three of us. Dewey was a pluralist, and we believe he would have welcomed alternative readings of his own as long as they were responsible as well as reflective. For a decade, the three authors have been involved in constructive dialogues, international collaborations, and exchanges with each other as well as with many other prominent contemporary Dewey scholars (see, e.g., Garrison 2008; Hickman, Neubert, and Reich 2009; Green, Neubert, and Reich 2011). They agree in seeing Dewey as the most important predecessor of constructivism in education in the twentieth century.

This book is an invitation for you, the reader, to rethink the Deweyan heritage for yourself, regardless of what you think about Köln constructivism, traditional pragmatism, Zygmunt Bauman, Michel Foucault, Pierre Bourdieu, Jacques Derrida, Emmanuel Levinas, Richard Rorty, or any other approach you may appreciate more. It remains for us to suggest that you will find many valuable resources for expanding and deepening your acquaintance with Deweyan pragmatism in the abundant new scholarship on Dewey that has been developed by a large number of researches during roughly the last three decades.[3]

Part 1

EDUCATION AND CULTURE—THE CULTURAL TURN

We see Dewey as a philosopher who already took a cultural turn in education long before this move became widespread in the second half of the twentieth century in new contexts of cultural diversity, multiculturalism, and questions of cultural identity. His perspectives on culture are indispensable for understanding his broader philosophy of experience and the relation of experience and education.

NATURE AND CULTURE

Since his early acquaintance with Hegel, Dewey had realized that nature and culture are not opposite but relational to each other. He was convinced that humans as cultural beings are a part of nature. They act within nature, with it, and partly also against it at the same time. For instance, Dewey observes about taste that it is not simply given by nature but represents an aesthetic experience rooted in culture: "The principles of taste are the product of the reflective analysis of the understanding as it goes over the action of aesthetic feeling...It follows that taste is something individual in its nature, depending upon the aesthetic capacity and culture of the one exercising it" (EW 2: 278).

This necessary relation is a recurring perspective that pervades Dewey's entire philosophy. On the Darwinian side, humans cannot evade nature and evolution. On the side of culture, this does not imply, however, that they are determined by nature and forced to act in predestined ways. Rather, nature is seen as an open and evolving universe: "Knowledge of nature does not mean subjection to predestination, but insight into courses of change; an insight which is formulated in 'laws,' that is, methods of subsequent procedure" (MW 4: 47).

In Western thought, however, there is a history of seeing nature as a realm from which supreme rights can be taken and justified—rights that seem to be more sublime than common human rights because they apparently are beyond human interests and power. This leads to the illusion of natural laws independent of cultural context and not constructed by humans. From this position we say about something, for example, "it is natural," thereby excluding from the start the possibility of any evidence against our claim. Dewey insists that we should be skeptical in face of any such position: "The function common to the differing senses of the term nature has been the demand for some standard or norm for the regulation and valuation of human beliefs. It designates whatever is taken to be intrinsic and inevitable in existence and thought, in antithesis to what is external, artificial, and factitious; leaving it to the culture of the time to determine just where the natural, the normal and normative shall be looked for, and just what, in contrast, shall be regarded as secondary and accidental" (MW 7: 287).

But how can we account for the fact that in everyday as well as in scientific thought and in the history of education there is a recurrent tendency to rely on nature and forget the import of culture? Dewey thinks that especially the eighteenth-century French philosopher and educator Jean Jacques Rousseau has articulated a fallacy that was handed on and became a common component in Western thought. Dewey says, "Rousseau confuses, as we do today, two unrelated ideas of nature: one meaning of native unlearned capacities and an order of development; the other meaning opposition to social life and to culture. Both of these confusions persist to this day" (MW 7: 377).

Let us try to dissolve this confusion following Dewey. Of course, we must concede that there is a natural basis of human life and development. Dewey in this connection speaks of native impulses and activities. For him, every individual is born with an inherited constitution. Nature is also the inescapable environment in which we live.

> Nature is the mother and the habitat of man, even if sometimes a stepmother and an unfriendly home. The fact that civilization endures and culture continues—and sometimes advances—is evidence that human hopes and purposes find a basis and support in nature. As the developing growth of an individual from embryo to maturity is the result of interaction of organism with surroundings, so culture is the product not of efforts of men put forth in a void or just upon themselves, but of prolonged and cumulative interaction with environment. (LW 10: 36–37)

Dewey distinguishes between environment and surroundings: "The environment of any organism consists of the sum total of conditions that enter in an active way into the direction of the functions of any living being. Environment, therefore, is not equivalent merely to surrounding physical conditions. There may be much in the physical surroundings to which an organism is irresponsive; such conditions are no part of its true environment" (MW 6: 438).

The environment is never independent of the developing experience of the individual. As we will see this idea has a crucial consequence for education and learning. The individual and its environment stand in continual transaction and grow in coevolution. Therefore, we have to distinguish between nature in the sense of mere surrounding existences and nature in the sense of an environment in which individuals are influenced by nature and also interact and coevolve with it. From a Deweyan perspective, learning environments can never be reduced to external conditions supposed to work by themselves. They have to be constructed in ways that allow for genuine transaction between organized contexts of education and the experience of learners.

Dewey explains, "Human life does not occur in a vacuum, nor is nature a mere stage setting for the enactment of its drama...Man's life is bound up in the processes of nature; his career, for success or defeat, depends upon the way in which nature enters it. Man's power of deliberate control of his own affairs depends upon ability to direct natural energies to use: an ability which is in turn dependent upon insight into nature's processes" (MW 9: 236).

This is another argument that we can turn against Rousseau. In the courses of their histories, humans change their own nature. This is so because changes brought about in the environment never remain without consequences for the very nature of humans themselves, as Dewey observes, "But the alleged unchangeableness of human nature cannot be admitted. For while certain needs in human nature are constant, the consequences they produce (because of the existing state of culture— of science, morals, religion, art, industry, legal rules) react back into the original components of human nature to shape them into new forms. The total pattern is thereby modified" (LW 13: 142).

We suggest that this is a strength of Dewey's approach that remains relevant. It is nonsensical to separate nature from culture or to view either of them in isolation because in our very experience and action they are always already involved together and interpenetrate each other.

The main fallacy of Rousseau was to conceive of man as a being with inborn natural conditions that of necessity determine certain social realities. According to him, man is essentially good by nature but becomes corrupted by society. This corruption depends on social conditions that prevent him from growing up in freedom and natural conditions. However, since man cannot return to the pure state of nature, Rousseau tries to develop an alternative way out. In his ideas about the social contract, he gives all men equal rights and obligations to overcome the social corruption. Dewey especially criticizes the extreme individualism implicit in this analysis and political vision: "The idea that human nature is inherently and exclusively individual is itself a product of a cultural individualistic movement" (LW 13: 77).

In other words, Rousseau projects his own individualistic wishes (as shown in the educational novel "Emile") and his social hopes (as shown in his essay "The Social Contract") into nature in order to justify his claims. But he remains oblivious to the cultural context that informs his specific perspectives on nature and makes it impossible to argue from a purely naturalistic standpoint.

Dewey's understanding of the relation of nature and culture truly remains relevant for today. Consider the following example. The dependence of nature from culture becomes evident when we think of the external consequences on nature produced by human cultures through pollution, exhaustion of natural resources, extinction of species, climate change, and many others. History shows that human cultures increasingly mesh with nature and especially put the life conditions of other creatures on the planet at risk. If we take the extraordinary effects into account that human activities have engendered on earth then we see that Dewey's interpretation is in no way exaggerated. The environmental crisis of our time evinces that humans may even act in overt antagonism to nature in ways that threaten their own natural resources of living.

Nature and culture are thus mutually intertwined. Both sides can be distinguished but not separated from each other. Whenever we talk about nature and culture, language is already used as a medium of representation. This involves linguistic codes and conventions that we apply to solve problems in our experience. Dewey is well aware of the import of language here: "'Culture' and all that culture involves, as distinguished from 'nature,' is both a condition and a product of language. Since language is the only means of retaining and transmitting to subsequent generations acquired skills, acquired information, and acquired habits, it is the latter. Since, however, meanings and the significance of events differ in different cultural groups, it is also the former" (LW 12: 62).

Against this background, we can say that although we often speak of the "nature" of things, events, characters, persons, and so on, in our everyday affairs, we can only do so from the perspectives of our own activities and involvements in culture. Here, we often take for granted certain ideas about nature that upon reflection turn out to be culturally determined and not naturally given.

But for Dewey this does not mean (as it does for Richard Rorty) that language fully exhausts experience. For him, language is an instrument for creating meanings in and from experience and we should never forget its importance. But we should also not confine our observation to language alone. Linguistic representations of experience, as we will discuss later in section 2, are not the same as experience in its primary and nonlinguistic forms. As we have seen so far, they always involve contexts of nature and culture that we rely on in our activities, articulations, and communications. This pragmatic view on language is important to understand Dewey's approach to the relation of nature and culture.

Furthermore, Dewey has a highly developed theory of habits in relation to cultural customs and institutions that has to be taken into account in this connection. Habits are generated as well as generating powers of behaving in culture. They have a biological basis—in what Dewey calls native impulses—but are not determined by nature: "Habit means that an individual undergoes a modification through an experience, which modification forms a predisposition to easier and more effective action in a like direction in the future" (MW 9: 349). Dewey's idea of habits is similar to the more recent concept of habitus developed by the French sociologist Pierre Bourdieu. Dewey especially emphasizes the connection between habits and intelligence in individual as well as social action. He talks about habits of action and habits of thinking. From the perspective of nature, they actualize potentials given by native constitution and environment. But only through social interaction, as we will see later in section on "Interaction, Transaction, and Communication," and the creation of meanings, it is possible to form habits of thinking and intelligent problem solving that contribute to the growth of cultures. Dewey observes, "Habit, apart from knowledge, does not make allowance for change of conditions, for novelty" (ibid., 349).

In the textbook *Ethics*, written with James H. Tufts, he explains more extensively,

> Any habit, like any appetite or instinct, represents something formed, set; whether this has occurred in the history of the race or of the individual makes little difference to its established urgency. Habit is second, if not first, nature. (1) Habit represents facilities; what is set, organized, is relatively easy. It marks the line of least resistance.

A habit of reflection, so far as it is a specialized habit, is as easy and natural to follow as an organic appetite. (2) Moreover, the exercise of any easy, frictionless habit is pleasurable. It is a commonplace that use and wont deprive situations of originally disagreeable features. (3) Finally, a formed habit is an active tendency. It only needs an appropriate stimulus to set it going; frequently the mere absence of any strong obstacle serves to release its pent-up energy. It is a propensity to act in a certain way whenever opportunity presents. Failure to function is uncomfortable and arouses feelings of irritation or lack. (MW 5: 309–310)

The quote shows that for Dewey habits emerge through the interaction of natural and cultural factors as they affect individual conduct. They are potentials that exist in different forms such as cognitive, emotional, social, communicative, and esthetic habits.

The term "instinct" that Dewey uses in this passage as a name for the biological basis of human conduct represents the common language of his day, but has become obsolete in our time. In later writings, for example, in *Human Nature and Conduct*, Dewey prefers the more contemporary term "impulse."

Habits are active tendencies that turn native impulses into culturally relevant behavior. They are generative powers that from themselves drive activities in certain ways, but environments that further or weaken the development of habits also influence them. In culture, habits not only emerge in individual ways but they also appear in collective forms as customs. Very often customs represent social conventions and duties. In this respect, they exemplify the necessary conservative dimension of habit that can be a hindrance to appropriate readjustments in cultural development. "Habit and custom tend rapidly to fixate beliefs and thereby to bring about an arrest of intellectual life" (MW 6: 453–454). If environments change, these fixations can become problematic or even dangerous for social life (ibid.).

Dewey thinks that in a dynamic world like ours, habits and all other cultural constructions must be flexible enough to respond to unavoidable and unforeseeable changes. Dewey says, "Even a thoroughly good habit needs to be kept flexible, so that it may be adapted, when the need arises, to circumstances not previously experienced even by way of anticipation" (MW 6: 466). Habits as flexible powers not only contribute actively to changes of environments but they are also always connected with ideas, imaginations, and ways of acting rooted in traditions and cultural, social, and historical experiences.

Dewey gives his most elaborate account of habit in *Human Nature and Conduct*. In the introduction of this book, he claims "that an understanding of habit and of different types of habit is the key to social psychology, while the operation of impulse and intelligence gives the key to individualized mental activity. But they are secondary to habit so that mind can be understood in the concrete only as a system of beliefs, desires and purposes which are formed in the interaction of biological aptitudes with a social environment" (MW 14: 3).

When we meet with difficulties and problems, in our actions, so far unproblematic habits are challenged and intentional problem solving and reflective intelligence set in. On this new level of thought and reflection, though, there are habits, for Dewey, like in all other activities.

We can talk about habits of observation, perception, communication, learning, appreciation, criticism, and so on, which help us to solve all kinds of problems when our more simple habits of everyday practices fail us. Dewey distinguishes between what he calls active habits and passive habituations (MW 9: 52). Active habits for him are dynamic and flexible powers of adjusting situations to our intentions. For example, if you find yourself in a foreign place like a city in a foreign country and find ways to orientate yourself, you use and develop some of your active habits in order to fashion the situation. In your own town, you get orientation mainly through the more passive habituations to a familiar environment that you have already acquired. Likewise, Dewey distinguishes between habits and routines. For him, habits must to a certain degree remain flexible and open to development in order that learning and growth can continue. Routines in contrast are "fossilized habits" (EW 2: 103) that may be indispensable, to some extent, in social life, but that are often problematic from the educational point of view. Further important in Dewey's terminology is the distinction between habits and routines as remarked above. Habits are powers of the individual acquired through social exchange and transactions, while customs are collective habits that always precede the individual acquisition. Customs are often based and manifested in institutions such as families, educational systems, administrations, bureaucracies, business and industries, and so on. Even science is based on institutions that inform members and discourses, decide about conditions of inclusion and exclusion, language games, practices, and routines. For instance, the organization of scientific disciplines is institutionalized and cannot be subjected to the casualness of personal wit and will. But this very institutionalization always also runs the risk of separating theory from practice. For science, therefore, it is important always to question given forms of institutions, and to ask for their weak points with regard to experience and practice. Even more generally, we can say that, for Dewey, it is always crucial to judge institutions, customs, and habits according to their benefit for human growth and the solution of actual and relevant problems. In a democracy, this task can only be achieved through active participation of all involved in all the diversity of their life-experiences. Therefore, critical reflection and judgment is a recurrent and often very complicated process if we follow Dewey's radically democratic commitment. For philosophy, this perspective involves that there can be no last words with regard to science as well as to morals or ethical norms and principles. Dewey is especially critical of universal claims separated from the context of experience (LW 6: 3–21). In our actions, as individuals or communities or whole societies, we ourselves shape the contexts of our experience and thereby construct and produce new habits and environments that continue to influence and transform each other.

To fully understand the background of this crucial insight one has to realize that Dewey himself lived in an age of huge and unprecedented social, economic, technological, cultural, and political transformations. Here, we come back to very important questions about the relation of culture and nature. Industrialization has led to new forms of thinking because through its processes of using and changing natural forces it has made it more obvious than before that culture and nature can only be understood as a relation of transaction. Dewey already saw this very clearly: "The state of knowledge of nature, that is, of physical science, is a phase of culture upon which industry and commerce, the production and distribution of goods and the regulation of services directly depend" (LW 13: 69). This also applies to social and political life: "For every social and political philosophy currently professed will be found upon examination to involve a certain view about the constitution of human nature: in itself and in its relation to physical nature. What is true of this factor is true of every factor in culture" (ibid., 72).

In his criticism of traditional philosophy, Dewey strongly rejects dualisms such as nature and culture, body and mind, theory and practice, and similar oppositions that have been influential in the history of thought. For him, experiencing and knowing are processes that are as natural as any physical event. "That meant that it was as natural for a thing to be known as it was for it to grow and change, and as natural for it to be changed purposely as a result of its being known as it was for it to decay or erode. It also meant that mind and consciousness lost any non-natural spiritual quality and became organic functions

or relations of knowing and awareness, rather than private entities"
(Ralph Ross: Introduction, in MW 7: xi–xii).
    Dewey understood this as processes of emergence or evolution.

> It seemed obvious to him that the evolutionary function of mind had
> been to guide behavior so that people could adapt themselves to their
> environment and adjust that environment to themselves in the interest
> of surviving and living better. That the mind should now be a knower
> for the sake of knowing, with no trace of its original function, struck
> him as untrue. Civilization had, of course, liberated the minds of
> some, especially in a leisure class, from a host of immediate perils, and
> that liberation had perhaps brought an exuberance which made pure
> knowledge, thinking for its own sake, seem an ideal fulfillment. The
> spectator of affairs, not the participant, the understander of action, not
> the actor, not even the intelligent actor who understood in order to act
> more effectively, was celebrated as ideal types. Against this type of phi-
> losophizing, Dewey pitted an acute awareness of the continuing perils
> and problems of men, which reflection might resolve, and accused the
> "knowers" of being innocent of the values of knowing. (Ralph Ross:
> Introduction, in MW 7: xii)

As Murray G. Murphey characterizes Dewey's position, this means
for our understanding of life in culture in a more general sense,

> that human beings and human behavior had to be studied as natu-
> ral phenomena, just as one would study the nature and behavior of
> the stars, or apes, or plants. The proper approach to man was there-
> fore one which viewed him in evolutionary perspective, as one type
> of animal among many, situated in an environment which he both
> depends upon for the maintenance of life and alters by his activity. So
> viewed, it is simply a fact that human beings are always to be found
> in groups, never in isolation. This is not only a fact of biology; it is
> a necessity of a human mode of existence. (Murphey: Introduction,
> in MW 14: ix–x)

To summarize the main arguments of this part, we can learn from
Dewey about the relation of culture and nature that it is not enough
to have a position of a "spectator of affairs" because this relation
changes according to historical, social, and individual perspectives.
We run the risk of a narrow and deceptive naturalism when we see
human life as determined by nature or construct a dualism between
culture and nature that neglects the transactions between both. The
transactional perspective involves that we are always already participants in a context in which we identify ourselves through culture in

nature. This double relation to culture and nature pervades all our observations, participations, and actions. We can only observe nature by participating and acting in culture. This involves our commitment to certain conventions, rule, traditions, institutions, interest, and so on as well as our habits of responding to our world. It remains as a continued relevance of Dewey's approach that he has shown us to avoid dualistic misunderstandings that are too reductive but often seduce us in everyday life because they help us to simplify matters. His claim is to see nature and culture as more complex and transactional even though his talk about "generic traits" has left some problems to this perspective.

CULTURE AND EXPERIENCE

In one of his early essays, "The Metaphysical Assumptions of Materialism," Dewey rejects materialistic copy theories of knowledge as well as other traditional metaphysics of knowledge:

> If there be no knowledge of substance as such, there is either only knowledge of phenomena produced by the activity of the Ego (pure subjective idealism), or of phenomena entirely unrelated to any substance whatever (Humian skepticism), or of those related only to objective spirit (Berkeleian idealism), or of those related to an unknown and unknowable substance (H. Spencer), or of those brought into unity by the forms of knowledge which the mind necessarily imposes on all phenomena given in consciousness (as Kant). (EW 1: 4–5)

It is well known that Hegel had largely influenced Dewey in his formative period. In accord with that influence, he was fascinated by the attempt to overcome the dualistic split in epistemology between an inner and an outer world that were apparently disconnected from each other. In his *Phenomenology of Spirit*, Hegel had already established a way and method to think through the problems of dualisms and unite knowledge in dialectical steps. The influence of Hegel on Dewey was deep and lasting (see Good 2005). However, Dewey does not follow Hegel in important respects. He has a much stronger focus on action and culture. This includes his shift to an experimentalist framework of knowledge that excludes any final solution and therefore completely surrenders the Hegelian system of knowledge. Inspired by William James, Dewey found his pragmatist way to an antidualistic foundation of knowledge. He took the concept of action as the key to the solution of epistemological problems. Dewey says,

"Every vital activity of any depth and range inevitably meets obstacles in the course of its effort to realize itself" (MW 6: 230). Human acting is rendered meaningful through overcoming difficulties and problems. It is experience.

Dewey's use of the word experience differs from the common understanding. For him, experience comprises the aspect of *experiencing* as well as the aspect of the *experienced*. For example, if we reach with our fingers into a flame the subjective feeling of pain (experiencing) cannot be separated from the heat of the experienced object. Further, we have to distinguish between primary and secondary (or reflective) experience.

Primary experience happens if we reach with our fingers into this flame for the first time, unprepared, simply as part of our prereflective interactions with a given situation. It hurts. Here, we take our experience as simply given: we act, do and undergo, enjoy and suffer, and so on. Although such action seems to be immediate, innocent, naive, and "natural," a closer observation shows that it is already laden with meanings from cultural contexts that we have learned so far for granted through our acquisition of habits. For example, even the child that reaches for the first time in a flame already has the habit of reaching in order to learn about objects. But on this primary-level experience is not yet reflective. It becomes so if we ourselves define or perceive the situation as problematic, that is, as a situation that demands intellectual response.

Secondary experience is Dewey's term for the process of intellectual response to problematic situations. For example, we learn that fire is dangerous and that we have to approach it in ways different to other objects. If we live in a culture, we do not even have to have this experience ourselves first hand but can learn from what others tell us. The reflective experience helps us to avoid undesirable consequences of primary experience. But if we rely too exclusively on the secondary experience, especially that of others, we run the risk of losing vital contact to our world through primary encounters. We then easily become oblivious of the actual conditions and challenges of our actions. Dewey often criticizes one-sided forms of intellectualism because, caught in this trap, they forget about the realities of life.

For Dewey, a fundamental criterion of experience is interaction. Human individuals interact with their environments, which can be natural as well as social. To a certain degree, the concepts of experience, life, and culture, can be used synonymously. We can say that experience is lived culture, we can speak of life-experiences, and we can talk about culture only through the perspectives of experience. But for Dewey, experience is no confused mixture of nature and culture in general but a very specific term that can and must be broken down to concrete implications and actions with regard to their contexts.

For Dewey, experience comprises perception as well as awareness, but we must understand these terms in the transactional sense discussed above and not as mere subjective appearances. From perception and awareness to reflection, there is a long and complicated way, as we will discuss later in part 2 in detail. Here, we want to focus on some more basic features of experience.

Dewey explains that we only have experience in the full sense if we are involved in an activity that includes an active phase of doing as well as a passive phase of undergoing. Only if both aspects are connected we can speak of a meaningful experience. If they are separated, experience loses its vitality and degenerates either to a senseless routine or to an arbitrary or impulsive activism. This is what often happens in schools when learning is only academic and has no sufficient connection to actual life problems. Such connection can only be achieved through experimentation, real problem solving, and construction of solutions through learner activities. And they must be problems, too, that are taken from the learners experiences in the first place and not only from textbooks and academic discourses.

Experience as doing and undergoing always has stable and precarious aspects. To understand this, we can recall what we said before about habits. Habit means that any primary experience already contains something from prior experiences (continuity) that has become incorporated as familiar, well known, and taken for granted. In this sense, habit gives us stability in experience. But there is also the precarious side of experience because, as we said, all habits are of necessity open to further development and reconstruction in response to unexpected and new events. Learning, for Dewey, must take place in the tension of these two poles. If we only passively perceive a situation without experiencing the consequences in an emotional and reflective way, we will not seriously and with sustainability reconstruct any of our habits. Our experience then will remain superficial and does not contribute much to growth through learning. However, learning is the key to all meaningful experience, provided that we understand learning with Dewey as an active process of construction of meanings by the learners themselves.

At the end of his long life as a philosopher and educator, Dewey was ready to dismiss the very term "metaphysics" as a name for his

approach.[1] He was troubled with the identification of his own pragmatism with the metaphysical tradition in the wake of Aristotle, that
is, the search for immutable essences, universal truth, and last words.
"Aristotle acknowledges contingency, but he never surrenders his bias
in favor of the fixed, certain and finished" (LW 1: 47). Dewey's own
use of the word metaphysics as a part of pragmatic philosophy had
often been misunderstood in this way, although his whole experimentalist approach rejected the very possibility of attaining fixed, certain,
and finished truths. It is a current debate in pragmatism today whether
metaphysics should be used as a name for a pragmatic reflection on
"the generic traits of existence" (ibid., 50, 52) as Dewey suggested in
Experience and Nature or if it should be surrendered altogether. We
have already seen before that this issue of maintaining a pragmatic
metaphysics is intimately connected with problems of naturalism and
the potential traps and fallacies of naturalizing culture. Pragmatists as
well as constructivists strive to avoid these traps but they partly take
different ways in doing so. One way is to emphasize nature as a presupposition and necessary context of culture; the other is to insist on the
assumption that we can never approach nature but through culture.

Dewey can sometimes be seen as a proponent of this or that way.
He characterizes his own approach as naturalism but he also emphasizes culture very much, so much indeed that he was eventually ready
to exchange his philosophical core concept *experience* with the term
"culture." In this way, he shows that culture, for him, is the necessary
and comprehensive context through which we live our experience and
even approach nature. At the very end of his long career he wrote in
retrospect,

> Were I to write (or rewrite) *Experience and Nature* today I would
> entitle the book *Culture and Nature* and the treatment of specific
> subject-matters would be correspondingly modified. I would aban-
> don the term "experience" because of my growing realization that
> the historical obstacles which prevented understanding of my use of
> "experience" are, for all practical purposes, insurmountable. I would
> substitute the term "culture" because with its meanings as now firmly
> established it can fully and freely carry my philosophy of experience.
> (LW 1: 361)

Dewey does not give up the continuity of his thinking about experience, in this statement, but rather responds to repeated misunderstandings especially in the direction of a reductionist understanding
of experience as either objective or subjective. Such misunderstandings
did arise from the background of typical modern either-or dualisms

that were a lifetime object of Dewey's philosophical criticism. So, he insists that experience is always contextual and interactive. "If 'experience' is to designate the inclusive subject-matter it must designate both what is experienced and the ways of experiencing it" (LW 1: 362). Therefore, experience can never be approached from the side of nature or biology alone. It can also not be reduced to subjective ways of experiencing or perceiving and subjective dealings with the world. Dewey would have welcomed Piaget's analysis of the schemes (plans) of action, perception, and thinking and his theory of assimilation and accommodation, but he would have insisted that it is also necessary to take the cultural context and social interactions into account. Experience in his sense is broader than Piaget's learning theory. It cannot be approached by psychology alone no more than it can be reduced to biology.

In his comprehensive work, Dewey offers us a variety of perspectives for understanding action and different types of acting in contexts. Boisvert (1998, 149ff.) suggests that a crucial idea in Dewey is the metaphor of mapping or constructing maps. It is an important metaphor in Dewey's pragmatic criticism of copy theories of knowledge because it insists on the constructive activities of the knower. But it is also an important metaphor for learning and education, as Dewey elaborates in his discussion of Rousseau. With regard to an episode of *Emile* he observes, "Rousseau describes in a phrase the defect of teaching about things instead of bringing to pass an acquaintance with the relations of the things themselves. 'You think you are teaching him what the world is like; he is only learning the map.' Extend the illustration from geography to the whole wide realm of knowledge, and you have the gist of much of our teaching from the elementary school through the college" (MW 8: 218–219). In education, we often confuse maps and world. We often think that the world itself has changed and we do not recognize that what have changed are rather our own constructed maps (see LW 1: 125). Going with Rousseau, Dewey insists that the construction of maps always takes place in necessary contexts of acting. Going beyond Rousseau, Dewey is aware that the "voyage of discovery is summed up in the map which shows the limit, external and internal, of the activity" (EW 4: 338). He concludes that things and events are never simply given but always produced or constructed in our interactions with the world. Even apparently, hard facts and unambiguous data do not simply come to us from outside to be taken up like in a mirror. They are always actively selected through inquiry in which we choose specific ways of responding to a problematic situation and creating solutions. What is called mapping here can in more recent terminology be explained as constructing realities. Like in the case of maps, we always have to try out and apply our constructions in our contexts of acting. Our constructions, this too can be learned from Dewey, are hypotheses to be put at work. They time and again have to show their viability in application and we should be prepared at every stage that there can and will be changes, reconstructions, and modifications.

The foregoing discussion brings us to the question of truth and truth claims as an essential question for every philosophical and scientific discourse. Like other traditions, pragmatism has developed a specific account of truth. Dewey introduces the term "warranted assertability" to point to the temporal and experimental character of truth claims. He says that in his view "the term 'warranted assertion' is preferred to the terms belief and knowledge. It is free from the ambiguity of these latter terms, and it involves reference to inquiry as that which warrants assertion" (LW 12: 17).

In the history of sciences, there have been many theories about how to warrant assertions. Characteristic for pragmatism, among other things, is the insistence that the warrant of assertions is a necessarily open-ended process of construction that is always connected to inquiry. Dewey approvingly cites Peirce in this connection: "C. S. Peirce, after noting that our scientific propositions are subject to being brought in doubt by the results of further inquiries, adds, 'We ought to construct our theories so as to provide for such [later] discoveries...by leaving room for the modifications that cannot be foreseen but which are pretty sure to prove needful'" (LW 12: 17, footnote 1). Dewey further radicalized this pragmatist assumption of Peirce with regard to its implications about the construction of theories in time and the necessary limits of all truth claims that depend on selectivity, choice, and partial perspectives. He thus shows a strong similarity to constructivist approaches in our time.

Dewey's theory of experience represents an important cultural turn in philosophy and provides a perspective of knowledge as an instrument in culture. In experience, we find a lot of cultural tools and resources that we can use in thinking and acting to creatively shape our world. This is close to present-day constructivist assumptions that reality is a construction out of transactions with experienced events. For example, Dewey says, "The only way in which the term reality can ever become more than a blanket denotative term is through recourse to specific events in all their diversity and thatness" (LW 10: 39). However, while "all that happens is equally real—since it really happens—happenings are not of equal worth.

Their respective consequences, their import, varies tremendously" (MW 10: 40). Dewey's implicit constructivism is based on the insight that the multitude of events in experience can only be dealt with constructively through contexts of discursive practices—or what he calls "a universe of discourse." For him, there is always a circular connection between events as existence and meanings in discourse, and we can never completely separate one from the other. For instance, he argues in his *Logic*:

> The question may be raised whether meaning-relations in discourse arise before or after significance-connections in existence. Did we first infer and then use the results to engage in discourse? Or did relations of meanings, instituted in discourse, enable us to detect the connections in things in virtue of which some things are evidential of other things? The question is rhetorical in that the question of historical priority cannot be settled. The question is asked, however, in order to indicate that in any case ability to treat things as signs would not go far did not symbols enable us to mark and retain just the qualities of things which are the ground of inference. (LW 12: 61)

Experiencing and knowing take place in events and the question is to overcome the dualism between subject and world. Dewey observes, "But if it be true that the self or subject of experience is part and parcel of the course of events, it follows that the self becomes a knower. It becomes a mind in virtue of a distinctive way of partaking in the course of events. The significant distinction is no longer between the knower and the world; it is between different ways of being in and of the movement of things" (LW 10: 42).

The issue of different ways of being in movements is essentially a question of the relation of education and social life.

EDUCATION AND SOCIAL LIFE

In *Education from a Social Perspective*, Dewey wrote in 1913 that the social is an inclusive idea of all education. He distinguishes between two aspects of the matter as follows:

> The social concept must…propose a twofold goal: on the one hand, action, work, must no longer be considered servile and mechanical, but must become liberal and enlightened through their contact with science and history; on the other hand, education must no longer constitute the distinctive mark of a class. It must no longer be seen as a leisure pursuit, an intellectual stimulant, but rather as a necessity for all free and progressive social action. (MW 7: 120)

This twofold perspective implies, for one thing, the liberation from traditional ideas of learning, limits of contents, and discipline for learners. Those ideas were focused on the aim of passing down a canon of knowledge to be distributed to restricted groups of interest. In the interest of democracy, however, as Dewey never tires of reminding his readers, knowledge must not be divided with respect to particular classes who are supposed to have privilege claims to education. Education is an inclusive aim for all members of democracy. As a social task, education must struggle to achieve as much equity as possible between advantaged and disadvantaged groups.

In *Democracy and Education*, one of the most influential works in twentieth-century education, Dewey describes education as a "necessity of life." Education is necessary for life because it is the chief social medium of transmission without which a social group or society could not come into existence or survive. "Education, in its broadest sense, is the means of this social continuity of life. Every one of the constituent elements of a social group, in a modern city as in a savage tribe, is born immature, helpless, without language, beliefs, ideas, or social standards. Each individual, each unit who is the carrier of the life-experience of his group, in time passes away. Yet the life of the group goes on" (MW 9: 5).

If we conceive of education too narrowly as only consisting of the transmission of basic cultural skills and techniques—such as reading, writing, and arithmetic—or basic moral virtues—such as diligence, control, punctuality, and obedience—then we readily lose sight of the necessary social task of education and its broader cultural aims. Education as a social function can have no other and more ultimate end for Dewey than growth conceived of as a continual process of reorganization or reconstruction of experience (see MW 9: 82). Among other things, the democratic ideal implies that the growth of individuals is key to the prosperity and growth of the society at large. This is meant to say that control cannot only be imposed from above. In this connection, Dewey distinguishes between direction, control, and guidance.

> Of these three words...[d]irection expresses the basic function, which tends at one extreme to become a guiding assistance and at another, a regulation or ruling. But in any case, we must carefully avoid a meaning sometimes read into the term "control." It is sometimes assumed, explicitly or unconsciously, that an individual's tendencies are naturally purely individualistic or egoistic, and thus antisocial. Control then denotes the process by which he is brought to subordinate his natural impulses to public or common ends. Since, by

conception, his own nature is quite alien to this process and opposes it rather than helps it, control has in this view a flavor of coercion or compulsion about it. Systems of government and theories of the state have been built upon this notion, and it has seriously affected educational ideas and practices. But there is no ground for any such view. Individuals are certainly interested, at times, in having their own way, and their own way may go contrary to the ways of others. But they are also interested, and chiefly interested upon the whole, in entering into the activities of others and taking part in conjoint and cooperative doings. Otherwise, no such thing as a community would be possible... Control, in truth, means only an emphatic form of direction of powers, and covers the regulation gained by an individual through his own efforts quite as much as that brought about when others take the lead. (MW 9: 28–29)

The appreciation and realization of individual growth of all members of society is core condition for the development of democracy and a necessary precondition of furthering social chances and opportunities. It is also necessary for finding constructive solutions to social conflicts on a most inclusive as well as deliberative level. Education should be organized in ways that all involved in the educative process have the chance to experience themselves as participants and agents in a diverse or pluralistic as well as open and growing democratic community of learners.

With regard to Dewey's account of education and learning, it may be helpful to further specify important insights by using more recent constructivist terminology in order to highlight Dewey's implicit constructivism. In the Cologne program of interactive constructivism, we employ, among other things, the distinction of three perspectives. These are construction, reconstruction, and deconstruction. The first two concepts can also be found explicitly in Dewey, the third was not part of the vocabulary of his time but can be found by implication in his theory of critical and creative reflection.

Construction

In educational psychology today, it is widely agreed that constructive learning is key to successful learning. If we look into a typical introduction into the field, we find statements like the following:

> One of the most important principles of educational psychology is that teachers cannot simply give students knowledge. Students must construct knowledge in their own minds. The teacher can facilitate this

process by teaching in ways that make information meaningful and
relevant to students, by giving students opportunities to discover or
apply ideas themselves, and by teaching students to be aware of and
consciously use their own strategies for learning. Teachers can give
students ladders that lead to higher understanding, yet the students
themselves must climb these ladders. (Slavin 2006, 243)

If one reads a passage like this it seems astonishing that in our time
authors in educational psychology very often do not even explicitly
mention Dewey although their theories clearly stand in the line of his
educational and psychological approach. Proponents of constructivist education and psychology can, among other things, learn from
Dewey that construction implies a broad field of creative and productive activities that are necessary components in the self-organization
of learning in every learner. "I have used the word construction,"
Dewey says, to denote "the creative mind," that is the mind that "is
genuinely productive in its operations. We are given to associating
creative mind with persons regarded as rare and unique, like geniuses.
But every individual is in his own way unique. Each one experiences
life from a different angle than anybody else, and consequently has
something distinctive to give others if he can turn his experiences
into ideas and pass them on to others" (LW 5: 127).

Dewey uses the terms "to construct" or "construction" in many of
his works. These terms point not only to the construction of material
complexes like buildings or walls but also to the construction of ideas
and meanings. In this sense, Dewey suggests that one constructs
ideas, concepts, theories, values, and so on. These constructions differ from person to person and from culture to culture to a certain
extent. Constructions therefore are necessary processes in the development of experience. "We use our past experiences to construct new
and better ones in the future" (MW 12: 134). Constructions are not
arbitrary as Dewey explains with regard to the construction of theories and knowledge in social and moral matters: "When it is realized
that in these fields as in the physical, we know what we intentionally
construct, that everything depends upon determination of methods
of operation and upon observation of the consequences which test
them, the progress of knowledge in these affairs may also become
secure and constant" (LW 4: 149).

In this connection there are many debates about the role of subjectivity in processes of construction that always imply a certain degree
of necessary objectivity if they are to be viable in a culture. But what
degrees of subjectivity can culture concede to individuals and in

how far must we delimit arbitrariness in order to avoid unqualified relativism?

According to Deweyan pragmatism, in every process of inquiry there are subjects at work in communities with other subjects. All of them bring their own experience with their cultural as well as individual backgrounds to the process. Their subjectivity and diversity of standpoints and original perspectives is essential for growth in scientific research as well as in all areas of social life. For if subjects were only copies of their environment, nothing new could ever emerge. With his fundamental and path-breaking insights into the connections between action and construction and the relevance of cultural contexts, Dewey clears the ground for a constructive pragmatism or even a pragmatic constructivism as we may call this position today. It is a consequence of his views that constructions shape realities, and themselves become powerful forces in culture. They produce their own history, which is "culture as second nature." Here, it is difficult ever to draw a clear line between what is nature and what is culture because in construction both fields deeply interpenetrate. Constructions often give us the sense of order, regularity, and security. But Dewey forcefully reminds us that in culture and nature our constructions will always be limited and selective. Therefore, they cannot do away with the precarious character of our world.

> We live in a world which is an impressive and irresistible mixture of sufficiencies, tight completenesses, order, recurrences which make possible prediction and control, and singularities, ambiguities, uncertain possibilities, processes going on to consequences as yet indeterminate. They are mixed not mechanically but vitally like the wheat and tares of the parable. We may recognize them separately but we cannot divide them, for unlike wheat and tares they grow from the same root. (LW 1: 47)

In such a world constructions can always have positive and desirable as well as negative and undesirable consequences. Therefore, Dewey insists that construction must always be accompanied by criticism. Criticism "is judgment engaged in discriminating among values. It is taking thought as to what is better and worse in any field at any time, with some consciousness of why the better is better and why the worse is worse. Critical judgment is therefore not the enemy of creative production but its friend and ally" (LW 5: 133–134). Dewey thus describes both sides in their necessary interaction: "Production that is not followed by criticism becomes a mere gush of impulse; criticism that is not a step to further creation deadens impulse and ends in sterility" (ibid., 140).

Against the background of Dewey's radical democratic thought, such criticism has to respond to social conditions as well as cultural tradition, practices, and institutions. If we see only the side of construction and forget about social criticism, we run the risk that our constructivism becomes naive to the power of vested interests in societies that are largely characterized by social and economic inequalities.

Reconstruction

From the perspective of individual learners, each of them has to construct their own reality. But without further qualifications, this statement invites misunderstandings. In the process of construction, every individual already uses resources that are not individual but cultural like symbols, languages, meanings, rules, ideas, knowledge, and so on. They have to discover the world of culture in the very process of inventing their own learning through construction. A central problem of teaching is to connect construction with reconstruction on the basis of necessary cultural contexts. This always implies that there will be a certain amount of reproduction of learning contents. But as Dewey's concept of experience suggests for learning theories already in his time, it is crucial for learning that the learners have sufficient opportunities to actively use cultural resources and learning materials to construct their own learning processes in cooperation with other learners.

The terms "to reconstruct" and "reconstruction" can be found in many of Dewey's writings. Reconstruction for him always has to do with making things over or reinventing them. Construction and reconstruction are companions for Dewey in any learning experience. With regard to the necessary reproductive side of learning, Dewey's account of learning as problem solving is very instructive. As learners, we always start with an emotional response to a concrete situation before we begin to assimilate and appropriate cultural contents, events, or situations. If teachers insist too much on the side of reproduction, however, the danger is that learning will become boring, oppressing, and uninteresting.

Deconstruction

The words "to deconstruct" or "deconstruction" were not part of the vocabulary of Dewey's time. But the sense of these terms is not alien to him. There are many places in his work where he discusses the value and the limits of deconstruction in the sense of criticism. Criticism is discovering the self-consistency of arguments and scientific theories, with criticism one can analyze the backgrounds and viabilities of these theories in their contexts. In our time, the need for and emphasis on deconstruction as a form of criticism has increased to an extent that the term has become an explicit label for a broad field of social and cultural criticism. Speaking on a rather general level, we can say that the sensitivity to discontinuity, contingency, indeterminacy, omissions, fallacies, contradictions, paradoxes, and ambivalences is important for deconstructive criticism. Such criticism is not fault finding, it "is judgment engaged in discriminating among values" (LW 5: 133). Therefore, it is a necessary supplement to creativity and construction. And Dewey already suggests an insight that has become widespread today among all sorts of deconstructivists: "Thus we may say that the business of philosophy is criticism of belief; that is, of beliefs that are so widely current socially as to be dominant factors in culture. Methods of critical inquiry into beliefs mark him [the philosopher] off as a philosopher, but the subject matter with which he deals is not his own. The beliefs themselves are social products, social facts and social forces" (ibid., 164). At the same time, Dewey warns us against a criticism that contents itself with deconstructing everything whatsoever and does not sufficiently combine deconstruction with constructive and reconstructive efforts.

FORMAL AND INFORMAL EDUCATION

In the history of education, the distinction between direct and indirect forms of educative processes is very common. Today, educational theorists for most part use the terms "formal" and "informal" education to draw this distinction. Dewey already uses this terminology although he sometimes prefers words like indirect or incidental to characterize the more informal side, and words like direct or deliberate to denote the more formal side. For example, he observes the following about the necessity of this basic distinction:

> We are not, however, primarily concerned with the distinction between formal and informal education as a historic matter, but as a standing distinction of fundamental importance between out-of-school education and schooling. Children to-day, for example, get their initiation into and chief contacts with their mother tongue in their informal education; that is, they get it by partaking in certain forms of social life which exist on their own account, not for the sake of education. Other

matters, technical science, algebra, and "dead" languages, are mainly relegated to formal education; many other topics lie partly in both fields. Many of the most important problems of educational theory and practice are determined by this situation. There are certain obvious advantages in the type of education that depends upon securing the educative result not by subject-matter and method selected and arranged for the express purpose of education, but by actual direct participation in some form of contemporary life valued and performed on its own account. Genuineness, vitality, depth of interest and of assimilation, and consequent assurance of influence upon habit and character, are features of the incidental type of education. In contrast with these marks, school education tends to become remote and artificial (abstract in the unfavorable sense sometimes given that term), devoted to modes of technical skill and accumulation of knowledge with only a minimum effect upon character, because its affairs are not organized into the ordinary practices of daily life. (MW 6: 427)

The quote suggests that Dewey always takes pains not only to distinguish between the two forms but also to discuss and reflect them critically with regard to their relative advantages as well as risks. He emphasizes the importance to see the difference between both fields and not to underestimate their functions in society. At the same time, he makes an essential argument about the relation of education and democracy in pointing to the dimension of informal education as a criterion for evaluating the social worth of all institutions. In *Democracy and Education* he observes,

That the ulterior significance of every mode of human association lies in the contribution which it makes to the improvement of the quality of experience is a fact most easily recognized in dealing with the immature. That is to say, while every social arrangement is educative in effect, the educative effect first becomes an important part of the purpose of the association in connection with the association of the older with the younger. As societies become more complex in structure and resources, the need of formal or intentional teaching and learning increases. As formal teaching and training grow in extent, there is the danger of creating an undesirable split between the experience gained through associations that are more direct and what is acquired in school. This danger was never greater than at the present time, on account of the rapid growth in the last few centuries of knowledge and technical modes of skill. (MW 9: 12–13)

Dewey already insists that it is one core problem of educational theory and practice to find well-balanced ways of combining the formal and informal sides of education that are responsive to the changing social, societal, and cultural contexts of life. Solutions to this fundamental educational problem will always be temporal, selective, and incomplete. To find a good balance, we must avoid the temptation of overestimating one side at the disadvantage of the other. For example, there is a repeated danger in educational research to exaggerate the import of school education: "Schools are, indeed, one important method of the transmission which forms the dispositions of the immature; but it is only one means, and, compared with other agencies, a relatively superficial means" (MW 9: 7).

Language, or more generally speaking the use of symbols, is an intimate component in both forms of education. It is a medium of representation that opens ways to connect learning with experiences not immediately present to the learners. Already in informal education, communication through language is necessary as "a process of sharing experience till it becomes a common possession. It modifies the disposition of both the parties who partake in it" (MW 9: 12). But the role of language in formal education goes much further, because without it "it is not possible to transmit all the resources and achievements of a complex society. It also opens a way to a kind of experience which would not be accessible to the young, if they were left to pick up their training in informal association with others, since books and the symbols of knowledge are mastered" (ibid., 11).

The distinction between formal and informal education implies for Dewey that both sides must always be seen in continuity. Learning always connects both aspects. Although we can distinguish between formal and informal contexts of learning, we cannot completely separate both sides because we cannot divide our experience into formal and informal parts. For example, even in school learning—as intentional and formal as it might be—is always connected to informal resources and backgrounds from learners' experiences in everyday life out of school. In formal education, communication and social interaction builds on habits not only formed in school but also primarily developed out of informal interactions.

The development of modern societies shows an increasing tendency to depend on formal education and ever more specialized and diversified institutionalization of procedures like instruction, testing, examination, certification, and evaluation. Against this background, Dewey's insistence on the importance of informal processes and his plea to appreciate the inevitable educational quality of these processes is an important reminder against a too narrow understanding of education. In Dewey's comprehensive understanding of democracy and education, the reduction of learning to formal contexts contains the danger of misunderstanding the possibilities of growth. Growth is always a process that happens across and between the formal and informal areas of experience. Therefore, we should use the distinction cautiously not to freeze it into a fixed separation. Dewey insists that we should see the process in the first place and not reduce it into ready-made categories. The process of education is a process of growth that has conditions that relativize the distinction of formal and informal. Therefore, in his general account of education as growth the distinction is irrelevant:

> Power to grow depends upon need for others and plasticity. Both of these conditions are at their height in childhood and youth. Plasticity or the power to learn from experience means the formation of habits. Habits give control over the environment, power to utilize it for human purposes. Habits take the form both of habituation, or a general and persistent balance of organic activities with the surroundings, and of active capacities to readjust activity to meet new conditions. The former furnishes the background of growth; the latter constitute growing. Active habits involve thought, invention, and initiative in applying capacities to new aims. They are opposed to routine which marks an arrest of growth. Since growth is the characteristic of life, education is all one with growing; it has no end beyond itself. The criterion of the value of school education is the extent in which it creates a desire for continued growth and supplies means for making the desire effective in fact. (MW 9: 57–58)

We may, for example, use the contrast between school and family as an illustration to show how this general account of education reaches across the distinction of formal and informal education. Often, it is assumed that the school is an institution of formal and the family of informal education. If we look closer, however, and apply Dewey's core concepts to understand educational growth, we find that we can apply them equally to both fields. Need for others, plasticity, and formation of habits are traits of interaction that we find in school life as well as in family life. To say that education as growth has no end beyond itself suggests that formal education is always embedded in larger contexts of experience. The example also shows that it is important to take the advantages as well as limits of both sides seriously. Often, informal education occurs in an environment that is limited in its resources. "Informal education, however deep, is almost sure to be contracted, since the environment in which an individual can directly share is limited in space and time. Moreover, its incidental character is favorable to its being incidental in the bad sense, viz., casual and fragmentary" (MW 6: 427). To counterbalance this limitation we need formal education. Schools can partly compensate for shortcomings in informal education. In a democracy, such compensation is a necessary demand for equity as a form of solidarity with the disadvantaged and marginalized members of society. To neglect this demand would mean to destroy democracy in the long run because of growing social, economical, and political inequalities that put sufficient democratic participation of all at risk. For Dewey, it is a question of developing a morality that is responsive to the needs of democracy and education. He argues, "All education which develops power to share effectively in social life is moral. It forms a character which not only does the particular deed socially necessary but one which is interested in that continuous readjustment which is essential to growth. Interest in learning from all the contacts of life is the essential moral interest" (MW 9: 370).

INTERACTION, TRANSACTION, AND COMMUNICATION

Communication is a core concept in Dewey: "Of all affairs, communication is the most wonderful. That things should be able to pass from the plane of external pushing and pulling to that of revealing themselves to man, and thereby to themselves; and that the fruit of communication should be participation, sharing, is a wonder by the side of which transubstantiation pales" (LW 1: 132). Explaining participation Dewey says, "Communication is the process of creating participation, of making common what had been isolated and singular; and part of the miracle it achieves is that, in being communicated, the conveyance of meaning gives body and definiteness to the experience of the one who utters as well as to that of those who listen" (LW 10: 248–249).

The concept of communication is a key element in Dewey's theories of culture and education. We find it already in his early works although Dewey elaborated his comprehensive and systematic discussions of communication in his middle and later works (see, e.g., MW 9 and LW 1). From the perspective of his cultural instrumentalism, Dewey characterizes language as "the tool of tools" (LW 1: 134, 146) and he convincingly argues that communication in the sense of direct personal exchange and lived relationships is indispensable for the coordination of humans in society and thus for the sustaining of their living. Communication is the medium of social interaction and participation and as such it constitutes the primary medium of education: "Education, as we conceive it, is a process of social interaction carried on in behalf of consequences which are themselves social—that is, it involves interactions between persons and includes shared values" (LW 8: 80). For participation in education, it is crucial that all individuals have chances to articulate their own views, interests, desires, and intentions as effective components in the interactive process. It is a core principle of democracy in education, according to Dewey, that participation cannot only mean passive adaptation or even subordination, but must be considered as an active and liberal contribution of individuals with unique experiences. Therefore, there is always a tension in educational participation and communication between freedom and social commitment in developing communities of learning. Dewey points to the root *common* in the word *communication*: "There is more than a verbal tie between the words common, community, and communication. Men live in a community in virtue of the things which they have in common; and communication is the way in which they come to possess things in common" (MW 9: 7). From his perspective of democracy and education, processes of communication are indissolubly tied to questions of democratic rights like "free speech, freedom of communication and intercourse, of public assemblies, liberty of the press and circulation of ideas, freedom of religious and intellectual conviction (commonly called freedom of conscience), of worship, and...the right to education, to spiritual nurture" (MW 5: 399). Such rights live only in and through communication. They need education as a force for their maintenance and further development. Education and communication are inseparable because every process of communication, for Dewey, has educative power. "All communication is like art. It may fairly be said, therefore, that any social arrangement that remains vitally social, or vitally shared, is educative to those who participate in it" (MW 9: 9).

Let us now turn to the relation between communication and interaction. In Dewey, as well as in common usage interaction is the more general term. Communication is a part of interaction; it is the medium of all social interaction. Interaction in Dewey's sense comprehends relations of an agent with other agents or with objects of the natural and social world. It is always a case of establishing relations. "In art, as in nature and in life, relations are modes of interaction" (LW 10: 139).

According to Dewey, interaction is fundamental in all human experience since, as we saw above, experience is a continuum of doings and undergoings. Dewey characterizes interaction and continuity as two basic criteria of experience: "The two principles of continuity and interaction are not separate from each other. They intercept and unite. They are, so to speak, the longitudinal and lateral aspects of experience" (LW 13: 25).

In order to understand human interaction, especially from an educational point of view, we need to have a focus on actual situations because interaction in the concrete always occurs in a situational context. This is especially important for theories of learning. For Dewey, learning always begins in the middle of things. Learning contributes to growth to the degree that learners can interact with their contexts in situations that stimulate productive or constructive developments that connect with their life-experiences. This presupposes that the context of learning involves sustainable relationships with others, for example, other learners or educators.

George Herbert Mead and John Dewey collaborated on the role of social interaction and communication in the formation of the mind and the self for 15 years during their time together first at the University of Michigan and later at the University of Chicago. As Dewey once said, "I dislike to think what my own thinking might have been were it not for the seminal ideas which I derived from him" (LW 6: 24). Eventually, Mead went much further with the inquiry on the social construction of mind and self that Dewey and he had started together. Therefore, in the history of American pragmatism, the most famous proponent of the concept of social interaction and communication has been Dewey's colleague and friend George Herbert Mead. His distinction between "I" and "Me" as parts of the "self" of an agent in social interaction has become a classical concept in social science and philosophy. The distinction is helpful, among other things, to understand the basic structures of communication and social experience. It is astonishing that Dewey himself refers only indirectly and by implication to Mead's concept, but does not appropriate it systematically to his perspectives. Nevertheless, we think it is helpful and necessary here to elaborate shortly on Mead's original concept and to discuss its implications for the pragmatist understanding of social action. We will after this detour turn back to Dewey and look at consequences for Dewey's ideas of interaction and experience.

Mead's concept involves several basic ideas. We come to have a mind when we come to have meaning. Significant (linguistic) meaning for Mead involves interpreting the significant symbol as a triadic relation between the organism that is the agent of the gesture, the organism to whom the gesture is directed, and the emerging stimulus object that will be codesignated by the end of the social act. Vocal gestures are especially important symbolic mediators. Taking the attitude of another with regard to our own actions in a symbolically mediated social transaction is critical to the acquisition of meaning. Dewey and Mead agree that language, the use of significant symbols originating in symbolically mediated action, marks the emergence of the mind.

The self emerges when an individual may respond to her or his own gestures as another would. Vocal gestures are critical to this self-reflexive process according to Mead (1922):

> If an individual uses such a gesture and he is affected by it as another individual is affected by it, he responds or tends to respond to his own social stimulus, as another individual would respond...The vocal gesture is of peculiar importance because it reacts upon the individual who makes it in the same fashion that it reacts upon an other...The self arises in conduct, when the individual becomes a social object in experience to himself. This takes place when the individual assumes the attitude or uses the gesture which another individual would use and responds to it himself, or tends so to respond...He acts toward himself in a manner analogous to that in which he acts toward others. Especially he talks to himself as he talks to others and in keeping up this conversation in the inner forum constitutes the field which is called that of mind. (Mead 1922/1964, 243)

Our vocal gestures may act on us much as they act on others toward whom we direct them. They may call out the same responses on our part (i.e., the same meaning) as they would in the other toward whom they are directed.

When the agents act toward themselves as they would toward others, they become their own social objects. It is the vocal gesture that gives rise to the "me," that is, the empirical self as a social object among others. The vocal gesture is not strictly necessary; any source of self-stimulation would do:

> The vocal gesture is not the only form which can serve for the building-up of a "me," as is abundantly evident from the building-up gestures of the deaf mutes. Any gesture by which the individual can himself be affected as others are affected, and which therefore tends to call out in him a response as it would call it out in another, will serve as a mechanism for the construction of a self. (Mead 1912, 140)

Our minds emerge when we acquire sociolinguistic meanings. Selves emerge when we may take the perspective of others in interpreting our own symbolic acts, thereby becoming self-consciously aware of our minds (our system of meanings).

Mead (1903) develops a distinction between the "I" and the "me" in which the "me" is the individual self as a stimulus object of consciousness. The individual as a "me" is "an empirical self" that "belongs to the world which it is the function of this phase of consciousness to reconstruct" (Mead 1903, 53). There are many instances of the "me." For example, the same self can be a teacher, a student, a parent, and a child simultaneously. The "I" is the spontaneous, creative, transitory self, the self that constantly reconstructs its world. The multiple instances of the empirical "me" can serve as a stimulus object to the reconstructive "I." The "I," however, "cannot be an object" (ibid., 46). It is the function that appears "in the shifting of attention in the adaptation of habitual tendencies to each other, when they have come into conflict within the coordination" (ibid., 45). The "I" is the creative aspect of self capable of reconstructing the multiple instances of "me."

A self is comprised of an "I" as well as the multiple instances of "me." It is the "I" that provides reflective self-awareness of the empirical "me." The "I" is only operative when the established (i.e., habitual) functioning of the "me" is disrupted. The "I," however, never appears because it is the expressive functional "I can do" at the center of reconstructive action: It is only the "me"—the empirical self—that can be brought into the focus of attention that can be perceived. "I" lies beyond the range of immediate experience. The "I" therefore never can exist as an object in consciousness, but the very conversational inner experience, the very process of replying to one's own talk, implies an "I" behind the scenes who answers to the gestures, the symbols, that arise in consciousness (see Mead 1912, 140–141).

Thinking here is represented as an internalization of social dialogue. The "I" is the individual agent's basis of functioning from birth as a biological inheritance and evolves through the unique personal experience of the individual's life history. This is the basis of unique creativity in individuals. This uniqueness interprets, and resists the social roles that comprise the varied constructions of the "me." This brings us to the idea of role-play in Mead.

There are as many instances of the empirical "me" as social roles that the agent plays: It is also to be noted that this response to the social conduct of the self may be in the role of another—we present his arguments in imagination. In this way, we play the roles of all our group; indeed, it is only insofar as we do this that they become part of our social environment—to be aware of another self as a self implies that we have played his role or that of another with whose type we identify him for purposes of intercourse (see Mead 1913, 146).

For Mead, individuals are an internal plurality, a community. Initially, the role-play is very literal; later, it is possible to abstract from the specific roles: "The features and intonations of the *dramatis personae* fade out and the emphasis falls upon the meaning of the inner speech" (ibid., 147). Pragmatic social construction is dermatological. The construction and reconstruction of dramatic narratives are crucial to the emergent construction and subsequent reconstruction of the self. The culture at large provides narrative scripts for playing the various roles that constitute the different senses of "me" that make up the empirical self. For the most part, most of the time, all of us live socially prescripted lives.

Mead (1922) distinguishes between role taking in play and games. He begins with play:

> The self arises in conduct when the individual becomes a social object in experience to himself. This takes place when the individual assumes the attitude or uses the gesture which another individual would use and responds to it himself, or tends so to respond . . . It arises in the life of the infant . . . and finds its expression in the normal play life of young children . . . He acts toward himself in a manner analogous to that in which he acts toward others. Especially he talks to himself as he talks to others and in keeping up this conversation in the inner forum constitutes the field which is called that of mind. (Mead 1922, 243)

Playing with dolls is a classic example of children's role-play. The child may respond in tone of voice and attitude toward the doll as his parents respond to his own cries and chortles. Social construction is not a new educational idea. Play readily evolves into games: "For in a game there is a regulated procedure, and rules. The child must not only take the role of the other . . . but he must assume the various roles of all the participants in the game and govern his action accordingly" (ibid., 285). Mead's example is that of a baseball player who must understand the function of every other player, and their organized responses to her, in order to understand how she herself is to play. The rules, values, and norms of games are abstracted from play much as the agent abstracts the concepts and categories of thought from the dramatis personae. The abstraction of roles and norms leads to the notion of the "generalized other."

The generalized other provides the most socialized sense of self. The "generalized other" is simply an extension of taking the attitude of specific others and directing our responses to them and, self-reflexively, ourselves. Here is how Mead (1934/1967) describes it, "In taking the role which is common to all, he finds himself speaking to himself and to others with the authority of the group...The generalization is simply the result of the identity of responses" (Ibid., 245). The result is a, perhaps tacit, universal rule of action. As an example, consider the soccer player who must understand the function of every other player, and their organized responses to her, in order to understand how she herself is to respond. When the agent abstracts the rules, values, and norms of a social game, they have the notion of a "generalized other."

If we now turn back to Dewey, we may shortly quote from one of the very few essays in which he explicitly refers to Mead's work. Among other things, Dewey appreciates the way in which Mead helps us to think through the tension between the precarious and the stable in personal social experience.

> How are we to unite in a coherent way the presence of those relatively settled orders to which the name of all uniformities, laws, universals is given, with the unremitting occurrence of individuality, novelty and the unpredictable? The idea of continuity, of remaking, of reconstruction, was with Mr. Mead more than an idea in any abstract sense of the word; it was an immediate and living feeling. As such it provided the binding thread by which he interpreted the great variety and seeming disparity presented by the movements of nineteenth-century thought. (LW 11: 451)

In this sense, the "me" stands for the phase of stability in social experience, while the "I" introduces modes of unpredictability, openness, creativity, and novelty that imply aspects of precariousness.

In comparison to Mead, Dewey's has a weaker emphasis in his own writings on the inner opposition and tension between parts of the self. At least he does not give us a systematic and differentiated account of these affairs comparable with Mead's. Already in Mead, the understanding of the inner tensions of the self is framed and partly delimited through the perspective on the generalized other. In Dewey, with his meliorist orientation toward solutions in social and educational processes, the tendency to underestimate the potential contradictoriness of inner conflicts in social agents is even stronger. To be more precise, although Dewey observes and reflects the potential precariousness of personal experience and subjectivity in modern life and gives many accounts of concrete problems that individuals have to face, he seldom follows through with an account of the inner contradictions and ambivalences in personal experience especially from a perspective that acknowledges the extent to which parts of these conflicts may turn out to be insoluble in individual life. Given their strong orientation toward the generalized other as a perspective of democratic development and solution, it is not astonishing that Dewey as well as Mead did not turn—even critically—to alternative approaches for understanding the complexities of the self like psycho-analysis as one influential approach in their time. From the perspective of a cultural constructivism in our time, we suggest that here is a challenge for contemporary Dewey scholarship with consequences for psychology as well as social and educational sciences. In the context of postmodern society, it has become more and more focal that it is necessary always to combine perspectives on communication and understanding (the side of the generalized other) with equally elaborated perspectives on the contradiction within the individual (the side of the precariousness of the "I"). With regard to the latter, we need to have a stronger emphasis on the ambivalences of desire, imaginations, and the unconscious levels of interaction and communication. This becomes evident not only from current research in psychology but also from sociological analyses of postmodern life such as we will discuss in part 4.

In Dewey, especially in his later works, we find an important further development of the theory of interaction to a theory of transaction. He occasionally uses the latter term throughout his work, but gives a systematical distinction between interaction and transaction only in his later work. Transaction for him becomes a name for characterizing long-term effects of interactions and their emerging consequences that mutually affect all involved elements. Transaction stands for the idea that the "process of interaction is circular and never-ending" (LW 8: 103). Even in the more limited sphere of financial transactions in which the term is in common use we can observe the circular and emergent consequences that change the very contexts in which interactions take place:

> Rights...are...resulting from express or implied agreements of certain agents to do or refrain from doing specific acts, involving exchange of services or goods to the mutual benefit of both parties in the transaction. Every bargain entered into, every loaf of bread one buys or paper of pins one sells, involves an implied and explicit contract. A genuinely free agreement or contract means (i.) that each party to the transaction secures the benefit he wants; (ii.) that the two parties are brought into cooperative or mutually helpful relations; and that (iii.) the vast, vague, complex business of conducting social life is broken up into a multitude of specific acts to be performed and of specific goods to be delivered, at definite times and definite places. (MW 5: 405)

This example shows how the proceeding exchanges of goods indirectly, and often unintentionally, inform and change the very institutional frames that order the ongoing processes. As the example of economic transactions already suggests, such processes need forms of stability, such as liabilities, contracts, rules, and laws in this case. Dewey even uses the metaphor of economic transaction to describe aspects of teaching and learning. In *How We Think* he argues,

> Teaching and learning are correlative or corresponding processes, as much so as selling and buying. One might as well say he has sold when no one has bought, as to say that he has taught when no one has learned. And in the educational transaction, the initiative lies with the learner even more than in commerce it lies with the buyer. If an individual can learn to think only in the sense of learning to employ more economically and effectively powers he already possesses, even more truly one can teach others to think only in the sense of appealing to and fostering powers already active in them. Effective appeal of this kind is impossible unless the teacher has an insight into existing habits and tendencies, the natural resources with which he has to ally himself. (MW 6: 204)

This metaphor suggests that educational transaction is connected with intentionality as well as exchange. The transaction loses its very sense and meaning if intentionality is not sufficiently given on both sides and if it is not appropriately brought into mutual exchange with others. Even in the case of economic transaction, the mutual exchange implies that "both parties (the idiomatic name for participants) undergo change; and the goods undergo at the very least a change of locus by which they gain and lose certain connective relations or 'capacities' previously possessed" (LW 16: 242). In the educational as well as in the economic case, transactions, however, always involve phases of potential contingency. The stable never goes without the precarious. In the educational field, one primary source of precariousness lies in the individuality of teachers and learners that affects the liability, predictability, and control of intentional processes of exchange. The need to take this dimension of indeterminacy in educational processes into account has become an even more urgent challenge in our time than in Dewey's. Against the background of increasing sociocultural diversity, plurality of information and intentions, growing speed and globalization of information exchange, learning itself becomes more and more diversified in contexts, methods, and contents. On the one hand, we find an easier access to diversified resources of learning, while on the other hand, we are confronted with growing indeterminacies, contradictions, and ambivalences of orientation.

In his later rendering of transaction as a philosophical concept, Dewey develops a more abstract and general level of application that tries to do justice to both sides. For instance, he writes in his *Logic*, "As new modes of social interaction and transactions give rise to new conditions, and as new social conditions install new kinds of transactions, new forms arise to meet the social need" (LW 12: 371). This quote generalizes the circularity of practices and effects in all social interaction. He refers the idea of transaction to his philosophical core concept of experience and explains why experience is always of a transactive nature:

> An experience is always what it is because of a transaction taking place between an individual and what, at the time, constitutes his environment, whether the latter consists of persons with whom he is talking about some topic or event, the subject talked about being also a part of the situation; or the toys with which he is playing; the book he is reading (in which his environing conditions at the time may be England or ancient Greece or an imaginary region); or the materials of an experiment he is performing. The environment, in other words, is whatever conditions interact with personal needs, desires, purposes, and capacities to create the experience which is had. Even when a person builds a castle in the air he is interacting with the objects which he constructs in fancy. (LW 13: 25)

His most mature exposition of transaction, though, is found in the late book *Knowing and the Known* (LW 16), coauthored by Dewey and Arthur Bentley. Here, we find a discussion of transaction in a three-step model of the development of action. The first step is characterized as self-action in order to indicate that all transactions start from agents and their acts. The second step is called interaction because the acts and intentions of agents must be brought into an exchange with others. The third step is transaction proper. This is always more than actions seen in isolation. It is also more than a mere exchange between opposite sides. Rather, the term "transaction" refers to the very process of emergence and change of agents, acts, and exchanges within a comprehensive context of mutual relations. Dewey exemplifies this idea of transaction with regard to the theory of inquiry in science, philosophy, and education. In the following we pick up some important points from his list of definitions:

- "Transaction is inquiry of a type in which existing descriptions of events are accepted only as tentative and preliminary, so that new descriptions of the aspects and phases of events, whether in widened or narrowed form, may freely be made at any and all stages of the inquiry" (LW 16: 113).Transaction implies that "no one of its constituents can be adequately specified as fact apart from the specification of other constituents of the full subjectmatter" (ibid.).

- "Transaction develops the widening phases of knowledge, the broadening of system within the limits of observation and report" (ibid.).

- "If inter-action views things as primarily static, and studies the phenomena under their attribution to such static 'things' taken as bases underlying them, then *Transaction* regards extension in time to be as indispensable as is extension in space (if observation is to be properly made), so that 'thing' is in action, and 'action' is observable as thing" (ibid.).

- "Transaction is the procedure which observes men talking and writing, with their word-behaviors and other representational activities connected with their thing-perceivings and manipulations, and which permits a full treatment, descriptive and functional, of the whole process, inclusive of all its 'contents,' whether called 'inners' or 'outers,' in whatever way the advancing techniques of inquiry require" (ibid., 114).

- And finally, "Transactional Observation is the fruit of an insistence upon the right to proceed in freedom to select and view all subjectmatters in whatever way seems desirable under reasonable hypothesis, and regardless of ancient claims on behalf of either minds or material mechanisms, or any of the surrogates of either" (ibid., 114–115).

In inquiry, observed results of transactions are often claimed as facts. Dewey thinks this is appropriate if all observers actually have had the freedom and opportunity to control the claimed facts and if the process of controlling facts is open to future readjustments. "The 'transaction,' . . . is to be understood as unfractured observation— just as it stands, at this era of the world's history, with respect to the observer, the observing, and the observed—and as it is affected by whatever merits or defects it may prove to have when it is judged, as it surely will be in later times, by later manners" (LW 16: 97).

Dewey's elaboration of the concept of transaction has deeply influenced his views about communication and its educational implications. As a transactional process, communication cannot simply be understood on the basis of a sender-receiver model because this would reduce transaction to interaction in the narrow sense indicated above. To develop a sufficiently broad understanding of communication, we need a complex and circular perspective on interaction in evolving contexts, and this is precisely what transaction stands for. Such contexts always imply observation as well as participation and action. In inquiry, the observer must always take into account the cultural and linguistic contexts of his observations or the observations of others. In education, learners and educators must be given opportunities to make full use of their abilities as observers, participants, and agents—as we would say today in a constructivist interpretation of Dewey (see Neubert and Reich 2006; Reich 2007).

To speak of transactions helps us to take systemic contexts of interactions into perspective, which involves contexts of observation, participation, and acting in social and natural environments. In science as well as in other fields of social and cultural practices, it is crucial for critical reflection to analyze and specify such systemic conditions and interrelations. This is one of the most general lessons to be learned from Dewey's pragmatism. It points to an attitude of sensitivity for ambivalences and contradictions in experience that is especially important for educational theory and practice.

From Mead, we can learn that his concept of interaction helps us to specify more closely the intrapersonal tensions, ambivalences, and contradictions that go hand in hand with any experience of interpersonal communication. Thus, interaction is always a necessary part of transaction. In the decades after Dewey's death, we have witnessed the development of many newer theories of communication that are partly connected with Mead. Communication has altogether become a core concern in late twentieth-century thought. Against this background, it seems ironic that Dewey's approach to communication has not sufficiently been used as a resource of reference. Even though these newer theories have helped to clarify many details in understanding concrete communicative processes more deeply, they have operated upon the whole on a much more restricted scale and with a much narrower perspective on communication and its contexts than Dewey has. Especially, they tend to lose sight of the necessary connection between communication and democratic participation in culture that was so important for Dewey and that indeed is still important for education today. We will get back to this theme more specifically in part 3.

SELECTION OF TARGET TEXTS

Part 1 is keyed to the following texts.[2] Dewey's philosophical core concept, "experience," finds its most comprehensive and detailed discussion in the two later works, *Experience and Nature* (1925/29; LW 1) and *Art as Experience* (1934; LW 10).[3] In *Experience and Nature*, which some have labeled Dewey's metaphysics, he elaborates on the close relationship between his idea of experience and his understanding of nature, a connection that is indicated not only by the title of the work, but also by Dewey's characterization of his own philosophical position and method as "empirical naturalism" or "naturalistic empiricism" at the very outset of the first chapter (LW 1: 10).

It would be misleading, though, if the two characterizations of Dewey's position, naturalism and empiricism, were to be reduced to the conventional understanding of these terms in the tradition of Western philosophy. Dewey reconstructed both concepts and used them in a fundamentally new and extended way. So *naturalism*, in Dewey, does not refer to an understanding of nature as something essentially given, a fixed order of things, beings, or species. Following Darwin, Dewey's philosophical understanding of nature implies an open, dynamic, and contingent process in which identities and relationships emerge as the actualization of natural potentialities in the context of evolutionary interactions. Like all other natural affairs, human experience, too, emerges from natural interactions. This is why, for Dewey, "nature and experience are not enemies or alien"—as is so often suggested in the philosophical tradition. "There is in the character of human experience ... a growing progressive self-disclosure of nature itself" (LW 1: 5).

At the same time, Dewey's *empiricism* builds on a concept of experience that shows remarkable differences as compared to the classical understanding of that term, for example, in John Locke and the tradition of British empiricism. Experience, for Dewey, is not restricted to the subjective experiencing of an objectively given reality that is supposed to be principally independent from the process of experiencing itself and the one who has the experience. Nor is it, in the first place, a passive event, for example, of receiving sense impressions. Rather, experience is characterized for Dewey by the two criteria of continuity and interaction (see LW 13: 17ff.). The basic unit in his concept of experience is the act, "and the act in its full development as a connection between doing and undergoing" (LW 11: 214) wherein meanings are actively constructed.

Dewey's comprehensive criticisms of epistemology and his grappling with different models and traditions of Western philosophy draw heavily on these two ideas.[4] In *Experience and Nature*, he articulates these criticisms from the perspective of a "naturalistic metaphysics" (LW 1: 62) that deals with the "generic traits manifested by existences of all kinds" (ibid., 308). Metaphysics, in this sense, constitutes a kind of philosophical metacriticism that provides "a ground-map of the province of criticism, establishing base lines to be employed in more intricate triangulations" (ibid., 309). In the view of Dewey's naturalistic approach, such "generic traits of existence" are characters to be found in every comprehensive experience and every universe of discourse—traits like "[q]ualitative individuality and constant relations, contingency and need, movement and arrest" (ibid., 308) as well as, generally speaking, the relative precariousness and the relative stability of values. According to Dewey, though, even these basic metaphysical assumptions must be understood as philosophical hypotheses that time and again have to be applied and related to new experiences and thereby only gain meaning in the concrete life of human beings. "Barely to note and register that contingency is a trait of natural events has nothing to do with wisdom. To note, however, contingency in connection with a concrete situation of life is that fear of the Lord which is at least the beginning of wisdom" (ibid., 309). Even Dewey's metaphysics, therefore, is no "philosophy of the last word" but claims to be an integrated part of his comprehensive philosophical experimentalism.

Dewey further developed his concept of "experience" especially in his book on art and aesthetics, *Art as Experience* (1934; LW 10). It is primarily in the first three chapters of this book that one finds his most comprehensive account of the qualitative and aesthetic dimension of experience. Dewey thinks that this dimension particularly manifests itself in the work of art, provided that "work of art" means more than just the expressive object—namely, the interaction of that object in the experience of either the artist or the recipient. The perception of a work of art involves creative and poetic potentials. Furthermore, *Art as Experience* can be seen as a further important contribution to Dewey's philosophic theory of communication, since he regards art as the most universal form of communication. He stresses political implications as to the relation of art and democracy in a modern industrialized society and points out art's critical potentialities for the advancement of democratic ways of life. For "[a]rt breaks through barriers that divide human beings, which are impermeable in ordinary association" (LW 10: 249).

Like Dewey's philosophical notion of experience, his logic and theory of knowledge have been developed in several steps and over a number of decades. We will mention only the most important works here. In 1903, a group of authors from the University of Chicago department of philosophy published *Studies in Logical Theory*, under the lead of Dewey, inaugurating what would eventually be known as the Chicago School of functionalism and instrumentalism. Basic to their approach was the view that the test of validity of an idea lies in its "functional or instrumental use in effecting the transition from a relatively conflicting experience to a relatively integrated one" (MW 2: xvii). This involves a very fundamental rejection of the correspondence theory of truth and knowledge in all its traditional forms. "The truth of an idea or theory," writes Dewey's student and colleague Sidney Hook in his introduction about the position maintained in the *Studies*, "depends not on its agreement with an antecedently existing reality but on the 'adequacy of [its] performance' in bringing into existence a new state of affairs in which the situation that provoked thought is reconstituted" (ibid.). Dewey further elaborated on this and other ideas about truth and knowledge in a series of essays that were collectively published as *Essays in Experimental Logic* in 1916.[5] The book *How We Think*, published in 1910 and again in a revised edition in 1933 (MW 6: 177–356; LW 8: 105–352) concisely summarizes his approach and focuses on implications for educational theory. In his ninetieth year, Dewey published the book *Knowing and the Known* (1949; LW 16: 1–279), an extensive study coauthored with Arthur F. Bentley, which was to become his last major work. Dewey's most comprehensive and thoroughgoing discussion of logic and knowledge, though, is his book *Logic: The Theory of Inquiry* published in 1938 (LW 12). Today, this book can be seen as the standard work on this part of his philosophy.

Dewey's anthropology and his conception of human nature are comprehensively and penetratingly explained in his 1922 book *Human Nature and Conduct* (MW 14). The book carries the subtitle "An Introduction to Social Psychology" and indeed represents an important result of Dewey's extensive psychological and social psychological works that were in part influenced by ideas of William James and George Herbert Mead. Among Dewey's other important writings in this field are, for example, his 1887 book *Psychology* (EW 2), the path-breaking 1896 essay "The Reflex Arc Concept in Psychology" (EW 5: 96–109), and from the later works, the 1930 essay "Conduct and Experience" (LW 5: 218–235), to mention but a few. Dewey's approach to social psychology as laid down in *Human Nature and Conduct* builds on three crucial concepts, "habit," "impulse," and "intelligence." One central thesis of the book suggests that native impulses in man, although first in time, play a secondary role in human conduct compared to habits acquired and formed in the interactions with a cultural milieu.

Part 2

EDUCATION AS RECONSTRUCTION
OF EXPERIENCE—THE
CONSTRUCTIVE TURN

Dewey believes that we need "a theory of experience in order that education may be intelligently conducted upon the basis of experience" (LW 13: 17). Let us start by contrasting Dewey's theory of experience with the ancient account of Plato and Aristotle and the modern account of the British Empiricists. The classical account was close to what modern psychologist call learning by trial and error as opposed to learning from ideas. Over time, rules exhibited as habits of action build up that yields a general idea of objects, relations, and situations. The skill development of artisans is the best exemplar of learning from experience. Because such practical learning was contingent and uncertain, the ancients considered it deficient compared to pure conceptual contemplation. The modern philosophy of experience assumed that we passively experienced discrete sense data that requires us to wire them together like sausages using psychological laws of association. Such a view naturally led to the radical skepticism of David Hume whose work awoke Kant from his dogmatic slumbers and led to the birth of rationalistic, subjective idealism with its transcendental, a priori categories subsisting dualistically apart from experience.

According to Dewey, two historical trends rendered his new theory of experience and the relation of experience to reason feasible. First, whereas the British empiricists asserted the existence of discrete sense data that then required connection by a separate faculty of rationality not found in experience. Dewey denied the dualism of reason and experience. Influenced by William James's notion of "the stream of consciousness," Dewey develops an empiricism wherein the relations among things appear in experience along with the things.

Dewey completely rejects the notion of sense data. For him, rationality emerges over time in experience. As a result, rationality is as contingent, falsifiable, and evolving as every other meaning that we may construct from experience. Second, Dewey relied on Darwinism and the advance of a biological psychology. Let us begin with the second trend.

EXPERIENCE AND EDUCATION: THE BIOLOGICAL MATRIX

Living organisms must act to maintain a dynamic, transactional, and homeostatic unity with the environment. The adjustment involves either accommodation, where the organisms mostly alters its self, or adaptation, where the organism mostly alters their environment. Here, we have the first lesson educators may draw from Dewey's theory of experience. It is never necessary to motivate a living creature to act. Motivation always means coordinating the learner's ongoing activities with his or her world in an appropriate developmental direction by establishing an interest in specific objects and objectives.

Dewey identifies interaction and continuity as the two principles that best explicate the biological basis of experience from whence mind and self eventually emerge. We begin with interaction. For Dewey, existence is comprised of events in actual or potential interaction. For him, "there is no isolated occurrence in nature" (LW 1: 207). Experience occurs when sentient organisms interact with their world. All sentient beings form a functional unity. Dewey understood experience based on biological functioning. For him, a living function is any "process sufficiently complex to involve an arrangement or coordination of minor processes which fulfills a specific end in such a way as to conserve itself" (MW 6: 466). Hence, organisms have a "selective bias in interactions with environing things" (LW 1: 196). It is important to educate selective interest and attention. A living function is "a moving equilibrium of integration" (MW 13: 377). For Dewey, all living beings experience the rhythm of life (equilibrium, disequilibrium, and restoration of equilibrium) that establishes the cycle of need (disequilibrium), demand, and satisfaction (the restoration of equilibrium). All living functions must constantly strive to maintain a dynamic equilibrium or what the biologist call homeostasis. Biological growth is not so much about an increase in size as about development understood as an increase in functional complexity that allows the organism to discriminate and respond to the environment in ever more adaptive ways.

Dewey believed any "operative function gets us behind the ordinary distinction of organism and environment...It is primary; distinction is subsequent and derived" (MW 13: 377). The distinction of organism and environment is temporal. Since a function is a moving equilibrium at any moment, the factors that "represent the maintenance of the function" constitute the organism while those that intervene first as disturbing and then as restoring equilibrium establish the environment. Within the larger functional coordination, what is environment and what is organism alternate over time. Dewey's antidualism goes deep.

As already indicated in part 1, Dewey distinguishes environment from surroundings. The environment is what an organism experiences; that is, what they incorporate into their functioning. Educators often make the mistake of thinking that what surrounds the student is part of their environment when it is only a part of the teachers' environment. Another mistake is to assume that we are always consciously aware of what enters our functioning. Often, the most powerful learning involves becoming conscious of our functional or dysfunctional interactions involving such things as drugs and tyrannical people.

The interactions involved in performing life functions yield what Dewey calls "primary experiences" (see LW 1: 12ff.). By primary experience, Dewey means existential, qualitative, and immediately had experiences (see LW 5: especially 253). Dewey thought such experience provided our primary relation to reality and that it was important to educate environmental sensitivity. He used the phrase "the intellectualist fallacy" to condemn the notion that our primary connection to existence is the cognitive, knowing relation (LW 4: 232). Dewey thought that for animals in which "locomotion and distance-receptors exist, sensitivity and interest are realized as feeling" however vague. Having the ability to respond here and now to temporally and spatially remote sensations allows activities to become differentiated into the "preparatory, or anticipatory, and the fulfilling or consummatory" (LW 1: 197). This establishes the biological basis of inquiry, which mediates between immediate noncognitive experiences using cognitive meanings. Later, we will see that inquiry is artistically creative in resolving disrupted situations. When that occurs, the satisfaction yields the basis of immediate consummatory aesthetic experience.

Experience and Education: The Social Matrix

Dewey remarks that the social "interaction of human beings, namely, association, is not different in origin from other modes of interaction"

(LW 1: 138). Many species facilitate social interaction by communicating using nonlinguistic signals. Marking territory and mating rituals are common examples. Linguistic communication makes use of animal behaviors in a novel way. The same holds for Homo sapiens, and perhaps other animals, that can communicate linguistically. Rather than an immediate response to a stimulus-object, linguistic beings respond to a representative sign that refers to another stimulus-object perhaps entirely absent from the immediate situation. Dewey thought pluralistic, communicative democracy as the best form of social experience.

According to Dewey, the fundamental linguistic experience involves two beings taking the attitude of the other in responding to a third thing that they use to functionally coordinate their social interaction. Their minds and selves emerge along with the stimulus-object in the interaction. Instead of responding to the gesture of another in itself, linguistic organisms respond to the gesture from the putative standpoint of the other as an index of some third stimulus-object. Pointing using the index finger is a poignant example. This ability to take something and use it as a means to refer to something perhaps durationally extensionally remote is the ability to respond to stimulus-objects not only in their sensed immediacy but also as providing a mediating, representational, and significant meaning. Dewey is a social constructivist. We are not born with a mind. Instead, we acquire mental functioning by participating in sociolinguistic practices (see LW 1: Ch. 5). Dewey's approach to mental development accords well with contemporary empirical studies (see Tomasello 1999, 2008). Finally, the experience of the self (i.e., self-consciousness) is also social for Dewey, although it was his friend and colleague George Herbert Mead who worked out a sociolinguistic theory of the self in far greater detail as we saw in part 1. For Dewey, to have a mind is to have meaning and meanings always emerge in sociolinguistic transactions. Likewise, to have a self is to take the attitude of the other toward one's own actions.

Experience and Education: Growth

Having examined first biological interaction and then social interaction, let us now turn to continuity. Growth is the kind of continuity that most concerns Dewey who insists that "the educative process is a continuous process of growth, having as its aim at every stage an added capacity of growth" (MW 9: 59). Indeed, for him, growth is the aim of education: "Since growth is the characteristic of

life, education is all one with growing; it has no end beyond itself"
(ibid., 58). What Dewey means by growth has been terribly misunderstood over the years and many believe it is incoherent. However,
what Dewey means is what any biologist means by the term. Besides
the rather uninteresting instance of becoming a bigger version of
the present self, growth means development. Of course, unlike the
biologist, Dewey is also concerned with psychological, sociological,
and even cultural growth. The Deweyan philosopher Thomas M.
Alexander (1993) uses the phrase "the human eros" to express the
desire to live a life of expanding meaning and value through growth.
Developmental growth occurs when we are better able to discriminate more characteristics of our environment in greater detail and
respond more appropriately.

For growth to occur, we must have the capacity, the potential, to
change, "the ability to develop" (MW 9: 46). Dewey goes so far as
to say that "immaturity designates a positive force or ability,—the
power to grow" (ibid., 47). Potentiality for Dewey is not a teleological
concept. Acorns do not become oak trees because they have the latent
potential. What they become depends on with what they interact. To
become an oak tree, the acorn must interact with the nutrients in soil
and receive energy from sunlight among many other things. It must
also avoid interactions with squirrels, which also require nutrition to
grow.

Growth and the power to grow introduce the critical idea of
reconstruction in Dewey's theory of experience. Dewey writes, "We
thus reach a technical definition of education: It is that reconstruction or reorganization of experience which adds to the meaning of
experience, and which increases ability to direct the course of subsequent experience" (MW 9: 82). Continuity in reconstruction not
only requires an effective adjustment of organism and environment; it
must also increase the ability to adjust to our world, to control future
experience.

We need a proper theory of experience in part so we can determine
"what marks off educative experience from non-educative and miseducative experience" (LW 13: 31). We may learn how to be a very
good drug dealer, but that will obstruct or deform our future development. The principle of continuity reminds us that we must consider the future consequences of any educational process we elect to
employ in the present. Often in our efforts to teach some specific content, we fail to attend to the unintended consequences of our methods. The result is that sometimes what students actually learn is to
dislike learning and to approach it with a poor attitude. In addition,

some specific content of leaning might actually be miseducative. We have already discussed bad influences in formal and informal education in part 1. Miseducation eventually blocks the path of continuous growth and reconstruction (or re-creation) while genuine education expands future possibilities.

Dewey's notion of continuity in education and reconstruction in experience ultimately derives from his commitment to the continuous reconstruction required of Darwinism. Consider this comment, "As some species die out, forms better adapted to utilize the obstacles against which they struggled in vain come into being. Continuity of life means continual re-adaptation of the environment to the needs of living organisms" (MW 9: 5). "Life," Dewey remarks, "is a self-renewing process through action upon the environment" (ibid., 4). For human beings, renewal involves "the re-creation of beliefs, ideals, hopes, happiness, misery, and practices" as well as of biological habits (ibid., 5). In many ways, the terms "re-creation" or "renewal" express Dewey's philosophy better than "reconstruction." Dewey did prefer "reconstruction" to creation because he thought the former "less pretentious" (LW 5: 127). Human beings adjust to the environment by relying on their innate endowment of impulses and responses, which evolve very slowly. However, their remarkable success as a species has depended on the acquisition of habits and the use of tools, including cultural customs and institutions (e.g., schools) as well as language as "the tool of tools" (LW 1: 134).

Dewey's fundamental Darwinian intuition is that everything is in flux, everything changes, and everything is contingent. The cycle of construction, deconstruction, and reconstruction seeks to avoid the physical destruction of the species, the society, and the self. In his essay, "The Influence of Darwinism on Philosophy," Dewey discusses the source of his organic and evolutionary theory of nature: "In laying hands upon the sacred ark of absolute permanency, in treating forms that have been regarded as types of fixity and perfection as originating and passing away, the Origin of Species introduced a mode of thinking that in the end was bound to transform the logic of knowledge, and hence the treatment of morals, politics and religion" (MW 4: 3).

He should have added education. Later, Dewey would argue that "change rather than fixity is now a measure of 'reality'...change is omni-present," or again, "natural science is forced by its own development to abandon the assumption of fixity and to recognize that what for it is actually 'universal' is process" (MW 12: 114 and 260). Estimates are that 99 percent of all species that have ever lived are now extinct (Parker 1992, 570). A species is an essence, a form, or what the ancient Greeks called an *eidos*. Dewey's neo-Darwinian insight is to realize what holds for biological forms or essences also holds for individual habits, the mind, the self, cultural customs, logical forms (concepts, ideas, etc.), and Ideals (values) as well. What does not reconstruct itself will eventually undergo destruction. Dewey's theory of reconstruction has a biological imperative. Surprisingly, many educators have yet to learn the lessons of Darwin.

In our lifetime, we reconstruct ourselves by learning. Let us begin with the biological basis of learning. Dewey states that "habit introduces continuity into activity; it furnishes a permanent thread or axis" (LW 7: 185). Dewey asserts that a habit is a form of executive skill, of efficiency in doing, that introduces continuity into activity:

> Organic instincts [or impulses] and organic retention, or habit-forming, are undeniable factors in actual experience. They are factors which effect organization and secure continuity. They are among the specific facts which a description of experience cognizant of the correlation [interaction] of organic action with the action of other natural objects will include. (MW 10: 14)

Further, a "habit means an ability to use natural conditions as means to ends. It is an active control of the environment through control of the organs of action" (MW 9: 51). When we have experience, it modifies our habits of conduct thereby affecting future conduct. Dewey declares, "The dynamic force of habit taken in connection with the continuity of habits with one another explains the unity of character and conduct, or speaking more concretely of motive and act, will and deed" (MW 14: 33). For Dewey, when we act, we express the present self. However, since the consequences of our acts return to affect us in the future, we also form the future self (see LW 7: 288ff.). Habits for Dewey also include the formation not only of intellectual dispositions to act, but also of emotional attitudes and sensitivities as well as interests. Indeed, "the union of the self in action with an object and end is called an interest" (ibid., 29). Actually, "an interest or motive is the union in action of a need, desire of a self, with a chosen object" (ibid., 291). Again, we never need to motivate a live creature to act, but we do need to understand their needs, desires, interests, attitudes, sensitivities, and purposes as well as their cognitive dispositions so that we may know how to best direct them. Student-centered teaching means connecting the subject matter to the student in this rich embodied sense. It does not mean allowing students to do anything they like.

Dewey's theory of experience is extremely embodied. It places as high a premium on emotional learning and the development of appropriate attitudes as well as cognitive competence.

THE REFLEX ARC CONCEPT

Dewey's reflex arc concept paper establishes an organic theory of functional "co-ordination" immensely influential upon modern functionalist psychology. His basic objection to the standard stimulus-response schema is that it relates two separate things (i.e., stimulus and response) resulting in a false dualism. For him, stimulus and response are subfunctions of a single functional interaction requiring constant coordination.

Even today, the received version of the reflex arc concept assumes a passive organism that an external "stimulus" must prod into action. For Dewey, we always begin with an organism transacting with their environment to maintain dynamic equilibrium. The emergent stimulus redirects activity rather than initiates it; even then, the agent's motor responses to the larger situation actively *constitute* the stimulus that serves as a temporary telos for coordinating subsequent activity. There are two remarkable things worth noting immediately. First, the live creature never requires motivation to act; they act because they are alive. Motivational stimuli only redirect action. Second, the organism's motor responses "constitute" or creatively construct the stimulus that controls subsequent activity. Dewey's constructivism is primordial. Finally, because it is a functional coordination, we must realize the reflex arc is really a circle of coordination.

Dewey begins by identifying the dualism hidden in the traditional understanding of the reflex arc: "The older dualism between sensation and idea is repeated in the current dualism of peripheral and central structures and functions; the older dualism of body and soul finds a distinct echo in the current dualism of stimulus and response" (LW 5: 96). A similar statement holds for central processing information input-output representations of the mind built on computer models of cognitive psychology. Dewey describes the residual dualism this way: "The sensory stimulus is one thing, the central activity, standing for the idea is another thing, and the motor discharge, standing for the act proper, is a third. As a result, the reflex arc is not a comprehensive, or organic unity, but a patchwork of disjointed parts, a mechanical conjunction of unallied processes" (ibid., 97).

The stimulus, cognition (e.g., idea), and the response are actually phases within a larger transactionally unified durational-extensional

Stimulus (Behaviour-Object) → Central Mental Functioning → Embodied Response

(Sensation)   (Brain Process, Cognition, Idea, etc.) (Re-action, behavior)

Figure 2.1 Schema of the conventional linear reflex arc concept.

process of functional coordination. Figure 2.1 is the schema for the conventional interpretation of the reflex arc concept shared by Pavlov, Thorndike, Watson, and many others.

Reflecting on the conventional reflex arc concept, Dewey wonders what it really designates: "What shall we term that which is not sensation-followed-by-idea-followed by movement, but which is primary; which is, as it were, the psychical organism of which sensation, idea and movement are the chief organs? Stated on the physiological side, this reality may most conveniently be termed co-ordination" (LW 5: 97).

What is primary is functional "co-ordination" of the organism-environment transaction. Consider the example of a baby that reaches for a candle and receives a burn. The usual explanation is that the sensation of the light is a stimulus to the act of reaching as a response. The resulting burn is then the stimulus for withdrawing the hand as a response, and so on in a linear, mechanical sequence as in figure 2.1. Dewey disagrees, "Upon analysis, we find that we begin not with a sensory stimulus, but with a sensori-motor co-ordination, the optical-ocular, and that in a certain sense it is the movement [activity] of body, head and eye muscles determining the quality of what is experienced. In other words, the real beginning is with the act of seeing; it is looking, and not the sensation of light" (LW 5: 97).

The real beginning is a "sensori-motor co-ordination." The active motor responses, including acts of attention, discrimination, and individuation, depart from a prior coordination of activity and function to restore equilibrium to the transaction. Until the organism attends to, selects, and actively responds to aspects of a situation, nothing is a "stimulus" for that creature. For Dewey, "what precedes the 'stimulus' is a whole act, a sensori-motor co-ordination...[T]he 'stimulus' emerges out of this co-ordination" (LW 5: 100). The crucial realization is that a stimulus is the emergent consequence of an ongoing, active process.

Dewey insists, "It is the motor response or attention which constitutes [constructs] that, which finally becomes the stimulus to another act" (LW 5: 101–102). Attention, engrossment, interest, discrimination, and so on, are themselves responses leading to a fuller response or series of responses that "constitute" a stimulus for the transient telos around which the agent coordinates subsequent action. In our struggle to successfully coordinate our activities, rejecting aspects of a given situation as irrelevant to our purposes is as important as selecting aspects as pertinent, which is something the wise educator must always remember.

Stimulus, response, and cognition are jointly emergent phases within a single larger functional coordination. The permanency of the coordination is a cognitive habit of response to similar stimuli in similar situations. We learn when we acquire such habits. The goal is the continued survival and growth of an always already active organism-in-environment-as-a-whole. Figure 2.2 depicts the result of Dewey's reconstruction.

Figure 2.2 displays the archetype of Dewey's entire theory of experience. Dewey concludes, "It is the co-ordination which unifies that which the reflex arc concept gives us only in disjointed fragments. It is the circuit within which fall distinctions of stimulus and response as functional phases" (LW 5: 109). Stimulus, cognition (idea or ideal), and response are simply phases (subfunctions) within a larger interaction.

It is impossible to identify a stimulus, cognition (habit), or response for an individual organism outside of the ongoing interaction, which is inevitably organic, circular, and continuous. What is fundamental is the entire "co-ordination" of stimulus, response, and cognition. Dewey observes, "What we have is a circuit, not an arc or broken segment of a circle. This circuit is more truly termed organic than reflex, because the motor response determines the stimulus, just as truly as sensory stimulus determines movement. Indeed, the movement is only for the sake of determining the stimulus, of fixing what kind of a stimulus it is, of interpreting it" (LW 5: 102).

We might designate such organic circuits of functional coordination hermeneutic circles of activity. No subprocess, stimulus, response, or cognition is more fundamental in figure 2.2 than any other is; rather, each helps constitute the other two. What is fundamental is

Stimulus (Behaviour-Object)   Embodied Response

Teleological Objective of Action

Mental Functioning, Cognition, Idea, Ideal, or End-In-View.

Figure 2.2 The reflex circuit.

the continuous functional coordination of the organism-environment interaction.

As Dewey's critique of the reflex arc concept shows, we do not learn until we establish continuity between what we do, and what we suffer as a consequence. Dewey indicates,

> The nature of experience can be understood only by noting that it includes an active and a passive element peculiarly combined. On the active hand, experience is trying—a meaning which is made explicit in the connected term experiment. On the passive, it is undergoing. When we experience something we act upon it, we do something with it; then we suffer or undergo the consequences. We do something to the thing and then it does something to us in return: such is the peculiar combination. The connection of these two phases of experience measures the fruitfulness or value of the experience. (MW 9: 146)

There is a profound relationship between praxis and pathos in Dewey. When we make the connection, we learn. Dewey uses the familiar example of the child sticking their finger into the flame. Once the child makes the connection between the action and its consequence, then "sticking of the finger into flame means a burn" (ibid., 146). Being burned is "a mere physical change" if "it is not perceived as a consequence of some other action" (ibid., 146). He continues, "To 'learn from experience' is to make a backward and forward connection between what we do to things and what we enjoy or suffer from things in consequence. Under such conditions, doing becomes a trying; an experiment with the world to find out what it is like; the undergoing becomes instruction—discovery of the connection of things" (ibid., 147).

If we create a means-consequence connection, if we can create continuity, then we can grasp the meaning of our actions. Notice that we make the connection. We must take Dewey's constructivism literally. According to Dewey, cognitive meanings always involve a means-consequence connection and only linguistic organisms grasp significant, representational meanings, which are capable of abstract symbolization.

Dewey draws two important conclusions from the forgoing discussion. They are that experience is "primarily an active-passive affair; it is not primarily cognitive" and "the measure of the value of an experience lies in the perception of relationships or continuities to which it leads up" (ibid., 147). For Dewey, the principles of interaction and continuity are inseparable in experience.

Dewey rejects the notion that we are theoretical spectators with minds that "appropriate knowledge by direct energy of intellect" (ibid., 147). Instead, the energy comes from the body: "For the pupil has a body and brings it to school along with his mind. And the body is, of necessity, a wellspring of energy; it has to do something" (ibid., 147). Dewey's theory of learning has a robust embodied quality. Our bodies have innate, instinctive impulses and reactions to stimuli that impart the energy of our activity. However, of themselves, impulses are meaningless. Our impulses acquire meaning as we acquire habits of conduct that direct them. Impulses are constituents in all working habits. They provide the motives of action while the habit provides the form and focus. Impulses are first nature while acquired habits are second nature. We do not have innate free will, innate ideas, or innate rationality, only innate impulses. We learn from experience as we construct our habits of interaction.

HABITS, IMPULSE, AND INTELLIGENCE

Dewey states, "Habits may be profitably compared to physiological functions, like breathing, digesting...[H]abits are like functions in many respects, and especially in requiring the cooperation of organism and environment. Breathing is an affair of the air as truly as of the lungs; digesting an affair of food as truly as of tissues of stomach" (MW 14: 15). Similarly, knowing something is a lot like eating something. We must not construct a dualism where none exists. Stomachs and food are subfunctions of a single function. The same holds for habits like speech and the objects to which words refer. In both cases, they are "things done by the environment by means of organic structures or acquired dispositions" (ibid., 15). For him, "habits endure, because these habits incorporate objective conditions in themselves" (ibid., 19). That is to say that "functions and habits are ways of using and incorporating the environment in which the latter has its say as surely as the former" (ibid., 15). If we are going to change our habits, therefore, there "must be change in objective arrangements and institutions" (ibid., 19–20). For Dewey, we educate indirectly by means of the environment to which the learner responds. Ultimately, the learner decides to what in an interaction they will attend. The teacher's task is to functionally coordinate the subject matter with the needs, interests, and abilities.

For Dewey, "habits are arts," they give us skill in carrying out activities (MW 14: 15). When we think of good habits, we tend to think of "habits as technical abilities" and when we think of bad habits we tend to think of them as "the union of habit with desire" (ibid., 21). In fact, they are both. Dewey asserts, "All habits are demands for certain kinds of activity; and they constitute the self. In any intelligible sense of the word will, they are will. They form our effective desires and they furnish us with our working capacities. They rule our thoughts" (ibid., 21–22).

Habits provide skillful means while harnessing passionate impulses to execute them. That is why the self is the tool of tools, a means to any end they may chose, although they are, of course, much more than that. Moreover, character "is the interpenetration of habits," which is why it "can be read through the medium of individual acts" (MW 14: 29, 30). Habits yield the persistent individual, beliefs, attitudes, and dispositions of the self. They are the content of our character, our virtues, and our vices.

In human beings, habits are primarily social. We are born into society with certain sociolinguistic structures and institutions that condition our habits of conduct. Culture always has us before we have it. Socialization is unavoidable. The social construction of the mind and the self is unavoidable. To function in society, we must be potty trained, learn language, acquire table manners, and stop at red lights. We incorporate social rules and norms in the affectively charged habits of our body.

Modern liberal thought has the relation between the individual and society backward. The very idea of a social contract as Hobbes conceived it is nonsense. Dewey declares,

> We often fancy that institutions, social custom, collective habit, have been formed by the consolidation of individual habits. In the main this supposition is false to fact. To a considerable extent customs, or widespread uniformities of habit, exist because individuals face the same situation and react in like fashion. But to a larger extent customs persist because individuals form their personal habits under conditions set by prior customs. (MW 14: 43)

Cultural customs, the power of the norm, obedience to rules and laws, and more condition our habits and constitute the mind, the self, the will, and our artful responses to the world. The power of those who control cultural institutions such as the political system, the economy, and schooling proves immense. Dewey observes,

> Those who wish a monopoly of social power find desirable the separation of habit and thought, action and soul, so characteristic of history. For the dualism enables them to do the thinking and planning, while

others remain the docile, even if awkward, instruments of execution. Until this scheme is changed, democracy is bound to be perverted in realization. With our present system of education—by which something much more extensive than schooling is meant—democracy multiplies occasions for imitation not occasions for thought in action. (MW 14: 52)

Oppressive cultural customs and social institutions are so powerful one wonders how, if at all, free and democratic experience is even possible. The answer involves two things: passionate impulses and intelligent deliberation.

We have seen that instincts and impulses give us the dynamic energy, to act. When coupled with habits, they provide more or less intelligently directed motives of action. While habits are second nature, our "original native reactions to stimuli" are first nature and can never come fully under our control much less the control of others. Therefore, they have a critical role to play in conduct: "Impulses are the pivots upon which the re-organization of activities turn, they are agencies of deviation, for giving new directions to old habits and changing their quality. Consequently whenever we are concerned with understanding social transition and flux or with projects for reform, personal and collective, our study must go to analysis of native tendencies" (MW 14: 67).

Socialization requires the formation of habits that harness impulses. If we wish to escape socialization, we must release impulses. It is, of course, always dangerous, but totalitarian oppression is by far the greater danger. The young often rebel against socialization. They dance, they sing, they play silly games. Much of this is nonsense, but without it, we can never be free. Therefore, it is good for the elders to dance, sing, and, sometimes, play silly games. Maturity, however, should bring intelligence to the guidance of impulse. Impulse finds everything it desires immediately good in itself. Perhaps it assumes sex, drugs, and rock and roll are always good. The task is to educate the human eros to desire the genuinely desirable, to value the genuinely valuable, and to seek the truly good by engaging in intelligent reflection. Otherwise, we are simply slaves to our desire, which is far from freedom. Many are oppressed by their pleasures not their discontents. Those who create media advertising know this fact quite well even if educators do not. Instead of educating eros to desire the good, they educate it to desire material goods. Release from established patterns of social control is a necessary, if always hazardous, prerequisite for freedom.

For Dewey, "Intelligence is the key to freedom in act" and not some mystical innate free will (MW 14: 210). Indeed, the false belief that we are born with free will often binds us better than explicit forms of oppression because it misleads us into believing that freedom is given rather than earned, found rather than created. Freedom is the ultimate product of intelligent, reconstructive inquiry, which often requires deconstruction of established habits and customs. Dewey declares, "The office of deliberation... is to resolve entanglements in existing activity, restore continuity, recover harmony, utilize loose impulse and redirect habit. To this end observation of present conditions and recollection of previous situations are devoted. Deliberation has its beginning in troubled activity and its conclusion in choice of a course of action which straightens it out" (ibid., 139). Here is how he defines deliberation:

> [D]eliberation is a dramatic rehearsal (in imagination) of various competing possible lines of action. It starts from the blocking of efficient overt action, due to that conflict of prior habit and newly released impulse to which reference has been made. Then each habit, each impulse, involved in the temporary suspense of overt action takes its turn in being tried out. Deliberation is an experiment in finding out what the various lines of possible action are really like. It is an experiment in making various combinations of selected elements of habits and impulses, to see what the resultant action would be like if it were entered upon. But the trial is in imagination, not in overt fact. The experiment is carried on by tentative rehearsals in thought which do not affect physical facts outside the body. Thought runs ahead and foresees outcomes, and thereby avoids having to await the instruction of actual failure and disaster. An act overtly tried out is irrevocable, its consequences cannot be blotted out. An act tried out in imagination is not final or fatal. It is retrievable. (MW 14: 132–133)

So understood, we get a theory of intelligent choice instead of free will: "What then is choice? Simply hitting in imagination upon an object which furnishes an adequate stimulus to the recovery of overt action. Choice is made as soon as some habit, or some combination of elements of habits and impulse, finds a way fully open. Then energy is released. The mind is made up, composed, unified" (ibid., 134).

Deliberate, reflective, and intelligent choice involves embodied habits and impulses. Once we abandon the sense data theory of experience, we can see that experience is really a flux held together by internal relations rather than external relations imposed by decontextualized abstract reason. What actually connects and structures experience are the biological habits of functional coordination. These habits provide the biological basis for linguistic usage including the manipulations of abstract symbols. Embodied, impassioned habits take the place of abstract, decontextualized categories of rationality supposed to somehow exist in realm apart from experience. We no longer require the transcendent Forms of Plato, the transcendental categories of Kant and the post-Kantian idealists, innate psychological faculties, or the reified structures of modern logic. Biological structures (habits) work in conjunction with linguistic structures to provide all the forms we need to relate experiences and organize them meaningfully.

What Dewey means by "rationality" is radically different from something cold, disconnected, and dispassionate. He writes,

> The conclusion is not that the emotional, passionate phase of action can be or should be eliminated in behalf of a bloodless reason. More "passions," not fewer, is the answer. To check the influence of hate there must be sympathy, while to rationalize sympathy there are needed emotions of curiosity, caution, respect for the freedom of others— dispositions which evoke objects which balance those called up by sympathy, and prevent its degeneration into maudlin sentiment and meddling interference. Rationality, once more, is not a force to evoke against impulse and habit. It is the attainment of a working harmony among diverse desires...The elaborate systems of science are born not of reason but of impulses at first slight and flickering; impulses to handle, move about, to hunt, to uncover, to mix things separated and divide things combined, to talk and to listen. Method is their effectual organization into continuous dispositions of inquiry, development and testing...Reason, the rational attitude, is the resulting disposition, not a ready-made antecedent which can be invoked at will and set into movement. The man who would intelligently cultivate intelligence will widen, not narrow, his life of strong impulses while aiming at their happy coincidence in operation. (MW 14: 136–137)

In "Context and Thought," Dewey remarks, "The significance of 'experience' for philosophic method is, after all, but the acknowledgment of the indispensability of context in thinking when that recognition is carried to its full term" (LW 6: 20). He finds that first consideration of context "is the range and vitality of the experience of the thinker himself" (ibid., 20). We can, for instance, acquire the habit of reflecting on our habits and impulses as well as acquire a passion for inquiry. Dewey proclaims, "Processes of instruction are unified in the degree in which they centre in the production of good habits of thinking" (MW 9: 170). Reflective experience, intelligence operates in a continuous, critical-creative circle of interactions. It seeks to understand the environment, including especially other people, social customs (including rules of political, moral, and religious conduct), and institutions. We reconstruct the self by deconstructing and reconstructing environmental constructs and we reconstruct the environment by deconstructing and reconstructing the constructs of the habits of the self.

Intelligence, reason, and reflection are not separate faculties any more than habit, impulse, and imagination. Intelligence is the emergent capacity to carry out cognitive functions; that is, the ability to work out means-ends connections. It too is something we must construct, deconstruct, and reconstruct. Dewey indicates,

> Concrete habits do all the perceiving, recognizing, imagining, recalling, judging, conceiving and reasoning that is done. "Consciousness," whether as a stream or as special sensations and images, expresses functions of habits, phenomena of their formation, operation, their interruption and reorganization...Yet habit does not, of itself, know, for it does not of itself stop to think, observe or remember. Neither does impulse of itself engage in reflection or contemplation. It just lets go. Habits by themselves are too organized, too insistent and determinate to need to indulge in inquiry or imagination. And impulses are too chaotic, tumultuous and confused to be able to know even if they wanted to. (MW 14: 124)

Inquiry is intelligent reflection on and contemplation of experience in the quest for conscious understanding, insight, and knowledge. It does what habits alone cannot do in hopes of constructing and reconstructing habits that will allow us to continually grow and do more things better (and perhaps stop doing things we should not).

INQUIRY AND THE FIVE PHASES OF RESEARCH AND REFLECTIVE LEARNING

Let us now turn to some of the general features of reflection and inquiry that, for Dewey, are also the five phases of thinking in education (MW 9: 170). He insists that "thinking is the method of an educative experience" (ibid., 170). The purpose of thought or reflection is to discern the "relation between what we try to do and what happens in a consequence" (ibid., 151). It is the pursuit of cognitively meaningful experience. Dewey states, "Thinking is thus equivalent of an explicit rendering of the intelligent element in our experience. It makes it possible to act with an end in view" (ibid., 152). Cognition, meaning construction, makes experience intelligent. True meanings, knowings, or what Dewey preferred to call the "warranted assertion" of judgments, are the products of the process of inquiry that allows us to manipulate and modify the connections of nature.

The goal of inquiry is always the reconstruction of some indeterminate situation: "The ultimate ground of every valid proposition and warranted judgment consists in some existential reconstruction ultimately effected" (LW 12: 483). Reconstructing an existential situation sometimes requires deconstructing and even destroying many concepts and values. Often, it is the beliefs and values of the inquirer, which after all partially constitutes the situation, which must change as well:

> There are occasions when for the proper conduct of knowing as the controlling interest, the problem becomes that of reconstruction of the self engaged in inquiry. This happens when the pursuit of inquiry, according to conditions set by the need of following subject-matter where it leads, requires willingness to surrender a theory dear to the heart of an inquirer and willingness to forego reaching the conclusion he would have preferred to reach. On the other hand, the problem of reconstructing the self cannot be solved unless inquiry takes into account reconstitution of existing conditions. (LW 14: 70–71)

The developmental adjustment facilitated by reconstructive inquiry often requires both adapting the situation to our desires, interests, ideas, and purposes as well as accommodating our desires, interests, ideas, and purposes to the situation.

Since reflective inquiry is a living function, we may think of it as an organic function composed of five subfunctions or phases. These are located between the initiating "pre-reflective" disrupted, affectively disturbing doubtful situation and the "post-reflective" functionally coordinated, unified situation. Dewey insists, "In inquiry, the existence which has become doubtful always undergoes experimental reconstruction" (MW 4: 140). The pre- and postreflective situations are, in themselves, not primarily cognitive. Dewey defines inquiry thus: *Inquiry is the controlled or directed transformation of an indeterminate situation into one that is so determinate in its constituent distinctions and relations as to convert the elements of the original situation into a unified whole*" (LW 12: 108; emphasis in original). Dewey believes that the "biological antecedent conditions of an unsettled situation are involved in that state of imbalance in organic-environmental interactions" (ibid., 110). All situations are comprised of the convergent interactions of events that include the inquirer as a participant and not as a spectator. In a disrupted situation, our habitual functions of perceiving, recognizing, imagining, and so on that coordinate our responses to the environment fail us. We must stop to think, observe, and remember.

Inquiry, including scientific inquiry, begins with a disruption of functioning that determines a qualitative situation. We feel such situations before we think about them, and the feeling accompanies the thinking. Instead of starting with a problem, we start with a felt situation, with an unanalyzed whole wherein "intuition precedes conception and goes deeper" and the intuition "signifies the realization of a pervasive quality" (LW 5: 249). "Reflection and rational elaboration," writes Dewey, "spring from and make explicit a prior intuition" (ibid., 249). We begin with "perplexity, confusion, doubt due to the fact that one is implicated in an incomplete situation whose full character is not yet determined" (MW 9: 157). Unlike Descartes, for Dewey doubt is existential; we cannot be in a genuine doubt at will. In part, this is so because functional habits comprise our will not mystical psychic substances. Therefore, all inquiry is theory- and value-laden. Oftentimes, what requires deconstruction and reconstruction is the theoretical concepts along with the moral, aesthetic, and epistemological values that guide inquiry. What is wrong with many "school problems" is that they are not genuinely the student's problems because they do not feel them as their own. The doubt belongs to the book or the teacher that assigns the problem. The student's intuitions do not aid their conceptualization.

Before describing the phases comprising the reconstructive function of inquiry, it is important to realize that we may enter and exit any phase at any point, that there is no fixed sequence, we can sometimes omit steps, and often we can compress steps into one. The phases (1–5) are also recursive.

First Phase

The first phase of reflective thought is "suggestions in which the mind leaps forward to a possible solution" (LW 8: 200). Here, the "idea of what to do . . . is a substitute for direct action. It is a vicarious, anticipatory way of acting, a kind of dramatic rehearsal" (ibid., 200). "Suggestions," writes Dewey, "just 'pop into our heads,' because of the working of the psycho-physical organism, they are not logical" (LW 12: 114). Living, psychophysical, organisms will leap to conclusion using various habits of response we already have. We use ideas already in our possession to explore possible solutions, to systematically guide the determination of facts, to collect data, to engage in rational elaboration, to formulate new ideas (hypotheses), or engage in experimental testing. Sometimes, the ideas are so vague and inexact that they lead nowhere. This is a process of trial and error. Even if successful, the result is not a systematic organization of facts and ideas that will provide a cumulative development. Still, we cannot identify facts or collect data until we at least have some "idea" of what is going on, even if we are mistaken. All inquiry is concept-laden. We must start somewhere.

Second Phase

The next phase is "intellectualization" (LW 8: 201). This involves determining the problem. Dewey states, "There is a process of intellectualizing what at first is merely an emotional quality of the whole situation" (ibid., 202). We begin with an indeterminate situation of disrupted functioning, not a named problem. Dewey states, "It is a commonplace that a problem stated is well on its way to solution, for statement of the nature of a problem signifies that the underlying quality is being transformed into determinate distinctions and relations or has become an object of articulate thought" (LW 9: 249).

As given, the indeterminate situation is anoetic. The task is to transform it into a cognitively determinate situation. No matter how indeterminate a situation, there is no progress toward resolution unless there are some "constituents of a given situation which, as constituents, are settled" (LW 12: 112). That is, we are not in doubt about them just the larger whole of which they are a constituent part. Observation determines "the facts of the case" (ibid., 113). The facts of the situation "constitute the terms of the problem" (ibid., 113). Once we can name the problem, we can begin to grasp it cognitively, although we do not know exactly what the problem is until we know exactly what is the solution (ibid., 201). How we conceive (or misconceive) a situation influences what suggestions, hypotheses, and conceptual resources for solution are subsequently entertained as well as what facts we determine to constitute the situation and what data for inference we select or reject. Need, impulse, desire, and interest are at play in problem definition.

Pedagogically, the fact that thinking begins with an indeterminate situation wherein the student is in a genuine doubt and not with a determinate, stated problem has important pedagogical consequences. So too does the process of intellectualization. Different people entering the same context with different needs, desires, purposes, and making different "suggestions" might well identify different facts thereby constituting a different problem. When we simply assign problems to students there is often no impulse, no disrupted habits of conduct that internally motivate them to engage in inquiry. Dewey insists, "It is indispensable to discriminate between genuine and simulated or mock problems" (MW 9: 161). He offers two criteria. First, "Is there anything but a problem? Does the question naturally suggest itself within some situation of personal experience? Or is it an aloof thing, a problem only for the purposes of conveying instruction in some school topic? Is it the sort of trying that would arouse observation and engage experimentation outside of school?" (ibid., 161). Second, "Is it the pupils own problem, or is it the teacher's or textbook's problem, made a problem for the pupil only because he cannot get the required mark or be promoted or win the teachers approval, unless he deals with it?" (ibid., 161–162). Dewey writes, "Where schools are equipped with laboratories, shops, and gardens, where dramatizations, plays, and games are freely used, opportunities exist for reproducing situations of life, and for acquiring and applying information and ideas in the carrying forward of progressive experiences" (ibid., 169). Further, the students must be able to identity facts that constitute the situation as a problem for them. Therefore,

> The perplexing situation must be sufficiently like situations which have already been dealt with so that pupils will have some control of the means of handling it. A large part of the art of instruction lies in making the difficulty of new problems large enough to challenge thought, and small enough so that, in addition to the confusion naturally attending the novel elements, there shall be luminous familiar spots from which helpful suggestions may spring. (Ibid., 163–164)

If the student is to intellectualize the situation as their problem and not just a school problem, then there must be some parts of the larger whole that they are familiar with and may use to establish facts that "constitute the terms of the problem" (LW 12: 113). There must be data that the students can work with. That said, "It is a matter of indifference by what psychological means the subject matter for reflection is provided. Memory, observation, reading, communication, are all avenues for supplying data" (MW 9: 164).

To just turn students loose in the classroom does not mean that they have a genuine problem. Therefore, lecturing is fine as long as it helps the students to intellectualize their situation. While facts are important, educators too often think knowledge and understanding is just a heap of facts. When we treat facts as if they alone are the aim of education, as is usually the case with standardized tests and the like, the result is what Dewey calls the "cold-storage ideal of knowledge," which he thinks is "inimical to educative development" (ibid., 165). This ideal is the same as what Paulo Freire calls "the banking model," where teacher makes deposits of knowledge in the students mind. All of this pedagogical advice can reduce to a simple statement: Give students something to do and not something to learn, and then work with them to develop their inquiry.

Third Phase

The third phase involves imaginatively constructing a hypothesis to help systematically guide subsequent inquiry. Dewey states, "The possible solution presents itself, therefore, as an *idea*, just as the terms of the problem (which are facts) are instituted by observation" (LW 12: 113). "An idea is first of all an anticipation that something may happen; it marks a possibility" (ibid., 113). Whereas suggestions are just "the workings of the psycho-physical organism" that habitually "pop into our heads," hypotheses are logical. They occur when we stop and think. While organic "suggestions" are not logical, "they are both the conditions and the primary stuff of logical ideas" (ibid., 114). Hypotheses are ideas that we may use to collect further data for inference and to carry out abstract conceptual reasoning (the fourth phase) by linking the hypotheses with other concepts, and eventually testing for validity (the fifth phase). Hypotheses facilitate controlled inquiry.

Dewey makes an important distinction between existence and essence. Dewey avers, "Every existence is an event" (LW 1: 63). A situation is a convergence of events that includes the inquirer. The immediate existential situation is the only thing given in inquiry, all the rest (existential data, facts, etc.) are taken from the situation by the inquirer (LW 12: 127). Existence is the subject matter of inquiry. Dewey affirms, "Observation of facts and suggested meanings or ideas arise and develop in correspondence with each other" (ibid., 113). All inquiry is theory-laden. Existential modifications may require us to reconstruct our concepts as the inquiry unfolds. The converse also holds. An essence is the form, idea, concept, method, or such used to functionally coordinate the situation by organizing its constituent parts. Dewey notes, "[T]here is a natural bridge that joins the gap between existence and essence; namely communication, language, discourse. Failure to acknowledge the presence and operation of natural interaction in the form of communication creates the gulf between existence and essence, and that gulf is factitious and gratuitous" (LW 1: 133).

Experience is an organism-environment interaction. What we immediately experience is existence. However, the meaning of existence (a given situation or the facts taken from it) is a sociolinguistic construction. No one can create from nothing. Meaning is created from our immediate experience of existence. Here is an analogy. Existence is given like grapes on a vine. Like meaning, grape juice is a human construction. Knowledge concerns those meanings that inquiry establishes as true (Dewey prefers the phrase "warrantably assertible"). Knowledge is like wine, the distilled import of the grapes. "Essence is never existence," Dewey remarks, "yet it is the essence, the distilled import, of existence" (ibid., 144).

Meaning and knowledge are forms of existence that allows us to mediate between immediate experiences of existence. The immediate experience of existence is ineffable. Linguistic experience of existence is meaningful; we may express it using vocal gestures (e.g., speech) or symbols such as the words on this page. Warrantably assertible meanings yield knowledge of existence. There is reality as given, the immediate experience of existence, and then there is reality constructed from the materials given, meaning and knowledge that give linguistic and logical form to what is given. We must never construct a dualism out of the distinction between existence as given and existence as we meaningfully construct it for our human purposes.

Dewey did not understand induction and deduction in the traditional sense of moving from particular to universal (induction) or from universal to particular (deduction). Instead, for him, it meant movement from selected data (facts) to meanings while deduction or reasoning meant working out the logical implications of meanings. Meanwhile, "the connection between fact and meaning is made only by an act in the ordinary physical sense of the word" (MW 13: 63). Pragmatism derives from the classical Greek "pragma," meaning "deed" or act. Because intelligent action connects universal meaning (e.g., an idea) to particular facts, empirical reasoning never yields certainty, but only what Dewey calls "warranted assertability" (see LW 12).

What we must not do is construct a theory versus fact dualism. Instead, theory and fact are subfunctions of a single function of forming a judgment that allows us to successfully transform the original situation. Dewey concludes,

[P]erceptual and conceptual materials are instituted in functional correlatively with each other, in such a manner that the former locates and describes the problem while the latter represents a possible method of solution. Both are determination in and by inquiry of the original problematic situation whose pervasive quality controls their institution and their contents. Both are finally checked by their capacity to work together to introduce a resolved unified situation. As distinctions they represent logical divisions of labor. (Ibid., 115)

We must not ignore the "the function of ideas in directing observation and in ascertaining relevant facts" (ibid., 114). As concepts emerge and evolve, we may have to reconstruct our facts. Once we have ideas to work with, we may use them to assign meaning (to interpret) what we see. In that case, we do not just see things; we see them as something. We do not just see some lines and color; we see them *as* the face of our lover. All inquiry is concept-laden and the ideas or concepts (including those systems of concepts we call theories) may undergo reconstruction as novel facts emerge. Likewise, emergent concepts and fact may require us to reconstruct facts.

There is surprising educational insight that arises if we can appreciate the functional correlation of the material with the method of solution. In education, there is a bad tendency to separate educational methods from the content we wish to teach. The assumption is all we need is good teaching methods while the student or subject being taught is largely irrelevant. This is wrong. In Dewey's view, method is simply the functional coordination, the structure, of the subject matter most useful for the purpose of instruction. Therefore, he concludes, "Method means that arrangement of subject matter which makes it most effective in use. Never is method something outside of the material" (ibid., 172). More fully, the best method of teaching is one that functionally coordinates (arranges) the subject matter best for connecting to the needs, impulses, interests, desires, purposes, and cognitive state (habits, skills, beliefs, knowings, etc.) of each individual student. Similarly, we may construct different meanings from the same existential material of immediate experience.

Reflecting on the educational significance of the third phase, Dewey begins by declaring, "The correlate in thinking of facts, data, knowledge already acquired, is suggestions, inferences, conjectured meanings, suppositions, tentative explanations—ideas, in short" (ibid., 168). Inference, for Dewey, makes connections among data. For him, inference is an embodied activity that makes use of innate reflexes, but far more importantly, it relies on habits. Jumping to conclusions depends on what habits of response "pop into mind." Unconscious inferences occur when we are not aware of a given habit. Controlled inquiry seeks to render habits of inference conscious, and hence, controllable;

otherwise, they control us. Experts in a field make better unconscious and conscious inferences. So-called tacit knowledge involves good habits of inferential "know how" of which the knower is unaware. The transference of learning remains a largely unresolved problem in educational theory because few consider the role of habits. Embodied habits transfer learning from one situation to another.

Formulating a logical hypothesis is an imaginative, creative act. An idea concerns conceptual possibilities and not factual actualities. As such, it is a work of art. Even if the inquirer is only transferring an idea they already have to a new context, it involves creative imagination. Often, however, the inquirer creates a new idea by connecting or disconnecting the ones they already have. That is, we create ideas by using such poetic devices as metaphor, metonymy, simile, and such. Dewey writes,

> [A] thought (what a thing suggests but is not as it is presented) is creative,—an incursion into the novel. It involves some inventiveness. What is suggested must, indeed, be familiar in some context; the novelty, the inventive devising, clings to the new light in which it is seen, the different use to which it is put...The same is true of every striking scientific discovery, every great invention, every admirable artistic production. Only silly folk identify creative originality with the extraordinary and fanciful; others recognize that its measure lies in putting everyday things to uses which had not occurred to others. The operation is novel, not the materials out of which it is constructed. (MW 9: 165–166)

We would also understand the transference of learning much better if we would attend to the artistic, creative, and inventive component. The transference of learning is largely a poetic activity wherein we transfer old habits to new contexts. This often involves the release of impulse. The educational conclusion that follows from this is that "all thinking is original in a projection of considerations which have not been previously apprehended" (ibid., 166). All genuine thinking is creative. This is why discovery-learning approaches are so pedagogically important. Other approaches, such as the "cold-storage" method so dominant in schools, actually block creativity; hence, they block thinking. They are as mindless as they seem.

Children at every age can learn the joy of learning if we allow them to creatively discover the meaning of educational situations for themselves. As Dewey notes, children actually experience joy in discovery learning, which derives from actual intellectual creativeness. Interestingly, as important as these insights are, there is something else perhaps even more important, which is that "no thought, no idea, can possibly be conveyed as an idea from one person to another. When it is told, it is, to the one to whom it is told, another given fact, not an idea" (ibid., 166). Newton's second law states that force equals mass times acceleration (F=ma). Unless you have had experience using this law, you do not truly understand the idea. It is just simply a fact useful for a quiz show or a standardized test, but it is not an idea until you can use it to creatively solve a problem in the physical world around you. If you can use it to solve a problem in a book, you only have partial understanding.

The foregoing leads to the stunning conclusion that all teaching is by indirection and that that teaching does not imply learning:

> When the parent or teacher has provided the conditions which stimulate thinking and has taken a sympathetic attitude toward the activities of the learner by entering into a common or conjoint experience, all has been done which a second party can do to instigate learning. The rest lies with the one directly concerned. If he cannot devise his own solution (not of course in isolation, but in correspondence with the teacher and other pupils) and find his own way out he will not learn, not even if he can recite some correct answer with one hundred per cent accuracy. (Ibid., 167)

A parent or teacher may do everything they possibly can to provide the appropriate conditions for learning, but the hungry, abused, brain-damaged child may not learn. Perhaps, they simply just lack the capacity. Further, good education involves much than good teaching. Eventually, it is a social function, which means it is always political. Does society tolerate childhood hunger or abuse? Does the school system itself aid such practices?

Fourth Phase

The fourth phase of thinking is reasoning. It may involve symbolically developing the hypothesis in conjunction with the situation abstractly defined as a problem until we can arrive at a form that promises to restore functional coordination. Observations, facts, and data refer to what exists; they are existential. Hypotheses, concepts or ideas, are abstract, formal, and logical; they are essences we have extracted through prior or present inquiry. Working with ideas involves "thinking" in the narrow, confined sense that most people have in mind when they use the word. We work out abstract ideas "in the head" or perhaps symbolize them and work them out with pencil and paper. We may carry out logically valid implications that compound ideas with each other. Algebraic manipulations are a typical example. We can develop, connect, and modify ideas without rising up from our chair. In this way, we strive to explain and predict phenomena. The result is a plan of action, an explanation, or prediction of anticipated consequences.

Reasoning organizes and systematizes thought. Dewey provides an example that contemporary educators should appreciate when he discusses the use of measurement in education. Dewey points out that quantitative measures (e.g., test results, statistics, etc.) only yield scientific knowledge when they are capable of being developed by reasoning "into other and more fruitful forms" (LW 8: 205). In his day, he found such a consideration "fatal to the claim to scientific standing of many educational measurements" (ibid., 205). All too often, the same observation holds for a great deal of so-called educational research in our day as well, whether quantitative or qualitative. That is why it is often difficult to translate educational research into useful practice.

Although reasoning appears totally abstract and decontextualized, that is not correct (see Dewey's "Context and Thought," LW 6: 3–21). The course of reasoning that a person is actually able to carry out depends on the stockpile of knowledge they have already obtained. This knowledge not only depends upon the individual's previous experience and education, but also on the culture and condition of intelligent inquiry within that culture. While reasoning helps extend knowledge, it always depends upon what is already known as well as the degree to which what is already known is public and communicable. This is why good teaching must always know and connect to student's background knowledge. Dewey thought open, democratic societies always had an epistemological advantage over closed, autocratic societies. It is much the same with open versus closed-minded individuals.

In reasoning, we explore the valid possible consequences of our ideas. If our reasoning is sound, then our conclusions are actually true. Reasoning is designed to preserve a specified property, usually truth. Reasoning is said to be valid when if the property is in the premises then it is present in every conclusion drawn from the premises. A course of reasoning is called sound if the reasoning is valid in the sense just stipulated and all the premises have the specified property (e.g., truth). Determining soundness is the function of the fifth phase of reflective thinking.

Fifth Phase

The final phase involves a return to actual empirical material that tests the implications of hypotheses, reasoning, and conclusions to see if they are experimentally sound. Often direct observation is enough to corroborate the factual truth of a hypothetical explanation or prediction. However,

> In other cases...conditions are deliberately arranged in accord with the requirements of an idea or hypothesis to see if the results theoretically indicated by the idea actually occur. If it is found that the experimental results agree with the theoretical, or rationally deduced, results, and if there is reason to believe that only the conditions in question would yield such results, the confirmation is so strong as to induce a conclusion—at least until contrary facts shall indicate the advisability of its revision. (LW 8: 205–206)

Of course, sometimes the empirical test fails to confirm our hypothesis, or perhaps we made an error in reasoning. Even when either of these occurs, the inquirer learns a great deal. Because the failed prediction occurred as the consequence of reasoned thought, the thinker may systematically modify his or her thinking and try again rather that just guessing wildly. Learning to make good use of our mistakes is as important as learning to make good use of our successes. Either way, students may learn to reason well, but only if they have an opportunity to try experiments for themselves.

Summary

Properly understood, these five phases of reflective inquiry "make thinking itself into an experience," that is, the experience of thinking (MW 9: 157). It is the experience whereby we reconstruct our habits of action and, thereby, our minds, selves, society, institutions, and cultural customs.

Inquiry is artistically creative in harmonizing disrupted situations. Dewey declares, "Knowledge or science, as a work of art, like any other work of art, confers upon things traits and potentialities which did not previously belong to them" (LW 1: 285). When that occurs, the satisfaction yields the basis of consummatory aesthetic experience, which is why Dewey states, "Scientific thought is...in its turn, a specialized form of art" (LW 5: 252). He insists that "science itself is but a central art auxiliary to the generation and utilization of other arts" (LW 10: 33). In an earlier work, Dewey notes that "art, the mode of activity that is charged with meanings capable of immediately enjoyed possession—is the complete culmination of nature, and that science...conducts natural events to this happy issue" (LW 1: 269). Dewey further states, "Thinking is preeminently an art; knowledge and propositions which are the products of thinking are works of art, as much so as statuary and symphonies" (ibid., 283). In "The Sources of a Science of Education," Dewey concludes, "[I]n concrete operation, education is an art, either a mechanical [technological] art or a fine art, is unquestionable. If there were an opposition between science and art, I should be compelled to side with those who assert that education is an art. But there is no opposition, although there is a distinction" (LW 5: 6).

For the ancient Greeks, *techne* was the form of knowledge associated with poiesis, which meant making, creating, or calling into existence. The artistic practice of inquiry seeks to produce aesthetically pleasing artifacts. Thinking that inquiry uncreatively grasps antecedent existences apart from their interactions with us is such a serious error that Dewey calls it "the philosophic fallacy" (LW 1: 34). The fallacy occurs when we convert "eventual functions into antecedent existence" (ibid., 34). When this occurs, the human contribution to knowledge, including emotionally influenced selection of data in a situation, imagination, and reasoning is overlooked.

Inquiry includes moral inquiry. Here too, the goal is to produce aesthetically satisfying forms of functional coordination: "The Greek emphasis upon Kalokagathos, the Aristotelian identification of virtue with the proportionate mean, are indications of an acute estimate of grace, rhythm, and harmony as dominant traits of good conduct. The modern mind has been much less sensitive to esthetic values in general and to these values in conduct in particular" (LW 7: 271).

The Kalokagathos refers to the classical Greek notion that the good, the beautiful, and the harmonious are one. Dewey titles the opening chapter of *Art as Experience* as "The Live Creature" and concludes, "Because experience is the fulfillment of an organism in its struggles and achievements in a world of things, it is art in germ. Even in its rudimentary forms, it contains the promise of that delightful perception which is esthetic experience" (LW 10: 25). The animal pleasure of functionally coordinated consummatory experience obtained after long struggle is the basis of aesthetics. Chapter two is titled, "The Live Creature and 'Ethereal Things.'" There Dewey connects the struggle for life with the creation of "ethereal things," a term borrowed from Keats to designate things never before called into existence. Examples include the currently heaviest element in the periodic table, Ununoctium (atomic number 118), the United Nations Declaration of Human Rights, and van Gogh's, "The Starry Night." These would not exist without Homo sapiens. Human experience is part of the endless disclosure and actualization of possibilities within an unfinished, interactive, and continuously evolving universe.

RE-/DE-/CONSTRUCTION

Deweyan inquiry involves what today may be called phases of construction, reconstruction, and even deconstruction (although the latter was not yet part of the vocabulary of Dewey's time, he rather spoke of criticism in place of what we here term deconstruction). Construction, reconstruction, and deconstruction are three phases or subfunctions of a single critical-creative function. The emphasis shifts from moment to moment, but each interpenetrates the other two and none can be fully understood when isolated from the others.

Construction

Without meaning makers in the universe, there would be no meanings. Human beings construct their own meanings from their experience of existence. All meanings are products of sociolinguistic coconstruction as we saw in part 1. These constructions provide the inheritance of cultural meanings that are passed from generation to generation. As they are socialized, each individual incorporates these meanings in their own unique way, as they become part of a community of interpretation and practice. Individuals are biologically (genetically) unique and each has their own unique experiences. Also, because the common inheritance is so great, each individual only comes to posses a small part of the whole. Culture seizes no two persons the same. Therefore, each individual must construct her or his understanding for themselves within the larger interpretative community. To some extent, individuals must reconstruct cultural meanings in the very act of learning them.

Meanings that define operations, which when carried out secure the intended consequences, are true meanings (see LW 1: 128). That there is a poisonous snake underneath your feet right now is a meaningful statement, but, hopefully, when you carry out the operations you will learn it is false. Inquiry and the five phases of research and reflective learning allow individuals, communities of inquirers, and entire cultures to determine if constructed meanings are true or false. Likewise, human beings construct their own values. They may have an immediate experience of value, but much as we distinguish true from false meanings through inquiry, we may distinguish objects of immediate value from those that are genuinely valuable. The immediate value of unprotected sex is evident, but many would not find it valuable if they reflected upon such possible consequences as sexually transmitted diseases and unwanted pregnancy. Those values that prove upon reflection to be genuinely valuable provide good guidance to human conduct.

The reflective method allows individual learners and entire societies not only to appropriate cultural constructions of meaning, but also to validate them and, where necessary, reconstruct them. In an evolving Darwinian universe, meaning constructions are not only always falsifiable but they are also always contingent. Therefore, they are subject to reconstruction, deconstruction, and outright existential destruction.

Reconstruction

"Rekonstruction" in German refers to the more specific and limited sense of re-production of previously established constructions. It refers to imitation and reiteration rather than creative renewal such as Dewey requires (see Neubert 2003). Still, as previously indicated, there is some degree of Deweyan reconstruction when any individual succeeds in learning any cultural construction.

For Dewey, we engage in reconstruction whenever we find ourselves in a disrupted situation. Inquiry and the five phases of reflective thinking allow us to reconstruct such situations. These situations often arise when the existing cultural constructions fail an individual, a community of inquiry, or perhaps even the culture as a whole. As noted earlier, often it is the meanings or values of the inquirer that partially constitutes the situation, which must change to complete inquiry successfully.

Cultural meanings can expand and develop through a constant process of reconstruction. A good example is the very idea of "number." Negative numbers were in use by the sixth century B.C.E. in India and in Greece by the third century B.C.E. The ancient Greeks understood natural numbers and rational numbers, but were shocked and dismayed by the discovery of irrational numbers in the sixth century B.C.E. They were never fully comfortable with zero. Complex (or imaginary) numbers did not become prominent until the sixteenth century A.C.E. Many other numbers that have emerged over the millennia and the meaning of numbers continues to evolve. For instance, there is Chaitin's number, which is an irrational (or real) number that informally represents the probability that a randomly-chosen program will halt. It is a definable, but not computable, number.

What holds for the concept of number also holds for all concepts including scientific, political, and economic concepts. Any concept, any meaning, is a contingent construction subject to continuous reconstruction and deconstruction.

Deconstruction and Destruction

Dewey thinks we are participants in an endlessly evolving, unfinished and unfinishable, open, and pluralistic Darwinian universe wherein no construction will ever prove complete, fixed, and final. He writes, "The stablest thing we can speak of is not free from conditions set to it by other things...A thing may endure *secula seculorum* and yet not be everlasting; it will crumble before the gnawing tooth of time, as it exceeds a certain measure" (LW 1: 63).

In time, destruction will come to all that exists. Every construction will collapse. The task of reflective inquiry is to aid us in rendering some things (including ours species) relatively stable within the precarious flux of events. In this connection, we need capacities of deconstruction in order to save us from destruction and help us to reconstruct and adapt the stabilities that we need to live by in a continuously changing and precarious world. In such a world, deconstruction is not for dilettantes. It is playful, but it is serious play. For the purposes of understanding deconstruction, however, the fact that interests us most is that even the most stable things depend on precarious conditions.

Recall that for Dewey, everything is in actual or potential interaction. For growth to occur, we must have the potential to develop. When we grow, we actualize our potential by interacting with other things and individuals. "There are at a given time unactualized potentialities in an individual," according to Dewey, "because and in as far as there are in existence other things with which it has not as yet interacted" (LW 14: 109). If we properly understand Dewey's functionalism, then it becomes clear that our interactive relations constitute our very identity. They are the conditions of our being and our development. The idea that interactions with alterity, with others different from ourselves, allow us to grow is also critical to Dewey's thinking about pluralistic democracy. In "Creative Democracy—The Task Before Us," Dewey affirms,

> A genuinely democratic faith in peace is faith in the possibility of conducting disputes, controversies and conflicts as cooperative undertakings

in which both parties learn by giving the other a chance to express itself, instead of having one party conquer by forceful suppression of the other—a suppression which is none the less one of violence when it takes place by psychological means of ridicule, abuse, intimidation, instead of by overt imprisonment or in concentration camps. To cooperate by giving differences a chance to show themselves because of the belief that the expression of difference is not only a right of the other persons but is a means of enriching one's own life-experience, is inherent in the democratic personal way of life. (Ibid., 228)

Here, Dewey is concerned with symbolic as well as physical violence. He is also concerned that we recognize that otherness and difference enhance the life of a pluralistic democracy and preserve the permanent possibility of individual and social growth.

The word "deconstruction" is unavoidably entangled with the writings of Jacques Derrida who argues, "Deconstruction certainly entails a moment of affirmation. Indeed, I cannot conceive of a radical critique which would not be ultimately motivated by some sort of affirmation, acknowledged or not. Deconstruction always presupposes affirmation" (see Kearney 1984, 118). Derrida is quite clear about what he wants to affirm. Deconstruction, for him, is "an openness towards the other" (see ibid., 124). Deconstruction problematizes because it constantly points away from itself toward absence and otherness. It welcomes in advance the excluded other. Derrida states deconstruction's affirmation this way: "I mean that deconstruction is, in itself, a positive response to an alterity which necessarily calls, summons or motivates it. Deconstruction is therefore vocation—a response to a call. The other, as the other than self, the other that opposes self-identity, is not something that can be detected and disclosed within a philosophical space" (Derrida 1984, 168). Deconstruction urges recognition and respect for what is different, left out, or queer. It is this positive response to the other, to those persons and situations different from the "norm" that, in writing our paper, we want most to urge the community of educators to consider. We should view deconstruction as expanding and releasing constructive potential for creative human growth by permanently preserving the possibility for interaction with others different from ourselves.

The immense power of Dewey's philosophy as reconstruction goes beyond the power of the reflective method of inquiry alone: "Only a philosophy of pluralism, of genuine indetermination, and of change which is real and intrinsic gives significance to individuality. It alone justifies struggle in creative activity and gives opportunity for the emergence of the genuinely new" (LW 14: 101). Dewey's philosophy of reconstruction seeks to exercise not only critical and reflective intelligence, but creative intelligence as well. In some ways, it resembles Derrida's deconstruction in its openness to otherness and difference, although the similarity should not be overstated.

For Dewey, intelligence, including the reflective use of intelligence indicated by the five phases discussed earlier, is itself a contingent construction, hence subject to reconstruction and deconstruction. Dewey makes no appeal to supernal forms of rationality either transcendent (e.g., Plato) or transcendental (e.g., Kant). Because there is nothing antecedently existing outside of our sociocultural constructions, for Dewey, all critique is immanent critique and creative reconstruction of cultural meanings, beliefs, knowings, norms, and values in the hopes of positively affecting subsequent self-development and the education of future generations. Part 3 will discuss immanent critique further.

Deconstruction problematizes meaning, knowings, and values that seem indubitable to many. It questions, criticizes, and reopens what others think are settled, beyond reproach, and closed. It disrupts our habitual and customary way of doing things. It renews the human eros. Dewey understands philosophy as reconstruction in much the same way.

Dewey's philosophy as reconstruction is criticism in its generality, a "criticism of criticisms" (LW 1: 298). Dewey affirms Matthew Arnold's dictum that "poetry is criticism of life" and says, "A sense of possibilities that are unrealized and that might be realized are when they are put in contrast with actual conditions, the most penetrating "criticism" of the latter that can be made" (LW 10: 349). By poetry, he means creative, artistic activity of all kinds. Art aids morality by grasping the ideal possibility beyond the actual. Dewey wishes to harness the power of poetic trope to release the ideal possibilities within experience to go beyond good and evil as conventionally defined. He thinks that "the ideal factors of morality are always and everywhere beyond good and evil" (ibid., 351). Dewey also turns to the power of literature to explore the meanings that poetry creates.

However, Dewey also sought to simultaneously harness the power of science. We may explore meanings in literature while in science we seek truthful meanings. Literature playfully introduces and explores meanings and provides powerful vicarious experiences, but it need not make actual, concrete, and existential reference. Still, imagination is critical to inquiry. Dewey proclaims, "Philosophic discourse partakes both of scientific and literary discourse" (ibid., 304). We construct meanings and explore possibilities. We may strive to construct these possibilities in the actual world. What starts as a mere possibility may sometimes end up a factual truth, which is why we must not construct a dualism between literature (including poetry and other textual practices) and science. However, it is important to maintain the distinction. Poetry and literature as well as science and logic can cooperate in an endless cycle of critical and creative construction, deconstruction, and reconstruction.

SELECTION OF TARGET TEXTS

Part 2 focuses on three extraordinarily insightful fragments of Dewey's work. The first is chapter 4, "Changed Conceptions of Experience and Reason" of *Reconstruction and Philosophy*, which is among the works that most influenced Richard Rorty. Experience and reason are critical concepts for any educator to comprehend since they are so crucial to the process of education. Being an empirical naturalist, Dewey does not think we are born with reason. Indeed, he would rather completely change the educational and philosophical conversation so that we could talk about "intelligence," which for him includes emotions, imagination, embodied habits, and, in the case of social intelligence, sympathy. For him, experience occurs any and everywhere sentient organisms interact with their environment. As educators, we are usually most interested in human experience. Because all experience involves transactions with the environment, Dewey thought we could only educate indirectly through the environment, even when we give dry lectures. The mind is not a computer. Ultimately, the student decides on what he or she wishes to attend, understand, and reflect upon. The teacher may offer rewards or punishments, but the student may always refuse, and many either refuse or drop out.

The second fragment is from his classic, *Experience and Education*. The book was written to correct many of the misreadings of his work, especially by his so-called "progressive" supporters. It is from chapter 3 titled, "Criteria of Experience." There Dewey discusses what is required for an experience to be genuinely educative, instead of miseducative. Many still misunderstand the chapter because they do not comprehend the profound philosophy of experience that sustains the insights he provides.

Dewey was particularly interested in cultivating reflective experience, by which he meant intelligent inquiry that arises when human action encounters obstacles that we cannot overcome or when we wish to examine and perhaps critique received customs, habits, knowledge, and values. The final target text is from chapter 7 of *How We Think*, which is titled "Analysis of Reflective Thinking." The fragment itself is called, "The Essential Functions of Reflective Activity." These functions include suggestions (guessing), formulation of the problem from inchoate experience, the construction of a hypothesis, thinking, and test. They have complicated reticulated and recursive structures with many subfunctions. They are hardly ever worked through in linear fashion. Far too many educators have failed to notice the recursive, nonlinear character of Dewey's analysis of reflective thinking.

Part 3

EDUCATION, COMMUNICATION, AND DEMOCRACY—THE COMMUNICATIVE TURN

In the preceding parts of this volume, we have seen that educational growth, for Dewey, consists of the continual reorganization or reconstruction of experience. "The criterion of the value of school education is the extent in which it creates a desire for continued growth and supplies means for making the desire effective in fact" (MW 9: 58). Growth depends on our ability to form habits. Habits endow experience with continuity and anchor it within the body (see Kestenbaum 1977; Alexander 1987; Garrison 1998). Their range extends from relatively passive "habituations" to "active habits" (see MW 9: 46ff.). "Habituations" are accommodations to usual contexts of living that are largely taken for granted in everyday practices and seldom rise to the level of reflection. "Active habits" are dynamic and flexible forces of intentional control—for example, powers of practical manipulation, intellectual grasp, and constructive organization—that we rely on in our attempts to adjust the environment to our needs. Although we can never completely transcend the habitual contexts of our experience, education as a process of continual growth depends on our ability to use habits as flexible resources in specific and changing situations and thereby partly to transform them in accord with the demands of the situation. This implies the extension or reorganization of old habits as well as the creation of new ones.

Educational growth is a constructive process that develops from within experience. It feeds on interaction with others in a sociocultural as well as natural environment. It can be furthered by others, but it cannot be imposed from outside. Learning from experience basically means learning through one's own activities ("doing") and the activities of others (e.g., within a learning community or a classroom) in connection with an observation of the effects produced by the activities ("undergoing"). It is successful to the degree that it "adds to the meaning of experience" and increases the ability "to direct the course of subsequent experience" (MW 9: 82). "An ounce of experience is better than a ton of theory," writes Dewey (ibid., 151). Without vital connection to the experience of learners, learning soon degenerates into a merely symbolic procedure, because any theory only gains significance and verifiable meaning in its application to experience. Even a "very humble experience" is "capable of generating and carrying any amount of theory," whereas "a theory apart from an experience cannot be definitely grasped even as theory" (ibid.).

EDUCATION AND COMMUNICATION

Dewey thinks that it is crucial for education to provide learning environments that offer a sufficient amount of opportunities, occasions, resources, and inspirations for the active reconstruction of the experience of learners (see MW 9: 82). We cannot educate directly because we cannot vicariously have experiences for others.[1] They themselves must have the opportunity of experimenting with their world (see ibid., 147). We educate indirectly through the environments we shape (see ibid., 23). And it is important to see that communication is a basic component of such learning environments. We ourselves, as educators and learners in mutual relationships, are part of these environments.

Dewey therefore believes that we need a theory of communication in order to understand the practice of education and conduct it intelligently. Communication is at the heart of the educative process. Earlier in this volume (part 1), we have seen that Dewey praises communication as the most wonderful "of all affairs." Communication makes participation possible. "Communication is the process of creating participation, of making common what had been isolated and singular; and part of the miracle it achieves is that, in being communicated, the conveyance of meaning gives body and definiteness to the experience of the one who utters as well as to that of those who listen" (LW 10: 248–249). Through communication, events change from the level of external push and pull to that of revealed and transparent meanings. They become elements in a universe of discourse. They can be reflected upon and manipulated in thought. They can be scrutinized and contextualized in many news ways. They can be seen in new and multiple perspectives shared by a community of understanding. Through communication, natural events are readapted to meet "the requirements of conversation, whether it be public discourse or that preliminary discourse termed thinking. Events turn into objects, things with a meaning" (LW 1: 132). They can henceforth be referred to even when they are not present or do not exist. They can be "operative among things distant in space and time, through vicarious presence in a new medium" (ibid.).

In so far as it involves participation and sharing, all communication, for Dewey, is "educative" (MW 9: 8). It has "educative power" (ibid., 9). This is true not only because it provides the participants within a mutually shared relationship with opportunities to learn from each other's experience, but also because it makes it necessary for them to take the perspective(s) of the other(s) with regard to their own actions and experiences. The imaginative projection into the position of others leads to an extension of the horizons of one's own experience—be it as far-reaching or as modest as the case may be. Dewey insists that communication is not only a means for conveying information. It is also a quality in and of experience that is directly had as an end. Communication has an instrumental as well as a consummatory (i.e., immediately fulfilling) dimension. With regard to the latter, Dewey also uses the term "final." We find his most elaborate philosophical discussion of the matter in the fifth chapter of *Experience and Nature*. Among other things he writes,

> Communication is uniquely instrumental and uniquely final. It is instrumental as liberating us from the otherwise overwhelming pressure of events and enabling us to live in a world of things that have meaning. It is final as a sharing in the objects and arts precious to a community, a sharing whereby meanings are enhanced, deepened and solidified...communication and its congenial objects...are worthy as means, because they are the only means that make life rich and varied in meanings. They are worthy as ends, because in such ends man is lifted from his immediate isolation and shares in a communion of meanings. (LW 1: 159)

Communication relies on the use of signs. Dewey did not develop a systematic approach to the theory of signs (semiotics). However, he clearly appreciated the work of his former teacher Charles Sanders Peirce who embraced a potentially infinite three-part semiotics comprised of sign, interpretant, and object. Here is how Peirce defines a sign: "Anything [is a *sign*] which determines something else (its *interpretant*) to refer to an object to which itself refers (its *object*) in the same way, the interpretant becoming in turn a sign, and so on *ad infinitum*" (CP 2: 303; cited in Derrida 1974, 50). Peirce's pragmatic semiotics differs dramatically from the two-part semiotics advanced by the pioneering structuralist Ferdinand de Saussure in which the sign is comprised of a formal signifier (i.e., a sound pattern) and a signified (the concept).

Against the background of what has been said about the importance of communication in Dewey's philosophy, it will, maybe, not surprise the reader that Dewey repeatedly calls attention to an aspect of Peirce's semiotics that many other interpreters virtually ignore. Peirce insisted on the primacy of concrete actions (structured operations) necessary to bring about the movement of semiosis and to construct the referent of signs and the role of embodied habits involved in all generality. Dewey also reminds us that for Peirce, "linguistic signs are modes or forms of *communication*, and thus are intrinsically 'social'" (LW 15: 151; emphasis changed). Unlike Dewey and many other pragmatists (including Mead and Peirce), almost all structuralist and poststructuralist underestimate the social acquisition of language.

Dewey's rich and thick understanding of communication is essential to his educational thought. Following him, we can speak of a principle of shared activities (see MW 9: 18ff.) that is of fundamental significance for education and learning. According to this principle, education occurs in everyday lifeworldly practices as a side effect of shared activities with others. These activities engender a vital interest in their joint execution because they appeal to the learners as immediately meaningful and rewarding. The resultant communities of action are a precondition for all genuine social life. They are constitutive for democracy as a lived experience. As we also already saw earlier in this volume (part 1), Dewey observes that the verbal connection between the words "common," "community," and "communication" is not incidental. The participants in a community have many "things" in common because of the communication through which they partake in shared possession of meanings (see MW 9: 7). These "things"—like common aims, beliefs, hopes, knowledge, and understanding—cannot be transmitted directly (physically, as it were) from one to another. They depend on communication as an educative process of active involvement in shared activities that entails like emotional, intellectual, and practical habits in those who participate. Communication is necessary to coordinate human activities and to secure human survival. Language is its tool. The fruit of communication is education through which the social and cultural life is transmitted and to which we owe all our opportunities for leading a humane life. Communication, in school as outside, must be mutual in order to be educative. If the individuals cannot have their own active share in communication and cooperation—which implies articulating their own views and taking their own responsibilities—if there are merely subjected to the wit and will of others, no community of action can emerge.

Dewey believes that even in highly complex societies many basic learning experiences occur through immediate forms of participation in the social life of a culture. He speaks of "indirect or incidental education" (MW 9: 21)—elsewhere he even uses the more modern term "socialization" (ibid., 88)—to denote processes through which our experience is always already embedded and interwoven through communication with the experience of others. "Active connections with others are such an intimate and vital part of our own concerns that it is impossible to draw sharp lines, such as would enable us to say, 'Here my experience ends; there yours begins'" (ibid., 194). Formal education in school or other educational institutions should connect with this educational potentiality of communication. Because of their larger and richer life-experience, teachers and educators have the responsibility to supply the necessary resources for the growing experience of learners, which will enable them to develop their own activities in viable directions of culturally relevant learning. The viability of these resources (like information, knowledge, skills, and values) is measured by the extent to which learners can put them into service of their own constructive learning processes. "The place of communication in personal doing supplies us with a criterion for estimating the value of informational material in school. Does it grow naturally out of some question with which the student is concerned? Does it fit into his more direct acquaintance so as to increase its efficacy and deepen its meaning?" (Ibid.). Information is educative if it meets these two requirements. Communication, in school as outside, must be mutual in order to be educative. This even implies the possibility of role change so that, in shared activity, the teacher becomes a learner and the learner becomes, "without knowing it," a teacher (ibid., 167).

LEARNING AND JOINT ACTIVITIES

In accord with his overall concept of experience, it is a basic assumption of Dewey's pragmatic understanding of education that "[e]very educative process should begin with *doing something*; and the necessary training of sense perception, memory, imagination and judgment should grow out of the conditions and needs of what is being done" (MW 4: 185; emphasis in original). Rather than an arbitrarily imposed task, the starting point for learning should be joint activities in communication with other learners that appeal to them as inherently significant and worthwhile. This is the way in which learning in itself takes places even before any specific instruction and schooling sets in. Formal education in school should connect with these informal learning processes by providing learning environments—a "miniature world" (ibid., 186)—that appeal to the natural life functions of pupils and offer them diverse opportunities for active and constructive learning experiences.

The more intellectual aspects of education, too, should develop out of the needs and potentialities of joint activities. The necessary contents of learning, the ideas and principles, the store of information and knowledge, as well as the necessary habits of deliberation and reflection should be organically connected with the learner's activities. "All thinking at its outset is planning, forecasting, forming purposes, selecting and arranging means for their most economical and successful realization" (MW 4: 187). Pedagogical communication should cluster about what Dewey calls "occupations."[2] This didactical concept stands for activities whose significance transcends the mere context of schooling. The primary aims lie in the activity itself and its respective motifs, objects, ends, and requirements. Instead of information being "driven into pupils" and accumulated in isolation just for the purpose of schooling (see ibid., 187–188), learning takes place as a side effect of joint activities because these activities cannot be successfully fulfilled without extension of the horizons of the learners' experience and knowledge. It is a by-product of solving real and relevant problems. Therefore, occupations must be sufficiently social, complex, comprehensive, stimulating, and suggestive for multilayered and continuously growing experiences. Drawing on the experiences of his own famous school experiment, the Laboratory School at the University of Chicago (1896–1904), Dewey gives us examples like gardening, horticulture, cooking, weaving, and shop work with different materials (see ibid., 189)—activities that, he insists, afford manifold opportunities for scientific, geographic, historical, economical, and societal learning as well as affective, aesthetic, and artistic dimensions of human experience (see MW 1: 1–109). But one may also think of theater projects, ways of participation in the self-administration of schools, explorations into local neighborhoods and production spheres, and activities in the reconstruction of school life or in the construction of club houses for pupils (see the broad array of examples in MW 8: 205–404). Today, we might add, for example, learning projects in which students produce their own TV news program and thus learn to engage constructively and critically with the social production and proliferation of news through modern mass media (see Reich 2005, 118–145).

Dewey thinks that the educational significance of such occupations lies, among other things, in the fact that they inspire learning through one's own explorations, inventions, constructions, and applications in communication with other learners and thus educate them to take an experimental attitude toward their own learning. They learn to treat ideas, theories, and principles as working hypotheses for the solution of problems and not as fixed and dogmatic truths, established once and for all, whose validity is to be accepted without question from some form of higher authority. "An education based upon the pragmatic conception would inevitably turn out persons who were alive to the necessity of continually testing their ideas and beliefs by putting them into practical application, and of revising their beliefs on the basis of the results of such application" (MW 4: 188).

Further, Dewey argues that an education based on occupations introduces forms of pedagogical communication that have the potential to change the moral life of schools. The school "would lose the special code of ethics…which must characterize it as long as it is isolated." Instead of "egoism, social stratification, and antagonisms," it would nurture powers of cooperation, solidarity, social sympathy, and coordinated division of work (MW 4: 191).

THE DEMOCRATIC VISION

Dewey's philosophy of communication is of course closely connected to his political thought. His insistence that the educative process consists of a continual reconstruction of the experience of the learner, that "education is all one with growing," that it "has no end beyond itself" (MW 9: 58) and that "the aim of education" is "to enable individuals to continue their education" (ibid., 107) ultimately expresses his belief in democracy and democratic self-governance which underlies his whole educational theory. Dewey is today widely considered one of the most important fathers of the discourse of radical democracy in twentieth-century thought. According to him, democracy is much more than a specific form of government, constitution, or the state. And its meaning is not exhausted by a particular order of social institutions or a set of political ideas. Rather, democracy, is a way of life, which is to say that it must be "a personal way of life" (LW 14: 226) for all those engaged in democratic communications—a basic and effective attitude toward human living together. "The democratic faith in human equality is belief that every human being, independent of the quantity or range of his personal endowment, has the right to equal opportunity with every other person for development of whatever gifts he has" (ibid., 226–227). This implies faith in the intelligence of human beings to judge and act on their own behalf if the proper conditions are furnished (ibid., 227). It entails the rejection of any political doctrine or practice that appeals to some ultimate authority above and beyond the realm of lived and communicated experience. "So stated, democracy is belief in the ability of human experience to generate the aims and methods by which further experience will grow in ordered richness" (ibid., 229). This attitude and belief is called "meliorism." It tries to keep a critical as well as constructive balance between naive optimism and fatalistic pessimism. It is oriented toward the necessities and opportunities of democratic reconstruction. "Meliorism is the belief that the specific conditions which exist at one moment, be they comparatively bad or comparatively good, in any event may be bettered. It encourages intelligence to study the positive means of good and the obstructions to their realization, and to put forth endeavor for the improvement of conditions" (MW 12: 182ff.).

More concretely, democracy designates a way of living together in which "mutual and free consultation rule instead of force, and in which cooperation instead of brutal competition is the law of life" in a social order that supports the forces "that make for friendship, beauty, and knowledge" so that every individual may become what he or she—and he or she alone—"is capable of becoming" (LW 11: 417). Becoming is not only essential for democracy in the sense of individual growth, but also in the sense of social reconstruction. The democratic faith implies that we live in an essentially open and unfinished universe in which human decisions constitute differences that really make a difference—a universe "in which there is real uncertainty and contingency, a world which is not all in, and never will be, a world which in some respect is incomplete and in the making, and which in these respects may be made this way or that according as men judge, prize, love and labor" (MW 11: 50). Dewey insists that with regard to democracy the process of experience is always primary to and more important than any results attained. Special results achieved "are of ultimate value only as they are used to enrich and order the ongoing process. Since the process of experience is capable of being educative, faith in democracy is all one with faith in experience and education" (LW 14: 229).

As we saw in part 1, Dewey introduces two general criteria (in chapter 7 of his 1916 book *Democracy and Education*) for assessing the democratic quality of a given group, community, or society. The first criterion is an internal one. It asks, "How numerous and varied are the interests which are consciously shared?" (MW 9: 89). It points to the necessary pluralism and open-mindedness toward diversity of interests within a democratic group or society and signifies "reliance upon the recognition of mutual interests as a factor in social control" (ibid., 92). The second criterion is an external one. It asks, "How full and free is the interplay with other forms of association?" (ibid., 89) It observes the extent of interaction and communication between different groups or societies and points to the necessity of continuously readjusting social habits "through meeting the new situations produced by varied intercourse" (ibid., 92). Thus, while the first criterion interprets democracy as a pluralistic and participatory way of living together, the second points to democracy as an open and evolving society. The first stands against uniformity and the dangers of totalitarianism, while the second rejects isolationism and unilateral power.

If democracy depends on action and participation, this implies that, especially for the young, it is necessarily connected with education. "When the ideals of democracy are made real in our entire educational system, they will be a reality once more in our national life" (LW 6: 98). Belief in the potentials of education is an indispensable component in the democratic faith because it is only through realization in the life-experience of individuals in communities that democracy can flourish and be in turn enriched by a multitude of individual contributions. Dewey insists "that the relation between democracy and education is a reciprocal one, a mutual one, and vitally so" (LW 13: 294). He observes that democracy "is itself an educational principle, an educational measure and policy" (ibid.). In the closing chapter of *The Public and Its Problems* (see LW 2: 351ff.), he insists that the welfare and growth of local communities are necessary conditions for the prosperity of democracy at large. This bottom-up view on the necessary everyday practices of democratic communication is based on the belief that the educative potentialities of democracy can only be sufficiently actualized when it is experienced through direct forms of partaking in communities of shared interests that cooperatively solve joint problems. Local communities in neighborhoods, schools, social groups, networks, social and political movements, and so on can provide opportunities for direct democratic involvement. They can articulate the multitude and diversity of contextualized experiences by which democracy is enlivened. They are backbone of civil society. At best, they turn democracy into a firsthand experience of learning and educational growth that of itself shows its advantages as a way of life for all who participate.

Dewey thinks that modern education needs to more fully recognize the relevance of democracy as an educational process "without which individuals cannot come into the full possession of themselves nor make a contribution...to the social well-being of others" (LW 13: 296). "Even in the classroom we are beginning to learn," he continues, "that every individual becomes educated only as he has an opportunity to contribute something from his own experience, no matter how meagre or slender that background of experience may be at a given time; and...that enlightenment comes from the give and take, from the exchange of experiences and ideas" (ibid.).

The necessary appreciation of the experience of learners implies that education takes the democratic claims to self-government seriously. "If democracy is possible it is because every individual has a degree of power to govern himself and be free in the ordinary concerns of life" (LW 6: 431). Dewey here gives an important response to all those who object that you can only be as democratic as "the circumstances" allow. The potential for self-government is something that we must presuppose if we are not willing to surrender our democratic hopes altogether. But how far is the potential actualized and made use of—especially given those structural contexts that support or work against its realization?

Deweyan pragmatism insists that we ourselves are always already part of such contexts because we partake in their construction and reproduction. They are implicit in our daily living as well as our education. The only way for education to realize its democratic potentials is through immanent criticism and self-criticism that comes from within those experiences and contexts that are being scrutinized. In many ways, we live in a "system" or "structure" that constitutes different positions and delimits spaces for experience and action. Structural conditions like sharp economic inequalities, marginalization of individuals and groups, oppressive labor, unemployment, poverty, exclusion through cultural hegemonies, and so on represent important contexts that democratic education cannot ignore. But they never fully determine our experience and action. Dewey believes that it is crucial for democracy and education to understand that the actual never exhausts the potential. Faith in democracy, experience, and education necessarily implies that there are opportunities for change. This is true as long as we live in an open and unfinished universe—a view that pragmatists and constructivists alike endorse. Therefore, they are so much interested in education as a force for democracy: "Since education is the keystone of democracy, education should be truly democratic" (LW 9: 393). It is essential for education to initiate democratic learning processes from the very start (construction) and to uncover and address democratic shortcomings as a step toward increasing the chances for more democracy (criticism). This is only possible through forms of actually lived democratic participation that include the socially marginalized and disadvantaged and give them the necessary educational support for truly partaking in the life of their society. We will not reach equality of education, but we must fight for equity. Every success in this struggle will make democracy a lived and meaningful experience for those who participate in it. In education, teaching, and learning, not only do we need values like democratic participation and inclusion, but we also need diverse models of good practices and concrete examples of practiced democratic-learning cultures. This is why Dewey insists that a democratic society must continually experiment with education and educational institutions. The accounts of his Laboratory School at the University of Chicago (see MW 1: 1–111) as well as the progressive school experiments that he discussed in his 1915 book *Schools of To-Morrow* (MW 8: 205–404) provide examples from Dewey's own time and place.

Dewey's democratic ideal of a life of full and unconstrained communication has been accompanied by penetrating criticisms of the antidemocratic tendencies in educational, social, economic, political, and imperialist practices that he witnessed in his time. Communication and participation are intrinsically linked to democratic rights that we must secure and further in our societies. Among these are, "free speech, freedom of communication and intercourse, of public assemblies, liberty of the press and circulation of ideas, freedom of religious and intellectual conviction (commonly called freedom of conscience), of worship, and . . . the right to education, to spiritual nurture" (MW 5: 399).

Such rights only live in and through communication; they must be communicated to be effective. This goes hand in hand with another crucial insight that, too, has lost none of its actuality with regard to the present state of democracy worldwide: "The fundamental principle of democracy is that the ends of freedom and individuality for all can be attained only by means that accord with those ends" (LW 11: 298).

Dewey is very clear that the project of democracy is a permanent task rather than a struggle to be won once and for all. Of course, there are democratic achievements from past struggles that we can build on in our attempts to further develop democracy. But democracy itself is always a process of becoming. Every generation "has to accomplish democracy over again for itself;... its very nature, its essence, is something that cannot be handed on from one person or one generation to another, but has to be worked out in terms of needs, problems and conditions of the [changing] social life of which... we are a part" (LW 13: 298ff.).

On the negative side, this view of democracy as an open process implies that we must always be prepared to encounter recurrent challenges and risks of democratic decay that may become traps in our societies—in present times at least as much as in Dewey's. If democracy is not actively lived through communication and participation, it easily degenerates—for the individuals as well as for the society as a whole—to a merely external procedure. If the democratic order only rests on external representations and it is not lived in daily practices it will, perforce, decay. That is because it does not act in accord with its professed proclamations. For example, with regard to the tensions of democracy and capitalism, Dewey wrote in the early 1930s:

> The essential fact is that if both democracy and capitalism are on trial, it is in reality our collective intelligence which is on trial. We have displayed enough intelligence in the physical field to create the new and powerful instrument of science and technology. We have not as yet had enough intelligence to use this instrument deliberately and systematically to control its social operations and consequences. (LW 6: 60)

And it seemed clear to him that a crucial challenge for democracy in his time was to reconstruct economic relationships in a more democratic way lest democracy become the prey of capitalism: "In order to restore democracy, one thing and one thing only is essential. The people will rule when they have power, and they will have power in the degree they own and control the land, banks, the producing and distributing agencies of the nation" (LW 9: 76). Many of these issues remain unsettled to our present day, and many appear in our time on a considerably more complex global scene. Without doubt, there has been much disenchantment and disillusionment in comparison with the socialist hopes and dreams of the early decades of the twentieth century. But pragmatism and constructivism stand and fall with their struggle for radical democracy because, in the end, they themselves can only be practiced under democratic conditions.

PARTICIPATION AND DIVERSITY

Recent developments in Western democracies show the relevance and visionary quality of Dewey's democratic theory and criticism. Democracy seems weakened because it cannot communicate fully and in all fields of living what the claimed democratic rights and principles seem to promise: The participation of all in public decision making and social-problem solving. More and more people turn their backs to politics because they hardly see any opportunities for real participation. Following Dewey, we need to recognize more fully that in a pluralistic and complex world like our own the perception and appreciation of diversity in human experiences is of central significance for this difficult task. It demands that we are willing and able to communicate across differences. "To cooperate by giving differences a chance to show themselves because of the belief that the expression of difference is not only a right of the other persons but is a means of enriching one's own life-experience, is inherent in the democratic personal way of life" (LW 14: 228).

To communicate across differences is always a risk, but it also provides us with unique opportunities for educational growth and can enrich our constructive powers of learning (see Garrison and Neubert 2005). In "Democracy and Education" (1916), Dewey suggests that a fundamental principle of democracy lies in the appreciation of "the intrinsic significance of every growing experience" (MW 9: 116). Educational growth is a necessary condition as well as an important touchstone of democracy.

According to Dewey, democratic communication and education must, among others things, release the imaginative powers of learners to respond in constructive and critical ways to the changing challenges of social and individual life and to realize new possibilities of observation, participation, and action in experience. "Imagination is the chief instrument of the good," he writes in an allusion to Shelley (LW 10: 350), because only imaginative vision "elicits the possibilities that are interwoven within the texture of the actual" (ibid., 348).

Dewey had a very positive view on communication that took its starting point from the direct face-to-face intercourse in small groups and local communities. "All communication is like art. It may fairly be said, therefore, that any social arrangement that remains vitally social, or vitally shared, is educative to those who participate in it" (MW 9: 9). However, he also considered and critically analyzed the broader and more anonymous communication spheres characteristic of modern life. He witnessed and theoretically reflected the beginning age of mass media communications (see LW 2: 235–372). When he wrote that "[t]he means of public communication—press, radio, and theater—are powerful instruments of instruction and influence" (LW 11: 538), he was already aware of the ambivalent insight that beneath their educative power modern mass media also involve an unprecedented power of manipulation. Of course, he could not foresee that modern society would eventually erect the completely fictitious worlds of participation and action that recent media like the internet, including Blogs and especially social media like Facebook, Twitter, and whatever the future may hold, make possible—a counter world to the realm of face-to-face communications that involves completely new opportunities for education and manipulation, participation and isolation. But his warning that "[t]he mass usually become unaware that they have a claim to a development of their own powers" (ibid., 218) gains new actuality and urgency against this background.

Today, it seems all the more important for us to learn the Deweyan lesson that only a cultural universe that combines communication with participation secures the necessary conditions for democratic engagement on a sufficiently large scale. Another of Dewey's essential visions about democracy lies in his willingness to imagine it as an open und unfinished process. "To my mind, the greatest mistake that we can make about democracy is to conceive of it as something fixed, fixed in idea and fixed in its outward manifestation" (LW 11: 182). This goes hand in hand with his crucial insight that democracy can only be attained by means that are themselves democratic. Such visions today still provide us not only with democratic hope, but also with a sense of direction for where to look for necessary improvements and how to define the aims of our own actions. As imaginations, they are ideal-typical in the sense that there are so many concrete situations to which they can be applied and in which their potential contents may be experienced that they themselves can never be completely exhausted or fulfilled. They require *our* imaginative powers, habits, interests, emotional sensitivities, and visions in order to become and remain vivid components of democratic culture (see also Eldridge 1998; Campbell 1992; Caspary 2000).

As Dewey already saw very clearly, practices of capitalism repeatedly tend to put democracy at risk. In the early 1930s, he wrote in "American Education Past and Future" (the draft of a radio lecture) that in earlier times "the aims of political democracy were easily understood, since they were in harmony with the conditions of soil and occupation. Now there are vast and concentrated aggregations of wealth; there are monopolies of power; great unemployment; a shutting down of doors of opportunity, a gulf between rich and poor, and no frontier to which the hard put can migrate" (LW 6: 95–96). There are considerable historical differences in the development of capitalism and its relations to democracy between North America and Europe. These differences have contributed to somewhat different democratic traditions. In Europe, the movements toward democracy have, upon the whole, been much more troublesome and continually threatened by setbacks and or even temporal defeats. (Things have been even more treacherous in Asia, the Middle East, Africa, and South America.) If democracy as a moral ideal combines "two ideas which have historically often worked antagonistically: liberation of individuals on one hand and promotion of a common good on the other" (LW 7: 349), then in Europe especially the "promotion of a common good" was a considerably more contested affair than in America. Capitalist production with all its contradictory implications between economic exploitation and emancipation struggles for social and democratic rights has had a more controversial and uneven development. In this connection, "promotion of the common good" has historically always been split into separate camps of interest that were competing for political influence. Therefore, in the processes of democratization there was a comparatively large premium put on the resolution of conflicts through mechanisms of representative democracy. However, traditions of direct democratic participation (or what today may be called "deep democracy") seem to be weaker or at least more dispersed than in America.

Not only against this background, Dewey's insistence that the prosperity of local communities is a necessary condition for the prosperity of democracy at large poses a crucial challenge that still seems topical today for many reasons. In a time of increasingly globalized economies, societies, and politics there is the standing (and maybe growing) danger that people turn their backs to democracy because they find the political processes too formalized, remote, intricate, or inscrutable and feel that even their voting does not make much difference to decisions that are made because of allegedly factual constraints. If democracy is only seen as a formalized system of representational politics, the democratic principles easily lose their substance and become hollow. To remain vivid and inspiring forces, they must be experienced through democratic participation in day-by-day practices and human interactions in all relevant areas of social living-together. Only then can we realize democracy as a "personal way of life" and as an educational process that furthers the growth of individuals as well as the prosperity of communities and societies. And only on that condition can there be the chance of an informed, diverse, articulate, and critical public sphere that has an impact on political decisions. New and extended forms of direct and self-organized democratic participation—in neighborhoods, schools, social movements, civic councils, NGOs, and other ways—can offer promising examples for the vitalization of democratic culture through multiple forms of bottom-up community organization. They constitute "local" communities in the sense of communities that allow for direct participation in transactions based on personal intercourse or face-to-face acquaintance. Even if today in many cases the internet is used as a means for connecting local communities to increasingly globalized communities that respond to increasingly globalized challenges, the level of direct personal contacts and exchanges remains an essential strength of such global and local communities. They can be communities of learning, of developing joint interests and cooperatively solving common problems. If they are fostered in ways that increase the opportunities for participation, cooperation, communication, and diversity, they can give substance to the ideals of democracy and root them in experience:

> In a word, that expansion and reinforcement of personal understanding and judgment by the cumulative and transmitted intellectual wealth of the community which may render nugatory the indictment of democracy drawn on the basis of the ignorance, bias and levity of the masses, can be fulfilled only in the relations of personal intercourse in the local community...Vision is a spectator; hearing is a participator...We lie, as Emerson said, in the lap of an immense intelligence. But that intelligence is dormant and its communications are broken, inarticulate and faint until it possesses the local community as its medium. (LW 2: 371ff.)

Direct democracy is, of course, not opposed to representational democracy. It is "because I believe in democracy that I believe in this principle of just representation," says Dewey, "especially when it is backed up by proportional representation that gives the minority its full voice" (LW 9: 318).[3] The quote shows that he is not willing to identify democracy with sheer majority rule, but wishes to recognize and secure minority rights. His understanding of "just representation" is directly connected with his insights into the uniqueness of each individual and the resourcefulness of each cultural group or community. In his reflections about the relationship between philosophy and democracy, Dewey writes that the democratic principle of equality demands recognition of "the incommensurable"—that is, the otherness of others—in a world "in which an existence must be reckoned with on its own account, not as something capable of equation with and transformation into something else" (MW 11: 53). Democratic communication presupposes that all individuals, groups, or communities have the right and opportunity to speak for themselves and demand consideration on their own behalf.

These insights connect with Dewey's insistence on the democratic necessity to recognize and appreciate differences as a means for enriching one's own life-experience (see LW 14: 228). This even implies respect for others whose beliefs and convictions we consider wrong. The "mechanics of democracy can function only when there is a clear understanding of the community of interest that the membership has, and likewise a deep, sympathetic understanding of one another's weaknesses, shortcomings, and proneness to error" (LW 9: 344)—writes Dewey together with other members of Grievance Committee of the Teachers Union in a 1933 report. These and other similar principles are necessary preconditions, according to Dewey, for the emergence and articulation of a social intelligence that in the end will decide upon whether we succeed in living together democratically at all. Dewey believes that this problem, among other things, poses a fundamental challenge for education—the problem of providing sufficient opportunities for all learners to develop social intelligence and to make constructive use of their democratic rights for learning.

SOCIAL INTELLIGENCE AND DEMOCRATIC RECONSTRUCTION

One necessary condition for the provision of opportunities for democratic communication and participation in the great societies of modernity is the emergence and articulation of democratic publics. In his 1927 book "The Public and Its Problems," Dewey extensively discussed the chances and difficulties of the democratic public sphere in his time. What is the public? Dewey gives the following definition:

> We take then our point of departure from the objective fact that human acts have consequences upon others, that some of these consequences are perceived, and that their perception leads to subsequent effort to control action so as to secure some consequences and avoid others. Following this clew, we are led to remark that the consequences are of two kinds, those which affect the persons directly engaged in a transaction, and those which affect others beyond those immediately concerned. In this distinction we find the germ of the distinction between the private and the public. (LW 2: 243ff.)

The democratic public sphere, accordingly, is the political realm where processes and transactions within a society that have indirect consequences for people who are not directly involved can be brought to open political discussion, deliberation, and decision making. "Indirect, extensive, enduring and serious consequences of conjoint and interacting behavior call a public into existence having a common interest in controlling these consequences" (LW 2: 314). But there are substantial difficulties and problems that stand in the way of the emergence and flourishing of democratic public spheres in modern society. Dewey observes that the "machine age" with its increasing formations of social interdependence and rather impersonal structures of social relations in work, social organization, administration, and government has "enormously expanded, multiplied, intensified and complicated the scope of the indirect consequences" (ibid.). Social interest groups like employers, trade unions, stakeholder, and markets have formed "consolidated unions in action" that tend to focus on their own limited ends. In their struggles against each other, they often obstruct a more generous appreciation of democratic welfare and interests. As a result, the democratic public cannot easily identify and distinguish itself. Yet, "this discovery is obviously an antecedent condition of any effective organization on its part" (ibid.). The public appears as too dispersed and disconnected, as too many disintegrated publics with specific interests and "too much of public concern for our existing resources to cope with. The problem of a democratically organized public is primarily and essentially an intellectual problem, in a degree to which the political affairs of prior ages offer no parallel" (ibid., 314).

Dewey observes that there is a tensional relationship between the democratic public sphere and the democratic state. This tension is a constitutive component of the democratic process. In any democratic society, there is the recurrent need to mediate between existing institutional structures like the agencies of the state on the one hand and the current interests and needs of the public on the other. At no time are concerns and problems of the public completely or finally represented by the already established institutional structures of the political system. As public interests and issues emerge and develop, political institutions as well as political conceptions are in need of recurrent reconstruction (see Campbell 1992, 46ff.). "By its very nature, a state is something to be scrutinized, investigated, searched for. Almost as soon as its form is stabilized, it needs to be re-made" (LW 2: 255). For instance, the great changes in social life that have been engendered by the processes of industrialization in Dewey's own lifetime have produced essentially new public concerns and interests because they have created completely new consequences in human affairs. These changes were extrinsic to the political forms and institutions that had been established in an earlier period: "The new public which is generated remains long inchoate, unorganized, because it cannot use inherited political agencies. The latter, if elaborate and well institutionalized, obstruct the organization of the new public" (ibid., 254ff.). To form and articulate itself, the public therefore has to partially break established political forms. "This is hard to do because these forms are themselves the regular means of instituting change" (ibid., 255). Modern democracy is therefore characterized by an inevitable ambivalence between the representative structures of institutionalized politics and the direct articulations of public interests and concerns.

The effective realization of a democratic public sphere is a crucial challenge for social intelligence in modern society. This brings us to a consideration of Dewey's notion of social intelligence. Dewey surrenders the traditional philosophical concept of reason "as the highest organ or 'faculty' for laying hold on ultimate truths." He suggests that we use the more contemporary word "intelligence" instead—not as something ready-made, but as "a short-hand designation for great and ever-growing methods of observation, experiment and reflective reasoning" (MW 12: 258). He rejects the extremely individualistic idea of intelligence that has become influential in the twentieth-century mainstream psychology as well as common consciousness through concepts like the IQ (Intelligence Quotient) or the standardized intelligence test. Dewey uses the term "social intelligence" to indicate that intelligence, for him, is not so much an individual possession but rather the product of processes of communication and participation in sociocultural environments. Intelligence is a factor in social practices that depends on cultural contexts and resources as much as on individual achievements. It is something that has been developed out of human experiences in a long process of cultural history.[4] According to Dewey, it does not primarily designate an individual possession, but rather a quality of human inquiries carried out by communities of interpreters. Dewey treats theory as instrumental and not as an end in itself. As we saw above, he thinks that theoretical formulations and even truth claims should be regarded as working hypotheses for conducting further inquiries based on observation that put theory to experimental test. The primacy of experimentalism against any claim to an allegedly superior or ultimate access to knowledge or truth is an essential characteristic of Dewey's notion of intelligence. He believes that the experimental method "is, in short, the method of democracy, of a positive toleration which amounts to sympathetic regard for the intelligence and personality of others, even if they hold views opposed to ours, and of scientific inquiry into facts and testing of ideas" (LW 7: 329).

The task of restoring the democratic public sphere is an "intellectual problem" in so far as it depends on social intelligence as socialized intelligence, that is, intelligence used as an instrument for social welfare and prosperity. "The problem of bringing about an effective socialization of intelligence is probably the greatest problem of democracy today" (LW 7: 365–366).[5] A crucial precondition as well as result of social intelligence lies in its liberation from narrow social constraints:

> Intelligence is, indeed, instrumental through action to the determination of the qualities of future experience. But the very fact that the concern of intelligence is with the future, with the as-yet-unrealized (and with the given and the established only as conditions of the realization of possibilities), makes the action in which it takes effect generous and liberal; free of spirit. Just that action which extends and approves intelligence has an intrinsic value of its own in being instrumental: the intrinsic value of being informed with intelligence in behalf of the enrichment of life. By the same stroke, intelligence becomes truly liberal: knowing is a human undertaking, not an esthetic appreciation carried on by a refined class or a capitalistic possession of a few learned specialists, whether men of science or of philosophy. (LW 10: 45)

In this connection, Dewey thinks that intellectuals have to play an important, but limited role. He strongly rejects any suggestion that a democracy can or should be ruled by experts. "A class of experts is inevitably so removed from common interests as to become a class with private interests and private knowledge, which in social matters in not knowledge at all" (LW 2: 364). The multitude of all people who participate in a democratic society must be involved, as far and comprehensively as possible, in the processes of political decision making and ruling. They must have an effective share in the government. After all, only the people themselves know where the shoe pinches. "No government by experts in which the masses do not have the chance to inform the experts as to their needs can be anything but an oligarchy managed in the interests of the few...The world has suffered more from leaders and authorities than from the masses" (ibid., 365). And, as Sidney Hook observes in his introduction to Dewey's *Democracy and Education*, "as for the rule of experts in any field, without disputing their expertise, Dewey holds that one does not need to be an expert in order to evaluate the recommendations of experts. Otherwise democratic government would be impossible" (MW 9: xvii). With regard to the crucial task of establishing a democratic public sphere, the substantial weight therefore lies on the part of the multitude of people in their processes of articulating public opinion through processes of discussion, consultation, and persuasion. Here, the establishment of majority rule is an important goal, but as Dewey reminds us, even more important than any majority are the "antecedent debates, modifications of views to meet the opinions of minorities, the relative satisfaction given the latter by the fact that it has had a chance and that next time it may be successful in becoming a majority" (LW 2: 365). All "valuable as well as new ideas begin with minorities," but they must be given the opportunity to grow and become a common "possession of the multitude" (ibid.).

But not all people can have direct access to the often highly specialized information and knowledge that are necessary to solve the complex problems of living in a modern society. Therefore, the democratic public needs experts to provide indispensable resources and tools. Interpreting Dewey's discussion in his 1927 book *The Public and Its Problems*, we can distinguish, among other things, four important functions to be performed by public intellectuals in fields like science, philosophy, education, art, literature, journalism, and the like: (1) to promote an experimental attitude toward social events, (2) to entertain systematic and continual inquiries into social and human affairs, (3) to further free access to information regarding issues that affect the public, (4) to cultivate forms of free and full intercommunication as well as multilayered articulation of knowledge of public import (including, e.g., artistic articulations) (see LW 2: 339–350). He does not claim that these are sufficient conditions for the recovery of the democratic public sphere, but he asserts that they at least are necessary and indispensable. Of course, Dewey's criticisms of the democratic public sphere refer to the social constellations of the "machine age" of his time and the type of capitalist production and organization commonly subsumed under the name of "Fordism." They do not include perspectives on more recent developments in post-Fordist, late-modern, or postmodern societies, as described and interpreted by more recent observers of changes in human affairs and social living-together like Zygmunt Bauman (1997, 1998, 2000). In many details, Dewey's accounts can and should be reconstructed as well as critically further developed today by combining them with observations of social thinkers like Bauman (see Neubert and Reich 2011).

But generally speaking, the four tasks just mentioned together with the criticisms and challenges they imply with regard to the prosperity of democratic publics have not lost their relevance in the present scene. Let us briefly specify them step-by-step.

1. Dewey thinks it is an illusion to suppose that effective freedom of thought and communication can be secured in the present simply on the grounds that certain juridical and political restrictions from former times have been overcome (see LW 2: 340). From his perspective, freedom of thought means the relative emancipation from the limitations of a given sociohistorical context rather than complete independence and detachment from all contexts of traditions, cultural customs, beliefs, and constraints. In particular, it goes hand in hand with a critical as well as experimental attitude with regard to the contents of actual human life-experience. This attitude implies unrestricted openness toward future developments and contingencies as well as the use of warranted concepts, instruments, and methods of thought and inquiry that can be tested, corrected, and further developed in and through application. The circle of constructions, deconstructions, and reconstructions that has been discussed in the introduction and parts 1 and 2 of this book characterizes—in the language of today—three fundamental and necessarily interconnected phases of this philosophical experimentalism. With regard to the needs of social intelligence in contemporary democratic practices, though, Dewey observes that in so far as the development of the instruments of thought and inquiry is largely confined to specific fields of academic discourse, while public (mass) communication mostly remains on the levels of *publicity* as represented by entertainment, advertisement, cliché, propaganda, sensations, and so on, the belief in intellectual freedom all too easily results in self-deception, complacency, and superficiality. The problematic thing about this state of affairs is the easy exploitability of the multitude by economical and other powerful interests that have the sufficient means at their disposal to manipulate public opinion according to their demands. From Dewey's perspective, the very exploitability of the multitude and their relatively low and undeveloped powers of articulating their substantial political interests are only possible on the basis that in modern industrialized societies strong emotional and intellectual habitudes are still predominant that are connected with deep-seated fears of experimentation in human affairs, especially with regard to social and political issues. "Men have got used to

an experimental method in physical and technical matters. They are still afraid of it in human concerns. The fear is the more efficacious because like all deep-lying fears it is covered up and disguised by all kinds of rationalizations." In "contemporary political life," there is an "unwillingness to think things through...which works powerfully against effective inquiry into social institutions and conditions" (LW 2: 341). Such unwillingness constitutes a withdrawal from reality; it manifests itself in ways like "querulousness," "impotent drifting," "uneasy snatching at distractions," "idealization of the long established," "facile optimism," "riotous glorification of things 'as they are,'" or "intimidation of all dissenters—ways which depress and dissipate thought all the more effectually because they operate with subtle and unconscious pervasiveness" (ibid., 341ff.). Tendencies like these constitute powerful social forces that counteract public inquiry and communication and restrict its constructive and critical potentials. They pose important challenges for democracy and render public promotion of an experimental attitude toward social events a necessary precondition of furthering social intelligence in human affairs.

2. Furthermore, Dewey claims that the methods and procedures of social inquiry must satisfy certain requirements and standards in order to contribute effectively to the formation of public opinion. Especially important, in this connection, are their continuity and actuality (see LW 2: 346ff.). He warns his readers that public opinion remains erratic as long as it is not the result of methods of inquiry and communication that are put to work permanently. "Only continuous inquiry, continuous in the sense of being connected as well as persistent, can provide the material of enduring opinion about public matters" (ibid., 346). This observation entails the claim for systematic, thoroughgoing and well-equipped programs of research and record. And what is more, Dewey insists that such inquiries must respond as timely as possible to current affairs in order to sufficiently maintain their public function and fulfill their public service. His diagnosis from the 1920s has still not lost much of its validity in our time: "Here, only too conspicuously, is a limitation of the existing social sciences. Their material comes too late, too far after the event, to enter effectively into the formation of public opinion about the immediate public concern and what is to be done about it" (ibid., 347).

3. According to Dewey, there is also a dilemma of the policy of "news" in modern industrialized societies that stands at the back of these problems, adding to their urgency. For the media of modern mass

communication—in Dewey's time these were the telegraph and telephone, the radio, accelerated mails, and the printing press, to which we today may add the television, emails, and the internet—have made possible the multiplication and dissemination of information to a degree unconceivable before. But, as Dewey observes, the materials that are being disseminated, the "news" that circulate in the new media, are upon the whole too scattered and too isolated to engender more than momentary excitements that easily end in triviality. They do not communicate social *meanings* in the full sense of the word "meaning," because they seldom lead to the apprehension of relations and connections of events with other events, which allows for a more differentiated insight into social processes and affairs. They present the "new" in many cases simply as a disconnected event, some real occurrence that triggers a sensational effect, which readily passes away as soon as the next disconnected "news" enters the scene. "The catastrophic, namely, crime, accident, family rows, personal clashes and conflicts, are the most obvious forms of breaches of continuity; they supply the element of shock which is the strictest meaning of sensation; they are the *new* par excellence, even though only the date of the newspaper could inform us whether they happened last year or this, so completely are they isolated from their connections" (LW 2: 347). What is missing, though, is sufficient communication of the symbolic means and resources that would allow for a constructive and critical integration of isolated bits of information into a more coherent and systematic grasp of social realities. Dewey suggests that here lies a kind of journalistic responsibility to which especially the social sciences must contribute: "a genuine social science would manifest its reality in the daily press, while learned books and articles supply and polish tools of inquiry" (ibid., 348). For it is only in and through application in "the daily and unremitting assembly and interpretation of 'news'" (ibid.) that social sciences can do justice to their function with regard to the democratic formation and articulation of public opinion and at the same time forge and sharpen the tools and methods of social inquiry in response to the needs of contemporary events. For Dewey, "knowledge is communication as well as understanding...and knowledge of social phenomena is peculiarly dependent upon dissemination, for only by distribution can such knowledge be either obtained or tested" (ibid., 345). He critically observes that under capitalist conditions such distribution is considerably impeded by the fact that publicity is practiced more as an issue of skilful management on behalf of particular interests of profit rather than as an opportunity and challenge for the comprehensive and democratic formation of public opinion. Therefore, publicity all too easily takes on forms of propaganda, hunting for sensations, manipulation, restriction, and control of opinion (see ibid., 348) which put the democratic project at risk because they weaken the formation of a sufficiently informed democratic public that can fruitfully respond to the diversity of social issues and interests. "Communication of the results of social inquiry is the same thing as the formation of public opinion. This marks one of the first ideas framed in the growth of political democracy as it will be one of the last to be fulfilled" (ibid., 345).

4. For Dewey, there is yet another side to the problem of sufficient articulation and dissemination of publicly relevant information, knowledge, and "news." To become part of a comprehensive process of democratic communications, public articulation and dissemination will have to fulfill an additional condition that has to do with the question of presentation. Especially, Dewey thinks that presentation of publicly relevant knowledge must not be confined to the rather academic articulations of scientific discourse if it is to be disseminated effectively throughout the diverse levels of the democratic public sphere and to reach the multitude of people. "A technical high-brow presentation would appeal only to those technically high-brow; it would not be news to the masses" (LW 2: 349). He argues that the issue of public presentation is essentially a question of art. It presupposes the liberty of arts as a necessary condition of the prosperity of democratic publics. "The freeing of the artist in literary presentation, in other words, is as much a precondition of the desirable creation of adequate opinion on public matters as is the freeing of social inquiry" (ibid.). Providing poetic articulation for the meanings and knowledge that the democratic public constructs, deconstructs, and reconstructs for and about itself and its common concerns, the artist paves ways for knowledge and meanings to penetrate into the deeper, more emotional and imaginative levels of the life-experience of those who participate in the public. In this way, her metaphors may provide new insights and enhanced forms of sharing in social meanings and communications. Dewey has the poetical power of the metaphorical dimension in mind when he writes that it has always been the function of art to "break through the crust of conventionalized and routine consciousness" (ibid.). He thinks that poetry, the drama, the novel, and so on give positive proof that the problem

of public presentation is not insoluble. "Artists have always been the real purveyors of news, for it is not the outward happening in itself which is new, but the kindling by it of emotion, perception and appreciation" (ibid., 350). In this sense, Dewey would have agreed with the more recent pragmatic philosopher Richard Rorty (1989) that democracy is of necessity a "poetic culture" in which shared values and achievements circulate through storytelling and other forms of artistic presentation by which communities imagine and narrate their own self-conceptions. To this end, they need public intellectuals as "strong poets" (Rorty) who produce insightful metaphors, images, and narratives.

We close the discussion of this part of the book with a lengthy quotation from Dewey's *The Public and Its Problems* in which he summarizes his democratic vision with regard to the needs of public communication, social intelligence, and the powers of a poetic culture. It is the vision of

> a society in which the ever-expanding and intricately ramifying consequences of associated activities shall be known in the full sense of that word, so that an organized, articulate Public comes into being. The highest and most difficult kind of inquiry and a subtle, delicate, vivid and responsive art of communication must take possession of the physical machinery of transmission and circulation and breathe life into it. When the machine age has thus perfected its machinery it will be a means of life and not its despotic master. Democracy will come into its own, for democracy is a name for a life of free and enriching communication...It will have its consummation when free social inquiry is indissolubly wedded to the art of full and moving communication. (LW 2: 350)

SELECTION OF TARGET TEXTS

The third part is keyed to the following texts.[6] Dewey's most important account of communication can be found in the fifth chapter of *Experience and Nature*—beginning with the gushing and succinct remark: "Of all affairs, communication is the most wonderful" (LW 1: 132). Here, the reader will find Dewey's philosophical theory of communication, which is so important for his educational theory. Dewey had already elaborated on that theme in the first chapter of *Democracy and Education* (1916; MW 9) and thus given a premonition of the central place the concept of "communication" was to acquire in his mature thought. In *Experience and Nature*, he takes up these earlier considerations and discusses them on an immensely broadened scale by comprehensively working out the fundamentally communicative structure of human experience and analyzing that structure in its pragmatic dimensions. Besides the instrumental phase of communicating meanings for the coordination of social interactions, he particularly exposes the qualitatively consummatory dimension of partaking in the construction of shared meanings. Communication, for Dewey, is at the same time means and end. Not only does it serve as a means for transferring ideas or information, but above all it is itself a process of constructing a universe of shared meanings that brings about an enhancement of the immediate quality of experience for those who participate in it. For Dewey, every genuine communication releases creative as well as educative potentialities of human experience.

The most comprehensive presentation of Dewey's pragmatist ethics and theory of morality is given in the 1908 textbook *Ethics* (MW 5), coauthored with James Hayden Tufts. The book was published again in a thoroughly revised edition in 1932 (LW 7). Between these two editions lie a number of important books like *Democracy and Education* (MW 9), *Reconstruction in Philosophy* (MW 12: 77–201), and *Human Nature and Conduct* (LW 14), in which Dewey, step-by-step, elaborates and develops his ethical positions.[7] Characteristic of Dewey's approach to ethics is his effort to find a middle position between absolutist-transcendentalist and relativist-subjectivist approaches. He rejects the attempt to establish a priori and universal norms and principles that precede concrete experience or are imposed, as it were, from outside. But he equally rejects positions that regard ethical norms as purely arbitrary determinations that eventually lack any normative force. For Dewey, moral reflection, like all reflection, begins in the context of immediate primary experience, that is, in the context of a specific, unique, and at first unanalyzed situation in which a moral problem appears and enforces a decision, for example, between two mutually incompatible claims. This situational context must always be taken into account lest we neglect the vitality and diversity of moral life. However, we do not have to confront every moral situation completely unprepared and unequipped. From the abundance of concretely experienced moral problems, there emerge well-entrenched moral principles and norms in a process that transcends generations. These principles and norms give us orientation. They play a *functional* role with regard to morality as a lived cultural practice. They are generalized moral ideas that draw their normative force not from themselves, but from their past successful application in experience. They time and again have to prove themselves in new situations where we always have to reckon with exceptions from the rule. This calls for a certain degree of moral flexibility as to the application, readjustment, and modification of inherited principles, "because life is a moving affair in which old moral truth ceases to apply" (MW 14: 164).

In a word, moral philosophy, for Dewey, is a function of the moral life. If it strives to do justice to the diversity and changeability of human experience it must not regard morality as mere application of universal and eternal truths, but rather as a social and experimental construction or practice that develops its own standards from within. Contrary to many other approaches, Dewey's ethical theory particularly stresses the affective, imaginative, and creative dimensions of lived human relationships.[8] It also draws attention to the genuine ambiguity and ambivalence of concrete moral situations in which it is often impossible to attain a complete dissolution of conflicting claims.

At the heart of Dewey's social philosophy is his notion of democracy. He gives a systematic and comprehensive account of that notion in *Democracy and Education* (1916; MW 9) and further develops it and broadens his perspective in successive political writings until the very end of his life. Dewey's democratic vision is characterized, among other things, by two central aspects. First, it implies the idea of a *participatory democracy*, which means that democracy is not just a form of government or a set of institutions, but denotes a way of life that relies on as comprehensive a participation as possible of all in the goods, values, and interests of society, on the same conditions and in all the areas of associated living.[9] Second, it involves the idea of a *pluralistic democracy*, which means that a diversity of different groups, communities, cultures, and societies does not represent a threat or a loss, but rather a gain for democracy provided that the institutional prerequisites for as free and comprehensive an exchange as possible between the different forms of associated living are secured (see MW 9: 87–106). In both respects, "democracy," for Dewey, means a meliorist project, not an account or description of societal reality.

Several of Dewey's major political works in the 1920s and 1930s gained considerable influence in the public discussions of his time and are still regarded as among the most inspiring philosophical works about radical democracy in twentieth-century thought. In *The Public and Its Problems* (1927; LW 2: 235–372), Dewey discusses the fundamental and still very important problem of how a democratic public capable of exercising an effective and sustainable influence on decisions of public import can be realized under the conditions of the "Great Society" of the industrial age. In *Individualism, Old and New* (1930; LW 5: 41–123), he addresses the necessity of a fundamental conceptual reconstruction of the traditional political notion of individualism. He explores the challenge of a similar conceptual reconstruction of the traditional notion of liberalism in *Liberalism and Social Action* (1935; LW 11: 1–65). In *Freedom and Culture* (1939; LW 13: 63–188) he elaborates on the menace of totalitarianism for democracy, focusing his criticism not only on the foreign fascist and Stalinist systems of the time, but also on several antidemocratic tendencies within American society itself. Here, we also find his most comprehensive discussion of Marxist political philosophy.

As target texts for part 1 to 3 of this book, we wish to point to the following educational texts of Dewey:

In the little book *The School and Society* (MW 1: 1–109), first published in 1899, Dewey provides an account of the pedagogical work in his "Laboratory School," founded at the University of Chicago in 1896.[10] Presenting his first systematic account of his theory of the school, the book would have a rapid and extensive international effect among educationalists of the time that were striving to reform and reconstruct the school. Dewey set out to rethink the relationship between school and society in theory and practice in the face of the fundamental and continuous social changes caused by the industrial revolution and the attendant urbanization in the second half of the nineteenth century. In his view, what was needed was to readjust the school to the life of the child and to avoid unnecessary waste of energy. Dewey's vision of the school as "miniature community" or "embryonic society" became famous. In the same context, he uses the phrase "the child's habitat" (ibid., 12). At another place, writing about the needed changes in school and classroom practice, he argues for a shift of the center of gravity, a pedagogical revolution comparable to the Copernican shift in astronomy: "In this case the child becomes the sun about which the appliances of education revolve; he is the centre about which they are organized" (ibid., 23). This is not a plea for a naive and one-sided child-centered education. Dewey's interactive approach and his emphasis on the primacy of the interactions between learners and their (natural and sociocultural) environments should have prevented such a misinterpretation right from the start. This also applies to his understanding of the relationship between "The Child and the Curriculum" (1902; MW 2: 271–291). For Dewey, learning always begins in the middle of things. This is why the school, above all, must be open to life in order to be a place for learning. In the ideal school, "the life of the child becomes the all-controlling aim…Learning?—certainly, but living primarily, and learning through and in relation to this living" (MW 1: 24). The school must be opened to the lifeworlds of the students and to the larger societal environment (see ibid., 39–56). As a place for learning, it is organized after the model of the "laboratory" (in the large sense of that metaphor), which involves opportunities for learning through active experimentation, observation, construction, testing, discussion, and artistic expression in cooperation with other learners.

Schools of To-Morrow (1915; MW 8: 205–404), a book that Dewey coauthored with his daughter Evelyn, is a highly interesting work not only for the history of education, but also for current discussions about school and classroom reform. The Deweys present and portray a selected number of progressive schools in different parts of the United States, combining theoretical explanations written by John with accounts of school and classroom practice mainly observed by Evelyn. Thus, they nicely keep the balance between the theory and practice of educational reconstruction.

One year later, Dewey published his major work on educational philosophy, *Democracy and Education* (1916; MW 9), in which he addresses the task of comprehensively and systematically working out the educational implications of the notion of democracy. He sets out to discuss the constructive aims and methods of public education from the perspective of his radical notion of democracy and to criticize those traditional theories of knowledge and ethics whose influence on education tends to hamper an adequate realization of the democratic ideal. He is concerned with the connection between the prosperity of democracy, the development of the experimental method in the sciences, the theory of evolution, and the industrial revolution, and wants to examine the educational consequences of these manifold processes of change (see MW 9: 3). It accords with his philosophical notion of "experience" and his concept of human nature explained above that he conceives of education on the most general plane as a continual process of growth that has no end beyond itself (see ibid., 46–58). The most comprehensive aim of education, according to Dewey, can only be more education. "Since in reality there is nothing to which growth is relative save more growth, there is nothing to which education is subordinate save more education" (ibid., 56)—in the sense of a continual and lifelong reconstruction of experience (see ibid., 82ff.) in the interactions of learners within a world characterized by change and diversity. "The criterion of the value of school education is the extent in which it creates a desire for continued growth and supplies means for making the desire effective in fact" (ibid., 58).

For reasons of brevity, we can only hint at two further writings from Dewey's later works.

First, the treatise on *The Sources of a Science of Education* (1929/30; LW 5: 1–40) deals with questions about the nature of a science of education and the appropriate methods for inquiring into the subject matter of education. Among other things, Dewey calls for a more direct and immediate participation of "The Teacher as Investigator" in the educational research process.

Second, the little book *Experience and Education* (1938; LW 13: 1–62) further elaborates Dewey's educational thought on the background of his mature philosophical approach and his then considerably broadened theory of experience. He also replies to common misunderstandings and misinterpretations of his pedagogy in the context of the Progressive Education movement.

Part 4

CRITICISM AND CONCERNS—
RECONSTRUCTING DEWEY FOR
OUR TIMES

In many respects, Dewey's groundbreaking introduction of a cultural, constructive, and communicative approach to democracy and education has started a turn that has yet to be fully completed. Hence, these ideas can still provide valuable orientations and guidance. However, especially with a philosopher like Dewey, who emphasized so much the necessary cultural, historical, and social contexts of education, we should at the same time take substantial steps to combine Deweyan pragmatism with more recent theoretical developments that respond to changes in our life and times. If we recall the expositions given in the three preceding parts of our book, we can say that the necessary reconstruction should connect productively as well as critically with the cultural, constructive, and communicative turns that Dewey's philosophy of education has already taken. All three aspects have been of fundamental importance for philosophy, the humanities, the social sciences, and education in the twentieth century and they are still relevant today. Even if the general tendency in these disciplines today is to regard great theories with some skepticism and give them an ironic twist, they still remain important and valuable. This particularly applies to Dewey. He did not develop philosophical positions that end up in mere speculation or serve merely as another metanarrative, because he always connected his observations and reflections with experiences in the dynamic and diversified contexts of life. It is this attitude, among other things, that we should take up today and make productive for our time.

In what follows, we want to put Dewey in constructive as well as critical dialogues with some more recent approaches that in one way or another articulate new developments in the contexts of the three turns. We do so by first introducing some core perspectives of interactive constructivism as our frame of interpretation. Our intention is to reconstruct Dewey. The readers should make a clear distinction: If they want to understand Dewey himself, they should address his own body of works, perhaps by relying on our introduction in the first three parts of this book. We think such an endeavor will always be valuable with a classic thinker like Dewey. But in doing so, the reader will have to interpret Dewey's works from his/her own contexts. Of necessity, we did so ourselves in the first three parts of this book, even as we took great pains to do justice to his comprehensive and genuine works. Here in part 4, we take more liberty for developing our own ways of possible reconstructions of the Deweyan heritage for our time. Dewey, the philosopher of reconstruction, would have expected us to do so. But our own position first needs to be made explicit to give the readers a chance to critically scrutinize our ways and motives of reconstruction. We have taken an explicitly constructivist turn in pragmatism. All three of us do not care much about whether our position is called pragmatism or constructivism, given that we see both in a line of continuity. Jim Garrison is well known as a proponent of constructivist pragmatism, and Stefan Neubert and Kersten Reich are proponents of the Cologne program of interactive constructivism that regards pragmatism as its most important predecessor. This part, then, is a recontextualization of Dewey from a specific position and with a specific interest, namely, a constructivist reconsideration based on core assumptions drawn from interactive constructivism. We believe the insights of interactive constructivism will prove valuable even for those that decide to pursue a different pattern of reconstruction.

Constructivists, in general, think that the production of realities—that is, the production of viable ways of world making in the sense of both knowing and the known—is a contingent and evolving, hence always falsifiable, process of construction. Interactive constructivism more specifically clarifies the meaning of construction by focusing on the roles of observers, participants, and agents in cultural contexts. At present, there are a variety of pragmatic and constructivist approaches that differ considerably from each other over this issue. In our view, philosophers as well as educational theorists and practitioners can profit a great deal from the perspectives of Deweyan pragmatism. But they have to respond to new challenges posed by the changes of time. The Cologne program of interactive constructivism tries to focus on such challenges while at the same time keeping the high level of pragmatist philosophical reflections and making them productive in new constellations.

From the perspective of interactive constructivism, observers should be understood at the same time as cultural participants and agents and not just as detached spectators. They partake in cultural practices, routines, and institutions before they are able to observe and to produce descriptions of the observations they make. Observing begins and ends in lifeworldly contexts—that is, what Dewey calls "life-experience."

> As observers, we see, hear, sense, perceive and interpret our world. We construct our versions of reality on the basis of our beliefs and expectations, our interests, habits and reflections. As participants, we partake in the larger contexts of the multiple and often heterogeneous communities of interpreters that provide basic orientation in our cultural universe. We participate in social groups, communities, networks and institutions of all kinds. Our partaking is an indispensable cultural resource, but it also implies commitments, responsibilities, loyalties, and the exclusion of certain alternatives. As agents, we act and experience. We communicate and cooperate and struggle with others. We devise plans and projects to carry out our intentions. We articulate ourselves and respond to the articulation of others. (Neubert 2008, 108)

Furthermore, as to observers-participants-agents in culture, we distinguish between self-observer positions and distant-observer positions. The self-observer observes her/himself and others from the *inside* of the practices and interactions that s/he, for the time being, finds her/himself immediately involved in. The distant-observer observes others in their practices and interactions from the outside. For every self-observer the presence of (potential) distant-observers implies a constant element of strangification, a constant challenge to relativize her/his own observation by trying to grasp the alien view.

Here, we want to invite the reader to try out the relevance of this distinction by looking at Dewey's perspectives first from an immanent position and interpretation (parts 1 to 3 in our book), and then to widen the discussion by connecting him with other positions (in this part). We thus combine Dewey studies with distant-observer perspectives that help us to recontextualize the pragmatic tradition. In liquid modernity, for instance, Zygmunt Bauman describes our age's philosophical discourses on difference and otherness. He emphasizes the importance of such contextualization as a necessary component of pluralist culture. The Cologne program of interactive constructivism understands itself as part of this recent "cultural turn" in contemporary thought. For interactive constructivism, observers are always located subjects involved in transactive relationships within specific cultural contexts—that is to say, they are at the same time agents and participants in culture, too. The aim of maintaining a constructivist observer theory is to refer knowledge claims to the *perspectives* of the observers-participants-agents who make them. It is to argue that all claims to knowledge be seen as viable and provisional cultural constructions of observers-participants-agents that on principle should be kept open to further re/de/constructions by other observers-participants-agents. This is not to say that all knowledge per se is relative for all observers at all times—which obviously it is not. Rather, it is to say that there is no claim to true knowledge that *necessarily* warrants the consent of all observers and thus evades the possibility of relativization. Such is the constructivist conclusion from a diversity of postmodern or liquid modern discourses on knowledge criticism that show the inherent paradoxes of the absolute and the relative in the field of truth claims (see Reich 1998, vol. 1).

The distinction between self- and distant-observer positions, interactive constructivism further suggests, is becoming more and more important for philosophical reflection in our times of liquidity. It is a marked trait of present-day discourses that they have diversified to a degree that no one self-observer can overlook the varieties of approaches even in a limited field of discipline. In proclaiming the end of the "great projects" and "metanarratives," postmodern criticisms of knowledge focus on how the pluralization of possible truth claims has rendered any single and comprehensive approach to knowledge questionable. Truth claims more and more seem to be stated by some only to be relativized by others. In the juxtaposition of approaches, plural knowledge gets relativized and deconstructed by itself, since discourses of knowledge have multiplied and differentiated to an extent that the *one* obligatory truth for all observers can only be seen as the fantasy of a long-lost unity of science. This situation suggests that a constant readiness to change perspectives between self- and distant-observer positions should be seen as a minimum requirement for knowledge today. We favor a discourse theory that draws on modern as well as postmodern theoretical movements (see Reich 1998, vol. 2; Neubert and Reich 2002).[1] From this perspective, discourses are never seen as fully accomplished, seamless, and unambiguous totalities. Rather, they appear as incomplete structures with open sutures that while being established are almost already in transition toward something else.

This view of discourses, first, draws on the (post)structuralist idea that discourses are largely characterized by semantic overdetermination (see Hall 1997; Laclau and Mouffe 1991, 144ff.). That is to say that discourses are always multilayered formations of meaning that allow for diverse and even antagonistic articulations. The shifting and never wholly stabilized relationship between signifier and signified makes possible condensations and displacements of meanings that lead to a potentially endless "game of differences." Hence, any given articulation allows for possible rearticulations and dearticulations that are at the most but temporarily delayed.

Second, discourses always involve power relations. Power, however, should not be thought of as monolithic force or substance, but as something relational that is disseminated throughout discourse. Following Foucault, power operates like a chain that goes through the individuals (see Foucault 1978). Accordingly, while there is no observer position within discourses that is beyond power, neither is there a position where the effects of power are total. Both arguments (overdetermination and power) stand in intimate connection. Taken together, they explain why the poststructuralist (and constructivist) proposition that subjects are *constituted* in and by discourse, is by no means equivalent to saying that they are wholly *determined* by discourse. On the one hand, any concrete discursive formation implies a limited set of subject positions that subjects may actively occupy as self- and distant-observers. These positions delimit their scope of possible observation and articulation. On the other hand, however, the overdetermined character of even dominant discourses always involves the possibility of new articulations that partly elude hegemonic interpretations by displacement. Hence, while always being pervaded by power, no discourse can in the long run block the possibility of counterstrategies that subvert established hegemonies. It is precisely this discursive suspense of re/de/articulations that allows for subjective agency in discourses.

Interactive constructivism, then, sees education as a reality socially coconstructed by observers-agents-participants in cultural practices, routines, and institutions. The focus here is on education and learning as a cooperative and constructive process engaged in and conducted above all by the learners themselves. Like Dewey, interactive constructivism argues that education and learning always begin in the middle of things. Learning is a constructive activity of children, students, learners, and teachers as observers, agents, and participants in their lifeworlds or social life-experiences. Learning begins when learners use and expand their constructive agencies to solve problems and create meanings in the concrete situations they find themselves in. Accordingly, the role of the teacher in pragmatist or constructivist education changes to that of a facilitator or assistant to the learning processes of his/her students. This implies rather indirect forms of stimulating, informing, and coordinating in the context of, for example, cooperative problem solving processes. Finding ways of "teaching with your mouth shut" (Finkel 2000) may oftentimes be more effective for teachers than direct attempts at pedagogical instruction. As Dewey observed as early as 1915, "The function of the teacher must change from that of a cicerone and dictator to that of a watcher and helper. As teachers come to watch their individual pupils with a view to allowing each one the fullest development of his thinking and reasoning powers...the role of the child necessarily changes too. It becomes active instead of passive, the child becomes the questioner and experimenter" (MW 8: 318).

For interactive constructivism, as for Dewey (see Campbell 1992), the questioning and experimenting of the individual learner is always informed by the interpretive communities to which s/he belongs. It is rooted in shared cultural preunderstandings. In our terms, this implies that the learning experiments as well as the constructed solutions that individual learners attain are expressions of cultural viability. Cultural viability means that these experiments and solutions "fit" and make sense within the frame of a given interpretive community. It does not deny that other learners in other interpretive communities may come to quite different learning experiences and construct different solutions and interpretations. Thus, the constructivist concept of cultural viability explicitly stresses an important presupposition of education today: that in our (post)modern and multicultural world learning takes place in a variety of cultural contexts and thus it is not advisable for educators to privilege in advance one cultural perspective over all others. This radical commitment to pluralism is constitutive for a pragmatist or constructivist ethics in education. It is part of an equally radical commitment to democracy that we should, again, share with Dewey. Education today should be education for an open and pluralistic universe based on the democracy faith.

The continuing relevance of Dewey's philosophy for a contemporary education for democracy can hardly be overestimated (see also Campbell 1992; Eldridge 1998; Garrison 1998). It is not at all diminished by the fact that many commentators today believe—justly, to our mind—that it is possible and appropriate to complement and critically enlarge his sometimes seemingly totalizing holistic vision of democracy—exemplified, for example, in the "Search for the Great Community" (see LW 2: 325ff.)—by more recent approaches that put a different and partly more critical emphasis on questions of power relations, dissent, antagonisms, and hegemonic struggles (see Laclau 1990; Fraser 1994, 1998; Mouffe 1996; Neubert 2002; for a pragmatist feminist criticism, see also Seigfried 2002).

In order to understand discursive and cultural practices, we need a theory of communication. Interactive constructivism uses the three registers of the *symbolic*, the *imaginative*, and the *real*[2] as conceptual tools and theoretical frames that pay attention to the broader cultural contexts and conditions of social and educational communications (see Reich 2010, Ch. 4). As we will see, the three perspectives are highly interrelated. They can never be separated from each other.

a. *Symbolic representations.* Partly influenced by poststructuralist theories about language, signs, and discourses, many recent approaches to cultural theory conceptualize culture by focusing on symbolic representations and signifying practices (see, e.g., Hall 1997). They analyze and theoretically interpret the symbolic orders of lived cultures. Similarly, for interactive constructivism, culture consists of discursive fields of symbolic practices where meanings are construed, articulated, and communicated between partakers. The production of cultural realities is insofar a matter of viable symbolic re/de/constructions within discursive fields. To be sure, different observers-participants-agents can interpret the questions of cultural viability quite differently. To an increasing extent, this seems to be the case in postmodern pluralist societies (see Bauman 1997) where a common denominator for partaking in culture is largely out of sight. Remaining claims to universal validity of cultural norms and standards are increasingly being overlaid by a diversity of heterogeneous and partly even contradictory claims to viability. However, there must at least be a minimum of symbolic meanings and resources common to the members of a cultural group or interpretive community if they are to be able to conduct and partake in discourses at all.

In this connection the poststructuralist concept of "over-determination" (already mentioned above) plays an important role. It is claimed that the pragmatic usage of symbolic meanings and representations in cultural practices, routines, and institutions is on principle characterized by ambiguity and an excess of meaning. For example, the following passage from an introductory text by Stuart Hall gives an illustration of what symbolic overdetermination implies for the use of meanings in language:

> If meaning changes, historically, and is never finally fixed, then it follows that "taking the meaning" must involve an active process of interpretation ... Consequently, there is a necessary and inevitable imprecision about language. The meaning we take, as viewers, readers or audiences, is never exactly the meaning which has been given

by the speaker or writer or by other viewers. And since, in order to say something meaningful, we have to "enter language," where all sorts of older meanings which pre-date us, are already stored from previous eras, we can never cleanse language completely, screening out all the other, hidden meanings which might modify or distort what we want to say. (Hall 1997, 32–33)

b. *Imaginative desire.* Interactive constructivism extends the analysis of lived cultures by taking into consideration the role of imagination in culture. As expressions of imaginative desire, cultural representations involve processes of semantic displacement and condensation (see Reich 1998, vol. 2) that underlie the very dynamics of symbolic overdetermination. "Home, for example, is more than just a place symbolically named and objectified. It is a feeling, a desire, maybe a longing that expresses a vision. Disgust with certain food is more than just a symbolically stated attitude. It is an imaginary process charged with emotion and desire" (Neubert and Reich 2001, 7). According to interactive constructivism, imaginative desire is always involved in mutual mirror experiences between self and others (see Neubert and Reich 2006; Reich 2010). Partly taking place in unconscious ways, these mirror experiences express a desire for the recognition, appreciation, love, and so on of others that cannot be fully represented in symbolic ways. Thus, the imaginative appears as a limit of symbolic communication. With regard to imaginative desire, there is always something left. Although the partakers in communicative interactions may often aspire and imagine that they can directly reach each other's imagination through ways of the symbolic, the two registers never completely coincide. This is because imaginative mirror experiences largely take place on an immediate and subliminal level compared to symbolic articulation and direct linguistic exchange. Here, an unexpected gesture or a peculiar tone may sometimes "say" more than a thousand words.

c. *Fissures and gaps of the real.* We can never completely seal off our imaginative and symbolic constructions of reality from unanticipated, novel experiences. Whenever the seal is broken by experienced events, interactive constructivism speaks of *intrusions of the real.* In this view, "the real (as an event) has to be distinguished from reality (as constructed). The real enters experience as a tear or discontinuity, a lack of sense and meaning. We use the term "real" to denote the contingency of the not yet symbolically registered or imaginatively expected lurking behind any construction of reality" (Neubert and Reich 2001, 8). Taking us by surprise and entering our experience and perception unexpectedly, real events time and again mark the boundaries of our symbolic and imaginative search for meaning and identity. "These events do not 'fit'. They are the real in its obstinate eventfulness that cannot be easily integrated and transformed into elements of a culturally viable understanding. They astonish us: there is something that could not be foreseen, something alien, strange, incomprehensible. They move us to change our symbolic thinking or imaginary horizon" (ibid.).

The fissures and gaps of the real represent important limiting conditions of any cultural construction of reality. However, interactive constructivists reject any attempt to devise ontology of the real. They speak of the real strictly in the sense of a void signifier that denotes a limit of our constructive capacities as observers. For interactive constructivism, there is no overall perspective, no best or final observer as to the real. That is to say, we cannot know what the real *really is* without incorporating and assimilating it into our symbolic and imaginative constructions of reality. The intrusions of the real are as much expressions of our cultural resources as are our constructions of reality. What can enter our experience and observation as a real event may therefore differ quite considerably from culture to culture, from person to person, and even from situation to situation.

In other words, "the real" is but a construct that we devise in order to remind us that there is a world of events independent of our constructions. Our relative openness to the real is a question of our being sensitive and vulnerable to the world in which we live. The intrusions of the real are often described as events of confusing, dumbfounding, perplexing loss, lack, or failure, like witnessing the unexpected death of someone we love or feeling a sudden pain in our body without having any explanation. What these examples highlight is the dramatic extent to which real events may take us unawares and render us speechless. But the beauty of a landscape that seizes the spectator or the sublime feeling that captures one in the presence of a work of art are quite as much examples of our being open to the real in our lives.

The three registers have a number of important implications for a constructivist theory of education. We will give a brief overview.[3]

a. *Development and constructive appropriation of symbolic realities.* As to the level of symbolic representations, constructivist educators should be attentive to the richness, diversity, and ambiguity of symbolic meanings in contemporary multiculture. They should strive to give their students as broad and manifold an access to the symbolic resources of their lifeworlds as possible. They should see learning as a cultural process of negotiation where symbolic resources are appropriated through constructive interpretations and applications by the learners themselves. And they should be responsive to the ambiguities, changes, and hegemonic effects of meanings in culture. The symbolic construction of realities never starts out of nothing, but presupposes a complex and in part even contradictory body of passed on meanings and hegemonic interpretations implied in the symbolic orders of language and culture. Constructivist educators should be ready to take into account the power effects that inhere in the very symbolic systems of representation in a society of diverse and often antagonistic interests. Such systems of representation should always be seen in historical contexts (see Popkewitz, Franklin, and Pereyra 2001) in which established relations, for example, of class, race, and gender are inscribed on all levels of representation (like language games, cultural myths, and discursive formations). This means that constructivist education implies the work of construction as well as criticism. (We like to think in terms of an endless cycle of construction, deconstruction, and reconstruction.) Dewey was already quite aware of this challenge:

> There is no one among us who is not called upon to face honestly and courageously the equipment of beliefs, religious, political, artistic, economic, that has come to him in all sorts of indirect and uncriticized ways, and to inquire how much of it is validated and verified in present need, opportunity, and application. Each one finds when he makes this search that much is idle lumber and much is an oppressive burden. Yet we give storeroom to the lumber and we assume the restriction of carrying the burden. (LW 5: 142)

b. *Development and cultivation of imaginative realities.* Constructivist educators must develop a sense for the construction and cultivation of the imaginative powers of their students and learners. They should provide educational contexts and environments that allow for the development of imaginative desire. Desire is a power that cannot be instructed. But it is possible to provide educational environments in which desire can grow and become intelligently shaped in such a way as to allow developing subjects (e.g., our students) to grow in and by appreciative mirror experiences (see Garrison 1997). Imaginative encounters between educators and learners can be motivating resources for self-esteem, initiative, autonomy, and responsibility on the side of all participants when they are embedded in projects of coconstructive learning. This is not at all an easy task for educators, and there are no ready-made precepts or symbolic rules that one can follow with secure success. This is because learners and educators are beings whose particular imaginative desires do not always "fit" into the prefabricated educational expectations and symbolic schemes. From the view of interactive constructivism, we can, however, identify at least some crucial preconditions—necessary, but not sufficient conditions— to be fulfilled if constructivist educators are to engage successfully in education as an imaginative encounter.[4] Among these are the following:

1. First, constructivist educators must develop and cultivate their own imaginative desire for shared learning processes in order to be able to communicate their educational intentions authentically to others and allow for genuine constructive participations of their own.

2. Second, they must cultivate a true respect and esteem for the otherness of the other's imaginative desires and be ready to accept and appreciate this otherness even when symbolical understanding fails or falls short.

3. Third, and as a consequence, they must be willing to have their learners take them by surprise by way of *their* imaginative constructions of reality. That is to say, they must cultivate a sense for the freshness and originality of imaginative encounters that comes to light only where the uniqueness of the imaginative other is given space.

4. Fourth, they must be able to reflect on the complexity and indeterminacy of imaginative mirror experiences in the sense described above. They must be willing to recognize the limits of symbolic communication and of their own perceptions and interpretations of educational situations. This recognition may in turn relieve them of the all too commonly felt obligation that educators must completely and accurately understand everything and everyone if they are to do their job well. Exaggerated expectations as to our possibilities of symbolic understanding may even be seen as a frequent source of burnout experiences in educational vocations.

c. *Sensibility to real events and the limits of reality constructions.* Learning through interactively coconstructing symbolic and imaginative realities always occurs on the fringes of "the real," as we described it earlier. To keep learning, we have to be vulnerable

to the world in which we live in the sense that we actively recognize that none of our reality constructions—comprehensive
and elaborated as they may be—is ever exhaustive as to the possibilities of future real events. Constructivist educators therefore
must cultivate a sense of openness and curiosity as to what might
surprise themselves and their learners in the cooperative learning
processes they are engaged in. This openness refers to the levels of
both contents and relationships. If we concede that there is no best
and final observer perspective as to *what* we should learn and *how*
we should learn together, we ultimately have to keep experimenting with the contents and relationships of learning. This is not
to depreciate the value of established educational theories, practices, and institutions that make up and sustain the educational
realities of a given time and place. Their relative worth as viable
resources for the solution of educational problems has to be evalu-
ated time and again in the context of changing societal and educational conditions. But it is to claim that no matter how positively
we assess their viability, these theories, practices, and institutions
are always limited reality constructions that cannot ever exhaust
our possibilities to learn from real events. Constructivist educators
should be ready to have their own theoretical certainties, practical routines, and institutional arrangements be challenged by the
real experiences they make in the concrete interactions with their
learners. And they should be eager to allow their students to have
their own real experiences within and beyond the framework of
theoretical, practical, and institutional expectations that make up
the cultural setting of the actual educational situation. This relative openness to the real in our world suggests that constructivist
education be seen as a continual process of conceptual, practical,
and institutional re/de/constructions on the part of both educators and learners.

With these introductory remarks on the Cologne program of constructivism in mind, we now turn to the selected theoretical approaches
that we have chosen for innovative exchanges with Deweyan pragmatism. These are very prominent and influential approaches in recent
philosophical and social thought. However, to a certain extent our
selection is of course arbitrary. We could have chosen other or further
dialogue partners. Indeed, we urge you to choose others for yourself. Still, we think that our selection offers promising perspectives
for reconstructing pragmatism because they show sufficient affinities with its core concepts and perspectives while differing in some

essential aspects. They can help to reintroduce Dewey's educational philosophy as a relevant position for our time. But how can such a project be successful? We suggest that we as authors can only take a few first steps here and leave it to the reader to think through the challenges and questions that will arise by themselves. For our part, we develop and briefly discuss some important educational implications against the background of interactive constructivism and leave it to the reader to further connect these perspectives with their own educational studies. In any way, doing Dewey today means reconstructing Dewey, from whatever perspective we take, with an eye to challenges of our own time and context.[5]

The six authors that we include in the following discussions—Zygmunt Bauman, Michel Foucault, Pierre Bourdieu, Jacques Derrida, Emmanuel Levinas, and Richard Rorty—articulate seminal positions in recent developments in philosophy, the humanities, the social sciences, and education. Many other researchers and approaches work in their wake today. It would be impossible here to name even the basic literature that deals with exposing and developing their traditions. We would hope that it might invite readers to think through possibilities of relating Dewey with other contemporary approaches. At least, though, we claim that our selection covers fields of reflection that have a large and pervasive influence on contemporary debates. We will indicate some directions and resources by posing open questions and giving suggestions for further reflection.

In the following attempts to recontextualize Dewey for our time, then, three main levels of tension come into play and pervade the discussion: First, there is the tension between Dewey's day and ours. Second, there is the tension between Dewey's texts and the writings of these six other authors. And third, there is the tension between our own interpretations and criticisms as pragmatist or interactive constructivists. We hope that, taken together, these tensions help to intensify the sense of actual challenges that are on stake and render part 4 for the reader as suggestive as it was enjoyable for us to write it.

ZYGMUNT BAUMAN

In his new introduction to the 1948 reprint of *Reconstruction in Philosophy* (MW 12: 256–277), John Dewey says that today—some 25 years after the original publication—he would prefer the title "Reconstruction *of* Philosophy."[6] Philosophy, as he points out, is in constant need of reconstruction because "the distinctive office, problems and subject matter of philosophy grow out of stresses and strains

122   JOHN DEWEY'S PHILOSOPHY OF EDUCATION

in the community life in which a given form of philosophy arises." Accordingly, "its specific problems vary with the changes in human life that are always going on and that at times constitute a crisis and a turning point in human history" (ibid., 256). Dewey cites the scientific, industrial, and political revolutions of the last few centuries as instances of crucial changes that amount to historical turning points in human life.

Dewey thinks that one great challenge posed to philosophical reconstruction is constituted by the fact that modernity, as he sees it, is still "unformed" and "inchoate" (ibid., 273), caught up in contradictions, uncertainties, confusions, and ambiguities between "an old and a new that are incompatible" (ibid.). He does not claim that the task of finding constructive solutions to this entangled situation is a work that can be achieved by philosophers or any other group of experts. Rather, it is a practical task that needs to be done by "human beings as human" (ibid., 277). This conviction of course reflects Dewey's deep commitment to democracy and democratic problem solving as the necessary response to the problems that arise in social developments. His commitment is closely related to his belief in the potentialities of social intelligence as a shorthand designation for the ideal of settling conflicts and solving problems by methods of experimentation, cooperation, and discussion under conditions of free and inclusive participation of all involved. "Intelligence," he claims about his use of the word, stands for "great and ever-growing methods of observation, experiment and reflective reasoning" that have revolutionized the physical and physiological conditions of life, but "have not as yet been worked out for application to what is itself distinctively and basically *human*" (ibid., 258). The split also applies, according to Dewey, to inquiry in the more specialized sense of science: "The science that has so far found its way deeply and widely into the actual affairs of human life," he complains, "is partial and incomplete science" (ibid., 269).

What is needed in this situation is, according to Dewey, more intelligent and cooperative inquiry into "matters of supreme significance to man" (ibid.)—that is, social inquiry and inquiry into human affairs. He believes that in this situation one crucial challenge for philosophical reconstruction lies in contributing to and furthering a general intellectual climate or "atmosphere" that is supportive to the further development of methods and practices of intelligent and experimental inquiry in social matters and human affairs: "Here, then, lies the reconstructive work to be done by philosophy. It must undertake to do for the development of inquiry into human affairs and hence into morals what the philosophers of the last few centuries did for promotion of scientific inquiry in physical and physiological conditions and aspects of human life" (ibid., 266). Among other things, he mentions the state of sociological inquiry in his time and criticizes its positivist reductionism: "When 'sociological' theory withdraws from consideration of the basic interests, concerns, the actively moving aims, of a human culture on the ground that 'values' are involved and that inquiry as 'scientific' has nothing to do with values, the inevitable consequence is that inquiry in the human area is confined to what is superficial and comparatively trivial" (ibid., 268). And he claims that "if and when inquiry attempts to enter in critical fashion into that which is human in its full sense," it will of necessity have to confront the present impact of traditions, institutional customs, and prejudices passed down from previous ages and have to respond to the deep contradictions and ambivalences that pervade modernity (ibid.).

Cultural and social theories are always constructions out of the contexts of their time. In accord with Deweyan pragmatism, we see the continual need of reconstruction and the need of taking into account the open-endedness of cultural and social developments in which we are involved. Against this background, we think that a dialogue between Deweyan pragmatism and the postmodern sociology of Zygmunt Bauman opens promising perspectives for philosophical reconstruction today. Our intention is not to give a comparison between Dewey and Bauman in the strict sense, because this seems to be impossible for us from the start. Their approaches are too different in methodological frames, conceptual foundations, and contexts of orientation. Unlike Dewey, Bauman does not provide a comprehensive and systematical philosophical approach, but his interest as a sociologist of postmodernity—or what in his more recent publications he calls "liquid modernity"—is to provide critical descriptions and diagnoses of social reality and human affairs. We can use Bauman's contributions to refresh and inspire the reconstruction of Dewey's pragmatism today. At the same time, we suggest that Dewey offers a broad and still relevant philosophical theory and perspective that can contribute to reflecting more comprehensively and systematically the grounds of critical social inquiry in our time. Therefore, what we intend is rather a mutually productive dialogue than a comparison.

Let us look first at modernity. According to Bauman, one of the most crucial features of modernity is its quest for order. More specifically, the order that modernity strives for is something that must be brought about, intentionally, something that must be produced and superimposed on the world through human endeavor. The quest for order therefore takes the form of a continual and progressive project. Modernity, according to Bauman, is marked by the discovery that order is not natural; it is a time when order is reflected upon and becomes a deliberate task (see Bauman 1993b, 4–6). Order is achieved by classification, which involves acts of inclusion and exclusion that often follow a binary code of opposition. Any such "operation of inclusion/exclusion is an act of violence perpetrated upon the world, and requires the support of a certain amount of coercion" (ibid., 2).

Order promises clarity, transparency, certainty of prediction, and control. Yet, ironically, the ordering work of classification also inevitably entails the emergence of ambivalence as a "side-product." Bauman tells us that this is so because no "binary classification deployed in the construction of order can fully overlap with essentially non-discrete, continuous experience of reality. The opposition, born of the horror of ambiguity, becomes the main source of ambivalence. The enforcement of any classification inevitably means the production of anomalies" (ibid., 61). Hence, he concludes that ambivalence is "the waste of modernity...arguably the modern era's most genuine worry and concern, since unlike other enemies, defeated and enslaved, it grows in strength with every success of modern powers. It is its own failure that the tidying-up activity construes as ambivalence" (ibid., 15). The modern quest for order of necessity goes hand in hand with struggles against ambivalence—the passionate endeavor to get rid of indeterminateness, ambiguities, undecidabilities, surplus meanings, and such. Since the task is itself impossible, modernity, according to Bauman, restlessly produces ever-new attempts at building order and purging ambivalence.

Seen from a Deweyan perspective, the modern quest for order and the more general intellectual quest for certainty that was a repeated target of Dewey's philosophical critique, both suffer from the same disease—namely, failure to recognize and fully accept human experience in all of its diverse qualities, dark and apparent, ambiguous and settled, precarious and stable. For Dewey, experience in an open and unfinished universe is of necessity characterized by order as well as contingency. Both are ineradicable traits of natural existence (see LW 1; LW 4). But modern thought, in its quest for order, rationality, and progress, often tends to neglect its necessary opposite. "Our magical safeguard against the uncertain character of the world is to deny the existence of chance, to mumble universal and necessary law, the ubiquity of cause and effect, the uniformity of nature, universal

progress, and the inherent rationality of the universe" (LW 1: 45).
Dewey observes (as Bauman does) that the most influential safeguard
for this neglect in modern thought is scientific and technological
progress. "Through science we have secured a degree of power of
prediction and of control; through tools, machinery and an accom-
panying technique we have made the world more comfortable to our
needs, a more secure abode" (ibid.). However, the very results of
rationality and progress remain ambiguous in that they produce new
solutions as well as new problems. The order they achieve cannot do
away with the precarious phase of human experience because their
solutions are always partial and selective. "Selective emphasis, choice,
is inevitable whenever reflection occurs" (ibid., 34). They of necessity involve omissions as to the possible consequences of constructed
and applied solutions. "Strain thought as far as we may and not all
consequences can be foreseen or made an express or known part of
reflection and decision" (ibid., 28). Therefore, "when all is said and
done, the fundamentally hazardous character of the world is not seriously modified, much less eliminated" (ibid., 45). Dewey points to
the destructive excesses of modern life—like the war and preparations
for future wars—to underline the inevitability of this concession.

Bauman's analysis and critique of modern culture bears important
affinities to this pragmatist cultural theory and critique. Similarities
are obvious, for example, when Bauman writes about the unfulfilled
claims of modernity and its contradictions:

> The ideal of the naming/classifying function strives to achieve is a sort
> of commodious filing cabinet that contains all the files that contain
> all the items that the world contains—but confines each file and each
> item within a separate place of its own...It is the non-viability of such
> a filing cabinet that makes ambivalence unavoidable. And it is the per-
> severance with which construction of such a cabinet is pursued that
> brings forth ever new supplies of ambivalence. (Bauman 1993b, 2)

In this connection, he argues that modernity regards "*fragmentation* of the world" as one of its most important achievements and
strengths (see ibid., 12). This is close to the following account given
in Dewey's *Art as Experience*:

> The institutional life of mankind is marked by disorganization. This
> disorder is often disguised by the fact that it takes the form of static
> division into classes, and this static separation is accepted as the very
> essence of order as long as it is so fixed and so accepted as not to gener-
> ate open conflict. Life is compartmentalized and the institutionalized

compartments are classified as high and as low; their values as pro-
fane and spiritual, as material and ideal. Interests are related to one
another externally and mechanically, through a system of check and
balances...Compartmentalization of occupations and interests brings
about separation of that mode of activity commonly called "practice"
from insight, of imagination from executive doing, of significant purpose from work, of emotion from though and doing...Those who
write the anatomy of experience then suppose that these divisions
inhere in the very constitution of human nature. (LW 10: 26ff.)

Affinities are not limited to occasional details of inquiry but apply to
the very core concepts that both authors use. They suggest a common attitude toward certain basic features of modernity as an open
and contradictory project. Like Dewey, Bauman takes his start from
concrete experience as it is lived by men and women in their times,
although he does not provide a philosophical elaboration of "experience" that is comparable to Dewey's. Writing as a sociologist, Bauman
rather concentrates on the description and interpretation of life-experiences in the changing contexts of society. Thereby he shows that
the solid grounds that modernity attempted to establish have been
subverted by the increasing fluidity of living that brings their inherent
contradictions to the fore. Bauman here speaks of the experience of
uncertainty that has become a major source of discontent in social life
today (see Bauman 1997). In his theory of modern culture, Dewey
already extensively reflected on the tension between the precarious
and the stable aspects of human life-experiences. For him, this tension was important for philosophical reflection in many aspects, and
he regarded "the precarious and the stable" as an important conceptual tool for philosophical perspectives on social as well as individual
developments, for example, in culture, communication, education,
and all kinds of practices, routines, and institutions. In comparison
to Dewey, Bauman does not put the same emphasis on the theoretical
reflection of continuity in experience, because he provides no theory
of social action that is comparable to Dewey's. His strong point rather
consists in his accurate and very detailed descriptions of the role that
contingency plays in social life in the transitions from modernity to
postmodernity. In many regards, he does for our time what Dewey
did in his, given Dewey's continuous and lifelong dealings with social
realities and human affairs in all their contingencies and contradictions. Yet Bauman's discourse is more descriptive and seems to fulfill a sort of "therapeutic" function in the sense defined by Richard
Rorty. He opens our eyes to often-neglected, hidden, and concealed
aspects of (post)modern life. Bauman interprets the development of

modernity and modern forms of individualization as a product of changes in social relations and structures rather than a mere product of enlightenment and liberal discourse (see Bauman 1993b, 6). Modernity can never reach the point of declaring the completion of its projects. As Bauman argues in his *Postmodern Ethics*, it cannot even achieve a "non-ambivalent, non-aporetic ethical code," which every rational man will choose as the best chance to live (ibid., 9). Yet this dream has always been a moving force in modern thinking. Its surrender is one central principle of postmodernity for Bauman. This is a point where Bauman clearly thinks beyond Dewey and Dewey's time.

From the viewpoint of interactive constructivism, however, it is noteworthy that both Dewey and Bauman have a great sensitivity to ambivalence and the contradictions of progress. But speaking from their different historical contexts, they show a somewhat different emphasis in these affairs and portray them against somewhat different horizons. For instance, Bauman, writing about the ambivalences of postmodernity, shows progress as a game of gains and losses: "You gain something, but usually you lose something in exchange" (Bauman 1997, 1). He refers to one of Freud's central messages in his famous critique of modern culture—published as *Civilization and Its Discontents*—which launched the skeptical diagnosis that modern culture's achievements of security and order had only been reached at the necessary expense of human freedom and happiness. According to Bauman, the same message still holds true for postmodernity, only that in the transitions from modernity to postmodernity "the gains and losses have changed places: *postmodern men and women exchanged a portion of their possibilities of security for a portion of happiness*. The discontents of modernity arose from a kind of security which tolerated too little freedom in the pursuit of individual happiness. The discontents of postmodernity arise from a kind of freedom of pleasure-seeking which tolerates too little individual security" (ibid., 3; emphasis in original).

Dewey, too, speaks of gains and losses in the context of social developments, for example, when he writes about American civilization:

> So it is possible to itemize with more or less accuracy certain gains and losses in American life, and yet not know what they import for the prosperity of our social body...I mean...that when we list items of gain and loss in opposite columns, we find paradoxes, contradictions of extraordinary range and depth; and...that these contradictions are evidence of what seems to be the most marked trait of our present state—namely, its inner tension and conflict. If ever there was a house of civilization divided within itself and against itself, it is our own

today. If one were to take only some symptoms and ignore others, one might make either a gloomy or a glowing report, and each with equal justice—as far as each went. (LW 3: 133ff.)

By comparison, Bauman's views especially on the losses and failures of modernity that extend into postmodernity are more comprehensive, more sober, and also more specific than Dewey's who sometimes shows a tendency to downplay the losses in light of his hopes for productive solutions and advancements of democracy. In *Liquid Modernity*, Bauman identifies five main traits of modernity that can exemplify the dark sides of modern life:

> Among the principal icons of that modernity were the *Fordist factory*, which reduced human activities to simple, routine and by and large predesigned moves meant to be followed obediently and mechanically without engaging mental faculties, and holding all spontaneity and individual initiative off limits; *bureaucracy*, akin at least in its innate tendency to Max Weber's ideal model, in which identities and social bonds were deposited on entry in the cloakroom together with hats, umbrellas and overcoats, so that solely the command and the statute book could drive, uncontested, the actions of insiders as long as they stayed inside; *Panopticon*, with its watch-towers and the inmates never allowed to count on their surveillants' momentary lapses of vigilance; *Big Brother*, who never dozes off, always keen, quick and expeditions in rewarding the faithful and punishing the infidels; and—finally—the *Konzlager* [concentration camp] (later to be joined in the counter-Pantheon of modern demons by the Gulag), the site where the limits of human malleability were tested under laboratory conditions, while all those presumed not to be or found not to be malleable enough were doomed to perish of exhaustion or sent to gas chambers and crematoria. (Bauman 2000, 25–26; emphasis in original)

According to this interpretation, the Fordist factory, bureaucracy, Panopticon, Big Brother, and the holocaust are not mere accidents of modernity but belong to its potentialities. The first four are necessary components of modern developments until today. The Holocaust stands for the worst catastrophes growing out of modernity (see Bauman 1989). Looking backward, Bauman is certainly more skeptical about the prospects of progress than Dewey who, looking forward, searches for opportunities of democratic reconstructions and consecutive steps to better life conditions.

From the perspective of interactive constructivism, we should expect from the very start that observations of human affairs depend on contexts of participation and action, and clearly the subject positions that Dewey and Bauman articulate differ considerably with regard to such contexts. Both articulations are constructions of reality that respond in viable ways to their respective contexts. Viability of observation is a core criterion in constructivism, but in interactive constructivism, we favor a cultural concept of viability that does not only focus on observation but at the same time takes account of participation and action in cultural contexts. If we compare Dewey and Bauman's position, we can say that Dewey is much closer to a traditional participant position in modernity. From this subject position, he—as a participant, agent, and observer—critically addresses the contradictions and ambivalences of his time with a view to democratic reconstruction. Compared to Bauman, he partly lacks the ironic distance of the latter that speaks in retrospection from the postmodern discourses in which he situates his observations and self-reflections as a participant and agent. As interactive constructivists, we think that Bauman's irony—like the irony of Richard Rorty—can help us today to live with the unfulfilled expectations and great dreams of the twentieth century. But nevertheless, the strong sense of democratic hope and vision that Dewey stands for, his acute sense for taking participation as a necessary foundation of lived democracy, his insistence on the relevance of action and agency, still seem significant in our time despite all ironic relativization.

Bauman's current influence is due not only to the large number of his publications but also to his extraordinary ability to illustrate and explain present social life conditions in many facets and largely accessible language. Speaking of "postmodernity," Bauman does not want to claim the end or abandonment of modernity. He thinks that the term "postmodern" is itself a transitional name given to a situation that lacks a more positive designation. In a 2002 interview, he observes,

> To start with, the concept of "postmodern" was but a stop-gap choice, a "career report" of a search... "Postmodern" has done its preliminary, site-clearing job: it aroused vigilance and sent the exploration in the right direction. It could not do much more, and so it shortly outlived its usefulness... About the qualities of the present-day world we can say now more than it is *unlike* the old familiar one. We have, so to speak, matured to afford (to risk?) a *positive* theory of the novelty. (Bauman and Yakimova 2002, 2; emphasis in original)

He believes that from the very start there was a certain weakness in using the term. It was pregnant with the potential misunderstanding that modernity is over and gone. The most serious proponents of postmodernity, like Lyotard and Bauman himself, have always tried to counter such misunderstanding, but protests "did not help much, even as strong ones as Lyotard's ('one cannot be postmodern without being first modern')—let alone my insistence that 'postmodernity is modernity minus its illusion'. Nothing would help; if words mean anything, then a 'postX' will always mean a state of affairs that has left the 'X' behind" (ibid., 2). There have been several other attempts to characterize the conditions and constellations of contemporary life by using names like "late modernity" or "reflective modernity." In his more recent books, Bauman himself prefers the term "liquid modernity." As we have seen above, modernity is of necessity an age of constant movements and changes. Bauman argues,

> *All* modernity means incessant, obsessive modernization (there is no *state* of modernity, only a *process*; modernity would cease being modernity the moment that the process ground to a halt); and *all* modernization consists in "disembedding," "disencumbering," "melting the solids" etc; in other words, in dismantling the received structures or at least weakening their grip. From the start, modernity deprived the web of human relationships of its past holding force; "disembedded" and set loose, humans were expected to seek new beds and dig themselves in them using their own hands and spades, even if they chose to remain in the bed in which they germinated. (Ibid., 4; emphasis in original)

There is continuity between forms of modernity in past and present. What is new today, in times of liquid modernity, is not this very quality itself but the fact that the contexts of its social containment have radically changed. "New is that the 'disembedding' goes on unabated, while the prospects of 're-embedding' are nowhere in sight and unlikely to appear" (ibid., 4). In liquid modernity, social relations and commitments are easily and quickly changed or even abandoned in favor of new opportunities. It might even turn out as a trap to stick too long and too insistently to them. Under these conditions, there is an increasing new pressure upon individuals to adjust themselves time and again to rapidly changing social bonds and ever-new rules that change while the social game goes on.

According to Bauman, we can observe certain important changes between the heavy/solid/condensed/systemic modernity of Dewey's lifetime and the more light/liquid/diffuse/network-like forms of modernity today (see Bauman 2000, 25ff.). Among other things, these changes have crucial implications for democracy and education. For instance, Bauman observes that the conditions, challenges, risks, and opportunities of individualization and emancipation have changed considerably:

> That heavy/solid/condensed/systemic modernity of the "critical Theory" era was endemically pregnant with the tendency towards totalitarianism. The totalitarian society of all-embracing, compulsory and enforced homogeneity loomed constantly and threateningly on the horizon...That modernity was a sworn enemy of contingency, variety, ambiguity, waywardness and idiosyncrasy, having declared on all such "anomalies" a holy war of attrition; and it was individual free-dom and autonomy that were commonly expected to be the prime casualties of the crusade. (Bauman 2000, 25)

Against this background, the main focus of emancipation projects in solid modernity was to liberate, safeguard, and empower individual-ity against the totalizing powers of surveillance, discipline, control, oppression, etc. that were threatening to normalize all appearances of "contingency, variety, ambiguity, waywardness and idiosyncrasy" by confining and reducing them to elements in an imposed and solid order.

In liquid modernity, though, the constellations between individ-uality and social order have changed in some important respects. Individuality and increasing demands of individualization are now seen as necessary components of a social order that has become more and more fluid. Instead of the older antagonisms between individu-ality and social order, there is now, according to Bauman, a growing gap between what he calls "individuality *de jure*"—that is, the tasks of individualization that men and women are socially required to take upon themselves—and "individuality *de facto*"—that is, their abilities, dispositions, chances, and resources to make, articulate, and realize the choices they really want to make. Being an "indi-vidual *de* jure means having no one to blame for one's own misery, seeking the causes of one's own defeats nowhere excepts in one's own indolence and sloth, and looking for no remedies other than trying harder and harder still" (Bauman 2000, 38). Bauman argues that in face of this situation, emancipation "in its present stage can only be described as the task of transforming the individual autonomy *de jure* into autonomy *de facto*" (ibid., 51), so that individuals can "gain control over their fate and make the choices they truly desire" (ibid., 39). Bauman clearly sees that this task is a crucial challenge for democracy today. Against the background of interactive con-structivism's perspectives on observers, agents, and participants in cultural contexts we may say that this social challenge is essentially a challenge for education. Individuals and social systems both have to respond in ways of construction, reconstruction, and deconstruction to the opportunities as well as limits and dangers involved in times of liquid modernity. With Dewey, we can observe more forcefully than Bauman himself does that it is a crucial task for education in our time. Interpreting Bauman through a Deweyan lens, we may say that claims about individuality de jure and individuality de facto constitute a tensional relation with important implications for educational theory today. Dewey's focus on experience in education indicates a necessary way for overcoming the gap that Bauman diagnoses between individuality de jure and de facto. Indeed, Bauman's account gives evidence for why a Deweyan approach to education based on the cultural, constructive, and communicative turns we talked about above, is today at least as significant as it was in Dewey's own time. If Bauman thinks that the gap is even growing in our time, we agree with Dewey that working against the gap is a social task that cannot be done without education.

From the perspective of interactive constructivism, we can observe still other tensional relations with important implications for education that appear in new light when we put Dewey's philosophy and Bauman's contemporary analyses into dialogue.

Consider the relation between stability and change in social life under present conditions. For both Dewey and Bauman, this issue is essentially connected with the ambivalent relation between democracy and capitalism. On the one hand, capitalism has produced social structures and conditions that partly sustain and support emancipation because they provide resources and platforms for producing wealth and prosperity as a necessary precondition for constructing and experiencing new ways and forms of freedom. This process has been a drive for modern reconstructions of democracy. But on the other hand, capitalism also repeatedly puts the democratic project at risk. Dewey and Bauman, recognize this ambivalence very clearly. For example, Dewey observes about the contradictions of emancipation under capitalist conditions,

> The democratic movement of emancipation of personal capacities, of securing to each individual an effective right to count in the order and movement of society as a whole (that is, in the common good), has gone far enough to secure to many, more favored than others, peculiar powers and possessions. It is part of the irony of the situation that such now oppose efforts to secure equality of opportunity to all on the ground that these efforts would effect an invasion of individual liberties and rights: i.e., of privileges based on inequality. (MW 5: 430)

In a broader sense, Dewey criticizes antidemocratic effects of capitalism like the reduction of work to labor, the compartmentalization of social life, the fragmentation of experiences, and the separation of thought and action, ideals and real conditions (see LW 10: 27–34). One of the "hard facts" of actual capitalism is competition. He observes that social life and economic relations in his day are characterized by extensive forms of precariousness. The great changes that went with the processes of industrialization led to the problem of millions of people having only a "minimum of control over the conditions of their own subsistence" (ibid., 300). Again, he combines his critical analysis with constructive orientations toward possible and more democratic solutions. For him, the essential problem is to further social intelligence, creativity, and imagination in order to find new and extended ways of reconstructing democracy to enlarge the possibilities of all for participation and better living. He believes that the democratic vision points beyond competitive individualism and the social risks involved in *laissez faire,* or what we now call neoliberalism. For instance, he observes about the financial and economic crisis of his own day, "The extreme individualism of laissez faire, with competition as the only regulator of the economic process, has been shown to be no longer tolerable in present conditions" (LW 7: 428). This sounds strangely familiar if we think of the recent global crisis that has considerably undermined the promised securities of late capitalism.

Bauman, too, observes aspects and dimensions of precariousness that arise from neoliberal competition on a global scale in our time. "Precariousness is the mark of the preliminary condition of all the rest: the livelihood, and particularly the most common sort of livelihood, that which is claimed on the ground of work and employment" (Bauman 2000, 160). Livelihood in postmodern or liquid times has become more fragile and less reliable. Flexibility is a core demand. Liquid life is a continuous succession of new beginnings, transformations, and reconstructions. Markets have become more fluid and extensive. What seems to be too stable does not sell. More and more people have to adjust their lives to it. Their world increasingly becomes liquid. Behind the curtains, capitalism has changed: "The present-day 'liquefied,' 'flowing,' dispersed, scattered and deregulated version of modernity may not portend divorce and the final break of communication, but it does augur the advent of light, free-floating capitalism, marked by the *disengagement* and loosening of ties linking capital and labour" (Bauman 2000, 149; italics in original). In the globalizing economies of today, new forms of capital have emerged, and most of them have taken a lighter character than in former times: "Having shed the ballast of bulky machinery and massive factory crews, capital travels light with no more than cabin luggage—a briefcase, laptop computer and cellular telephone" (ibid., 150). At the same time, the increasing disengagement and volatility of capital adds to the growing precariousness of life for all those who remain dependent on labor and are less mobile than the light travelers.

Modern sociologists like Max Weber and Norbert Elias have portrayed the capacities of acting in large perspective and postponing gratification or satisfaction on behalf of a comprehensive project as essential virtues of work in capitalism. Liquid capitalism tends to undermine these traditional virtues, depriving the individuals of a sustainable and stable form of orientation and disposing them to new risks and anxieties. "The most acute and stubborn worries that haunt such a life are the fears of being caught napping, of failing to catch up with fast-moving events, of being left behind, of overlooking 'use by' dates, of being saddled with possessions that are no longer desirable, of missing the moment that calls for a change of track before crossing the point of no return" (Bauman 2005, 2). Comparatively speaking, these anxieties and particular forms of worry are relatively new phenomena and consequences of capitalism. Following Bauman, they testify to a new constellation in which the tensional relationship between the precarious and the stable aspects of modern life appear today. From our perspective, this new constellation poses crucial challenges for rethinking the opportunities and prospects of democracy and education in our time.

Let us briefly look at a further tensional relation with important implications for democracy and education—the relation between diversity and solidarity. Both, Bauman and Dewey, recognize the necessity of communities for democracy as well as their potential ambivalences. Freedom and community are understood in a necessary correlation and tension. Bauman uses examples like nationalism, patriotism, and communitarism to show the need and the potential traps of the construction of a "we" as a collective agent that constitutes a community. Such communities can be very restrictive and have a homogenizing effect upon their members, like oftentimes in cases of communitarism that Bauman profoundly criticizes. Against such forms of community, he insists on the advantages of a democratic way that can be understood as "an emergent unity which is a joint achievement of the agents engaged in self-identification pursuits, a unity which is an outcome, not an a priori given condition, of shared life, a unity put together through negotiation and reconciliation, not the denial, stifling or smothering out of differences" (Bauman 2000, 178).

For Bauman as well as for Dewey, it is clear that the struggle for democracy is a struggle that must be fought out by all who want to live under democratic conditions. It cannot be won by one class or group, for example, of experts or elites, alone. Similar to Deweyan pragmatism, Bauman believes that the realization of freedom is only possible in and through social relationships, and one of the threads of capitalism to democracy is precisely that it puts human relationships at risk. If we want to develop and strengthen democracy under capitalist conditions, the hard questions have to do with unequal chances for participation and the need for solidarity. Bauman insists in all his critical diagnosis of social life in post- or liquid modernity that solidarity most of all has to do with fighting against poverty. Democracy cannot survive in the long run if the gap between those who have and get more and those who have not and stand in danger of losing all exceeds a critical level. Bauman especially warns us, in this context, against "the renunciation, phasing out or selling off by the state of all the major appurtenances of its role as the principal (perhaps even more monopolistic) purveyor of certainty and security" (Bauman 2000, 184). Democratic solidarity implies a basic income for all that is sustainable for active participation in social and cultural life. To give substance to solidarity, interactive constructivism insists on claims to equity in education to counteract antidemocratic tendencies in unequal societies (see Hutmacher, Cochrane, and Bottani 2001). The Deweyan tradition of democracy and education provides resources and ways that even today are indispensible for fulfilling this task.

Summary

Bauman helps us to understand some important implications of the challenges of democracy and education in times of liquid modernity and light capitalism. He shows us new forms of ambivalence that pervade projects of emancipation and individualism today. Interpreting Bauman, we have emphasized three tensional relationships that appear as especially relevant for education. All three respond to topics that have already been focal in Dewey, but they render and formulate these topics in a more contemporary context. Who today addresses educational theory and philosophy, such is our basic claim, must also address the paradoxes and ambivalences we discussed with Bauman and Dewey.

Questions for Discussion

What is your attitude toward our times? Are you optimistic, pessimistic, ironical, or something else?

How deep goes ambivalence in modern life? Are all social processes and developments necessarily ambivalent? Is genuine and unambiguous progress possible?

Can we still hold on to a critical ideal of emancipation today? What is your own understanding of emancipation? Can you combine Dewey's and Bauman's perspectives in this respect?

Can you identify concrete aspects or examples of precariousness in contemporary life conditions? Can education respond to these? How?

Do you think that the problems of poverty and unequal chances put the democratic project at risk? If so, how can contemporary societies respond to these challenges?

What institutional changes and reconstructions can compensate for the decline of the national state today?

Can we globalize democratic solidarity?

MICHEL FOUCAULT

As to the relationship of democracy and power, Dewey observes, "What the argument for democracy implies is that the best way to produce initiative and constructive power is to exercise it.[7] Power, as well as interest, comes by use and practice" (LW 11: 224). Here, power is the power of doing. This is astonishingly close to Michel Foucault's theory of power relations. Foucault, too, reconstructs power from the agents' actions and practices. This way, he arrives at an amazing differentiation of the aspects of power. But this differentiation does not mean, as has often been insinuated in simplified terms, that Foucault would dissolve everything only into power. He rather reflects power as a central dimension in discourses. He adds a new perspective without forcing everything into this new focus. Power in its different aspects is seen as part and parcel of scientific discourses.

Foucault's very complex theory of power seems to us to imply the following challenges for a reconstructed Deweyan understanding of democracy:[8]

1. Foucault's analyses help us to interpret historically the very subtle, changeable, complex, and sometimes violent (from torture to psychic pressure) effects of power and interests and describe their

continuous importance in all practices, routines, and institutions. Thus, Foucault provides us with criteria for the observation and interpretation of power relations. He thus opens perspectives of critical reflection on effects of power and conditions of democratic struggles to delimit hegemonic power.[9]

2. At the same time, Foucault helps us to overcome the illusion of a noncoercive, power-free space or a discourse free from domination. He shows that all practices, routines, and institutions contain aspects of power, even if their cultural and historical expressions are diverse. Observation, interaction, and partaking are always not only traversed by existing power but also themselves produce power on their part.[10]

3. Although Foucault never neglects the potentially brutal effects of exercised power, he rejects the simple schematizing in the common dualism of culprit and victim, of the powerful and the powerless. He also explains that there is a disciplinary power whose crudest expression is the execution of, for example, a sovereign's direct violence against subordinates. In the course of historic development, however, disciplinary power has been developed as a Panopticon, as a network of impersonal relations and an invisible gaze of power.[11]

4. The strength of disciplinary power lies in the fact that it does not only have an effect on actions but is connected structurally and invisibly with all disciplines (including the sciences) and orders (like systems of knowledge).[12] Disciplinary power implies that we normally perceive routines and institutions as a matter of course without observing the implicit power aspects in form of our own submission or the subjugation of others. Disciplinary power restricts the chances that the sources of power become visible. Therefore, reflective and critical resistance is necessary to have a chance to uncover parts of the invisible. For Foucault, such possible resistance or critical thinking is always part of the power struggles.

5. In his later works, Foucault discussed technologies of the self. He clarifies perspectives that show how the self is situated between aspects of power and resistance.[13] We have to come to terms with the powers surrounding us without ourselves becoming powerless. For the postmodern strategies of subjugation, it is important that those who are subjugated accept the effects of power upon them as their own free decision. Thus, the power of subjugation avoids the rise of resistance. Power thereby takes a hegemonic form. This represents a major risk of democratic chances in our time. If we want

to save democratic possibilities against hegemonic forces, we have to develop our own power in the context of hegemonic struggles to delimit hegemony.[14] But the new dilemma is to determine who and what belongs to "us." For Foucault this is only shown by the struggle itself.[15]

If we take on Foucault's theory of power we will be able to determine in how far the interpretations and versions of realities are themselves imbued with power or embody our own claims to power. The less we reflect on our claims in their cultural contexts the more naive we will be in our understanding of scientific approaches and their cultural conditions. Foucault demonstrates in detail, how orders, identifications, disciplinary actions, and systems of control set up a disciplinary frame to increase the efficiency of multiple and complex social developments. This frame always runs the danger of hegemony and a degeneration of democratic structures into an excess of power on just one side. But there is no alternative in the sense of communication free of domination as still dreamed of by Habermas as a counterfactual ideal.[16] Basically, Dewey and Foucault do not lie too far apart in this respect.[17] Dewey, too, has an extraordinary sense for power asymmetries as a menace for democracy.[18]

If we use Foucault to reformulate Dewey's understanding of power in regard to democratic conditions of living, we can ask the following question:

How much power is being played off against one another within the numerous and varied interests in a community and how can we prevent power from being acted one-sidedly in hegemonic forms against certain members of the community?

At this point, for example, the influence of Foucault's thoughts on gender or cultural studies and the discussion of underprivileged minorities show that there are very subtle mechanisms of suppression often concealed under the guise of the wish for mutually shared interests. These mechanisms are often underestimated in social movements. Their actions often demonstrate how the common interests invisibly dissolve into unequally shared results for several subgroups. Generally, this is also true for bourgeois liberalism sharing common interests while paying too little attention to the practical consequences of real power relations. Thus, the emergence of new inequalities is hidden.

Today, the exchange between different social groups in a society or between different societies is often discussed in the context of globalization. But this globalized world represents, to a large degree, the interests of global capitalism and provides the state and legal conditions necessary for supplying its demands. Behind this, however, there are local or national as well as ethnic and religious interests powerfully struggling against one another and again undermining the mutually shared interests we want to believe in. Even in themselves, these interests are often highly contradictory. If Huntington's "The Clash of Civilizations and the Remaking of World Order" (1996) expressed a rather one-sided and often undifferentiated view of culture, the impact of his ideas show that culture increasingly has become a site of political struggles. Huntington argues only from a narrow Western point of view, a position that Stuart Hall ironically called "the West and the Rest" (1992). From the viewpoint of global power, the emphasis on such cultural aspects often only touches the surface of power relations and conflicts. Here, Foucault's analyses can help us to reflect more deeply on the contractions between different claims in societies and the power relations that support them. Power penetrates all dimensions of society and is not restricted to culture. With Foucault, we are called upon to question all hegemonic claims, not only where they appear in universalistic forms but also where they are taken as expressions of common sense.

Dewey's arguments about power are limited. "Possibly the greatest objections to Dewey's work...is that he gave us so little attention to the problems of race, class, and gender and that he puts such great emphasis on the power of scientific thought to solve our problems" (Noddings 1995, 38).[19] With Foucault, then, Dewey's understanding of power and democracy may be stated more precisely. The crucial point is to regard even discourses about democratic criteria, as Dewey gives us,[20] as part of power struggles. As such, they contain presuppositions that have to be critically examined in order to reconstruct the criteria of democracy in accordance with changing social contexts.

But there remains one important commonality between Foucault and Dewey. Even though Foucault reflects on power relations more critically and soberly than Dewey, both insist that the only way to delimit hegemonic power lies in empowering the participation of the self. Democracy means to fight for conditions that give people the chance to develop their resources. Dewey here stresses the need of communities whereas Foucault puts more emphasis on the difficulties of power relations within communities and between them. Therefore, to live in a democracy implies the readiness to fight for democratic principles. If we take these principles for granted like something given to us from a higher authority, we will be disappointed in the end and lose the fight for democracy perhaps much quicker than we expected.

Although in his historical analyses Foucault time and again refers to educational institutions and their involvement in power games, he was not an educational theorist and has not developed a systematic approach to education. However, if we take his analyses seriously in our reflections on education today, we suggest from the viewpoint of interactive constructivism that one cannot overestimate the importance of a critical perspective on power in education. In educational philosophy, this point has often been neglected too much. Among other things, one crucial aspect should be noted. Deweyan educational theory, as we have shown in parts 1 to 3 of this book, has an especially strong and elaborated perspective on communication and community in context of democracy and education. With Foucault, we get a more sober and critical view on the construction of communities. According to him, all articulations of a "we" necessarily involve power as a constitutive and not only as an accidental factor. This puts a much stronger emphasis on the need to deconstruct communities and the common in all democratic interactions. It implies, for example, that we always have to question the contexts of our educational practices. Educators often tend to take their own theoretical, practical, or institutional contexts for granted and neglect the power dimension. Even if educational efforts try to realize emancipatory intentions, they at the same time involve power that pervades discourses and communications. Depending on the standpoint from which we look at education, we will not only find that we need to construct communities and the "we's" they rely on, but also always need to deconstruct the hidden power games and traps that we stumble into by doing so. The need to accept the limits and ambivalences of deconstruction belongs to the great challenges of social thought in what Bauman calls liquid modernity. Every context deserves being deconstructed and critically scrutinized, even though we ourselves as participants in our contexts can only do so to a limited extent. From Foucault we can learn that one important aspect of such limitation is our unavoidable involvement in interests and power games even if we follow emancipative aims in education. This belongs to the inevitable paradoxes of our time. Foucault clearly shows through not only his works but also in his life as a critical public intellectual, that to live productively with this paradox implies strategies of empowerment especially for those who do not fully participate in the opportunities of mainstream society. The challenges of deconstruction may help us to criticize a naive constructivism in education which claims that autonomy in learning is all about freedom and liberation and not also at the same time about discipline and exclusion. Democratic education implies a precarious and always ambivalent balancing out of power relations and not the illusion of overcoming power altogether.

From a Deweyan perspective, this is not a totally foreign and offensive view, but a perspective that could and should be emphasized and elaborated more forcefully. For instance, this would help us to avoid shortsighted idealizations of even the pragmatist and/or constructivist classroom, the facilitating teacher, the autonomous and self-organized learner, the well-balanced group without egoism, and so on. With regard to all these and other positions in educational and learning processes, we need to recognize that we have to critically reflect the ways in which we are ourselves involved in power relations. But there is no detached metaperspective and our self-critical observation is always part of our very involvement. As educators, we actively take part in power games. Even in our aspirations to overcome inadequate power asymmetries and in our hopes of finding an ideal constellation for democratic education, we remain culturally immersed observers, participants, and agents within contexts of interest. However, if power, with Foucault, is seen as ubiquitous, this is not to say that the struggle for more democratic forms of living and education that allow for increased equity, diversity, and growth of individuals and communities is useless or impossible. Educators have the responsibility to care for the empowerment of their learners, and they can do so best if they address together with their learners even the hidden and taken for granted contexts of power in human relations. Otherwise, even progressive movements in education as well as in society all too easily take the risk of establishing rigid new forms of hierarchy and suppression as a consequence of their forgetfulness of power relations in their own claims and actions.

Summary

Foucault insists more decidedly on an analysis of power and power relations. This view helps to question and criticize the seemingly excessive harmonic view of communities in Dewey. But with Dewey, we can recognize more clearly than with Foucault that in education we find an indispensible resource to use existing power relations in a democratic sense.

Questions for Discussion

Do you think that Foucault is right in observing that power is ubiquitous?

What dimensions and manifestations of power relations must a theory of democracy and education in our time take into account?

Do you believe that scientific discourses can have social and political effects that are strong enough to secure the prosperity of democratic living together and growth?

What moves do you think are necessary today in the struggle for a better and more democratic education?

Do you think that educators, struggling for more equity in education, themselves necessarily participate in power games? Can you distinguish good from bad consequences of such power games? Can one finally and unambiguously distinguish oppressive power from empowerment?

Do you believe that education has the power to change the world? What are the opportunities, limits, and risks of educational power?

PIERRE BOURDIEU

Dewey's conception of democracy is rooted in the optimism that social intelligence can and must criticize existing practices, routines, or institutions at any time to both realize the variety of democratic interests and open up viable ways for the development of democracy itself:[21] "The essential fact is that if both democracy and capitalism are on trial, it is in reality our collective intelligence which is on trial. We have displayed enough intelligence in the physical field to create the new and powerful instrument of science and technology. We have not as yet had enough intelligence to use this instrument deliberately and systematically to control its social operations and consequences" (LW 6: 60). Dewey was clearly aware, at this point, of the importance of "intellectual capital" (LW 5: 294) as necessary instrument for the solution of human problems.

Pierre Bourdieu is well known in our times for his use of the concept "capital" in understanding social relations. He distinguishes between different forms of capital. For him capital is not restricted to the field of material production and the exchange of goods, which determines the wealth of people (with material and immaterial values). Instead, capital today must be understood in a different way if we want to comprehend the structure and function of the social world. Therefore, Bourdieu's different forms of capital are essential for a description of democratic developments.[22]

Quite like Dewey, Bourdieu (1988) assumes that the social milieu and the fields of education, especially the family and school, constitute an essential role in the allocation of social positions. However, where Dewey focuses on the positive role of education balancing out and compensating for different social starting points, Bourdieu introduces the distinction between economic and cultural capital.[23] The economic capital represents the wealth and possibilities of action on the part of those possessing property. In modern societies, it is always supplemented by cultural capital.

> Cultural capital can exist in three forms: in the *embodied* state, i.e., in the form of long-lasting dispositions of the mind and body; in the *objectified* state, in the form of cultural goods (pictures, books, dictionaries, instruments, machines, etc.), which are the trace or realization of theories or critiques of these theories, problematics, etc.; and in the *institutionalized* state, a form of objectification which must be set apart because, as will be seen in the case of educational qualifications, it confers entirely original properties on the cultural capital which it is presumed to guarantee.[24] (emphasis in original)

As well as in the case of economic property, the possession of cultural capital is a criterion for the possibilities of the prospects of life. It is a basis for the access to positions of power. Especially through cultural heredity in the family and a selective school system, it is also a decisive point for social advancement or decline. "Fine distinctions" have taken the place of raw class differences.[25] Especially with experts and bureaucracies, cultural capital is connected with positions of power, with social and political dominance linked with economic profit in return.

Social capital for Bourdieu is a resource that represents relationship networks. It is the sum of cumulated effects both cultural and economic that result from being involved in social contexts of more or less institutionalized relationships. Mutual acquaintance and recognition are important for social capital. Equally, these networks must be maintained and nurtured continuously in order to be used as a resource readily.

All sorts of capital not only exist on a material but also on a symbolic level. "*Symbolic capital,* that is to say, capital—in whatever form—insofar as it is represented, i.e., apprehended symbolically, in a relationship of knowledge or, more precisely, of misrecognition and recognition, presupposes the intervention of the habitus, as a socially constituted cognitive capacity" (Bourdieu 1986, footnote 3; emphasis in original).

With Bourdieu, we get a perspective on the role of the habitus in producing social perceptions and knowledge. Symbolic capital is subject to complicated regulations for the production of new inequalities and power relations.[26] From this perspective, the free and independent intellectual standing in a neutral position toward society is an illusion. Economic and cultural capitals are crucial conditions for the realizations of social capital, that is, the networks of relations and liabilities that inform the habitus. This is true for the intellectual (as expert for the symbolic) as for everybody else. And as social sciences in the last decades have repeatedly observed, these networks actually rather tend to increase social inequalities than to delimit them. The state with its supposedly neutral position itself produces relations of dominance and sets up advantages for certain groups of interest.[27] In view of the school-systems worldwide and their development, numbers of graduates with academic degrees are rising. But almost everywhere in the world, in industrial nations in particular, the power and influence of elites is increasing too.

If we compare this situation with Dewey's hope for social intelligence and his warnings against the dominance of elites over democratic publics the result is sobering. Social intelligence fails very often in the face of egoistic interests of power and aspirations to economic and social advantages with no consideration for others.[28]

Where Dewey speaks of habits, Bourdieu uses the term "habitus." Generally speaking, habits are cultural resources displayed in the conduct of individuals. In a different way than Dewey, Bourdieu emphasizes the dependence of these resources on social fields of interests and power relations.[29] Like habits, the habitus is a system of dispositions, durably acquired schemes of perception, thought, and action directed toward a field of practice. It can be reinforced or weakened by changing social contexts. More decisively than Dewey, Bourdieu stresses the duration of a once acquired habitus even when the social, cultural, and economical fields are changing. But the main difference lies in Bourdieu's account of the relation between habitus and the forms of capital. In this view, we observe the subtle ways in which power is implicated in all social relations as the articulation of fine differences. The habitus is, for Bourdieu, the central key to the understanding of societal and individual reproduction of culture. It stands for the regulation of practices in a more or less durable way and for the organization and the deployment of the diverse forms of capital according to specific rules.

With regard to democratic development, Bourdieu's perspective suggests that we investigate more thoroughly and critically into the preconditions implicitly contained in the interpretive communities that define conditions of democratic living. If we accept Dewey's criteria of democracy, then consciously sharing numerous and varied interests within a social group or community already implies a specific habitus. For Dewey, there are two essential criteria in describing a democratic community (MW 9: 89ff.):

1. He points out that in any social group "we find some interest in common" (ibid., 89). But if we look for democracy, we have to ask an important question: How numerous and varied are the consciously shared interests within a community? Democratic growth presupposes the existence of diverse interests.
2. Dewey argues that in any social group "we find a certain amount of interaction and cooperative intercourse with other groups" (ibid., 89). Again, this involves an important question for democratic development: how complete and unhindered is the exchange taking place with other communities? Democracy can grow (in families as in nations) more efficiently if interaction takes place not only between social groups of one common interest, one nation, or one special society, but also when people continually create, and constantly readjust, new challenges within the frame of social change by means of different interactions with different interpretive communities, families, nations, or societies.

Freely and tolerantly exchanging viewpoints and interests between different groups equally presupposes a particular habitus. In the background of Dewey's criteria stands the ideal of the liberal, open-minded, and public intellectual. From Bourdieu's perspective, this ideal must be considered as rather utopian even for the academic circles in Western societies. If we set up criteria for democracy, we must at the same time investigate empirically in how far the symbolic ideal accords with economic, social, and cultural conditions of capital. It has to be inquired who benefits from these conditions. If the criteria are not used as an ideal but as perspective for empirical analyses, it has to be questioned in particular who gains economic profits, social recognition, and cultural benefits from the relations and hidden inequalities in and between communities. With this shift in perspective, we move from democratic vision or utopia to the sober and down-to-earth reality of competition, self-interest, and investing capital for surplus value.

Although Bourdieu thus observes more critically and precisely what the conditions and resources of democracy are in view of the distribution of capitals, Dewey gives us a more productive perspective as to democratic solutions. He insists that participation has to be developed in education if the project of democracy is to succeed at all. For example,

> The argument that teachers are not prepared to assume the responsibility of participation deserves attention, with its accompanying belief that natural selection has operated to put those best prepared to carry the load in the positions of authority. Whatever the truth in this contention, it still is also true that incapacity to assume the responsibilities involved in having a voice in shaping policies is bred and increased by conditions in which that responsibility is denied. I suppose there has never been an autocrat, big or little, who did not justify his conduct on the ground of the unfitness of his subjects to take part in government. (LW 11: 223–224)

In this connection, however, Bourdieu's critical perspective can be used to specify our views of the contexts of applying the two criteria.

If we want to further develop Dewey's perspective of solution, we must render explicit as a third criterion a notion that is already implied in his approach—namely the inevitable connection between democracy and education.[30] What is needed is education offered equally to all people in a society. Such education must provide sufficient support for all learners and has to compensate for unequal resources. It must enable all learners to actively participate in the contents and relationships of learning. Thus, a partaking in numerous and varied interests within a community and a vivid and unhindered exchange between communities must be recognized as fundamental principles in education. The claim for democratic education must require in all educational practices, routines, and institutions that the realization of the two criteria in educational communities is guaranteed. This is an educational principle of diversity that stands against the one-sidedness of elites' power, unequal distribution of resources, separation between public and private schools, egoistic or partial use of social networks, compartmentalization of lifeworlds, and lack of solidarity with the less privileged. Here, the democratic paradox between freedom (diversity) and solidarity[31] turns out to be an educational paradox: If all learners need adequate conditions and resources for individual growth in and between communities in order to realize diversity, this especially means that the socially deprived and marginalized need solidarity and compensatory support. It will be decisive for the survival and prosperity of democracy to meet this claim of balancing out freedom (diversity) and solidarity. The more advantaged groups and communities worldwide must do justice to this claim if they are willing to support democracy at all.[32]

In a word, Bourdieu helps us to understand the extent to which equality of chances in human living together is an illusion under the present constellations of capitalist society. From the perspective of interactive constructivism this is an important critical insight we have to take into account in contemporary education. The starting points of learning are unavoidably unequal in a society that is grounded on capitalist economy. In a society marked by inequality as well as diversity, we should suppose from the start that contexts of observation, participation, and action among the multitude of learners are important and highly different. From Bourdieu we can learn that the constructivist claim to take participation and agency as serious conditions of learning has to be observed carefully and always made explicit in the concrete. He shows that it is not enough to say and criticize in a general fashion that society is marked by inequality. What is needed, especially in education, is to recognize that this inequality appears in highly complex social forms and constellations, and his theory of diverse forms of capital illuminates important ways in which these forms and constellations are lived and have effects on living. Bourdieu's approach has had an international impact on social research in these respects. Today, many studies, for example, on poverty, equity, and development in societies rely on his work. This provides important results that show how different societies respond to the challenges of inequality in very different ways.

It is a measure for the social and democratic quality of societies in how far they further the delimitation of inequality by deliberate programs for increased equity especially in education. This is fundamentally a Deweyan intention. Bourdieu helps us to articulate it in a more precise way under present conditions. His distinction of different forms of capital gives us conceptual tools as well as theoretical frames to analyze existing forms of social inequality and legitimizes educational claims to more equity. Bourdieu as a sociologist has his main focus on the side of description and analysis. For the Deweyan educator his accounts can well serve as a starting point for raising concrete questions and to specify the hard and solid problems for democracy and education in our time. Empowerment in the concrete means appropriation and reconstructive use of economic, cultural, and social capitals. Education is always confronted with inequalities in these three main fields. The Deweyan educator cannot ignore this fact but must give constructive response on what democracy and education means with regard to it. Contemporary discussions

about inclusive education that we find on an increasingly international scale throughout the last decade represent possible connecting
points for a reconstructed Deweyan education in this respect. For
instance, the ethical claims stated by the Toronto District School
Board in its "Equity Foundation Statement" connect very well with
this need.[33]

Summary

Bourdieu analyzes different forms of capital and their effects on the
habitus. This habitus is always interwoven with the forms of capital
and the interests represented in them. With Bourdieu, we can critically reject idealized expectations of neutral expert roles and of a supposedly neutral science. This view helps us to reconstruct Dewey's
concept of habits. Like Foucault, Bourdieu gives a description of
practices, routines, and institutions but has no educational model.
Nevertheless, his work offers many resources that give orientation in
the struggles about equality and equity.

Questions for Discussion

Do you think that Bourdieu's forms of capital cover adequately the social and
cultural chances, resources, and limits for participating or being marginalized in society?

Do you think that equality of chances is possible?

What is the difference between equality and equity? Can you give a concrete
example in connection with your own experience?

Can you think of concrete examples or manifestations of the paradoxes
of freedom and solidarity? Can you think of a possible solution for these
problems?

What is the difference between Dewey's habits and Bourdieu's habitus?

Jacques Derrida

While Dewey's name is inextricably associated with the notion of
reconstruction, Derrida's is even more closely associated with that of
deconstruction.[34] Both agree that construction, deconstruction, and
reconstruction are phases of an endless cycle, although each places
the emphasis at a different place in the rotation. Their agreement
that there is no eternal, fixed, and final construction is profound, but
their divergence in emphasis points to an equally deep disagreement.
Let us begin with the remarkable insights they share regarding the

contingent, ever-changing process of meaning construction. They share these insights not only with each other, but also with interactive constructivism, which provides a theoretical frame to combine their focal perspectives.

Derrida rejects the metaphysics of invariable presence with its idea of an absolute and unalterable ultimate structure:

> The entire history of the concept of structure . . . must be thought of as a series of substitutions of center for center, as a linked chain of determinations of the center . . . It could be shown that all names related to fundamentals, to principles, or to the center have always designated an invariable presence. (Derrida 1978, 279–280)

Dewey also dissolves the notion of structurally static centers:

> Neither self nor world, neither soul nor nature (in the sense of something isolated and finished in its isolation) is the centre [*sic*], any more than either earth or sun is the absolute centre of a single universal and necessary frame of reference. There is a moving whole of interacting parts; a centre emerges wherever there is effort to change them in a particular direction . . . Mind is no longer a spectator . . . The mind is within the world as a part of the latter's own ongoing process. (LW 1: 232)

Dewey always emphasizes the reconstruction of transient structural centers while Derrida emphasizes their deconstruction.

Derrida deconstructs traditional Western metaphysics by showing that it can never produce the kind of immediate and indubitable presence it proclaims. Derrida pursues what he himself calls a quasi-transcendental approach. His philosophy is no doubt partly inspired by Heidegger's proposed "destruction" of Western metaphysics. His work aims at a transcendental move in the sense that he seeks to deconstruct the frames of experience through analyzing texts. It is quasi-transcendental in the sense that Derrida himself from the very start denies any possibility for the transcendental move to reach a final or absolute position that could serve as a foundation of experience. Therefore, he introduces his famous concept of *différance*. By doing so, he draws attention to his crucial insight that the symbolic articulation of identities and differences always involves a necessary and unavoidable game of supplements. This game plays with the tension between establishing absolutes (our necessary and taken for granted starting points in thinking) and dissolving them in the process of thinking that points beyond. Deconstruction presupposes that establishing an absolute is always a process of construction that at the same time produces limits that challenge us to think beyond. Here, "difference" may be articulated as "différance" in order to expose the limits and what they do to us. We must be careful not to confuse this quasi-transcendental strategy of deconstruction with traditional strategies of transcendental foundation.

Dewey rejects all transcendental a priori arguments because they seek to establish the conditions of possibility of experience or the contents of experience in advance. In this respect, we can say that there is an affinity between Dewey and Derrida's quasi-transcendental critique of foundations. But Dewey prefers empirical naturalism, which he believes provides the immanent conditions of possibility for the existence of semiotics. From the perspective of Derrida, empirical naturalism appears as an apparently self-evident starting point that, however, must be questioned about its unarticulated presuppositions. Otherwise, it stands in danger of establishing yet another absolute.

In *Of Grammatology* Derrida proclaims, "writing is not only an auxiliary means in the service of science—and possibly its object—but first,...the condition of the possibility of ideal objects and therefore of scientific objectivity" (Derrida 1974, 27). By ideal objects, Derrida means the objects of knowledge that provide immediate, intuitive, and indubitable knowledge through their very presence in thought or perception. Christopher Norris suggests that "Derrida's version of this Kantian [transcendental] argument makes writing...the precondition of all possible knowledge...His claim is *a priori* in the radically Kantian sense...that we cannot think the possibility of culture, history or knowledge in general without also thinking the prior necessity of writing" (Norris 1988, 95). As is typical of transcendental arguments from Immanuel Kant to Edmund Husserl and Martin Heidegger, Derrida seeks to thematize the transcendental conditions of possibility for all experience while at the same time deconstructing these foundations by showing supplements and thus relativizing the game of absolutes. In this sense, he arrives at the quasi-transcendental ground of différance upon which he bases his deconstruction. This ground, however, cannot serve anymore as a metaphysical foundation, but only as the orientation of a method.

Let us take a more specific view on the linguistic backgrounds of Derrida's deconstruction. The great structuralist Saussure declares,

> The conceptual side of value is made up solely of relations and differences with respect to the other terms of language, and the same can be said of its material side...Everything that has been said up to this

point boils down to this: in language there are only differences. Even more important: a difference generally implies positive terms between which the difference is set up; but in language there are only differences without positive terms. Whether we take the signified or the signifier, language has neither ideas nor sounds that existed before the linguistic system, but only conceptual and phonic differences that have issued from the system. The idea or phonic substance that a sign contains is of less importance than the other signs that surround it. (Saussure 1959, 117–118, 120)

Immediately after citing most of the forgoing passage in his essay "Différance," Derrida writes,

The first consequence to be drawn from this is that the signified concept is never present in and of itself, in a sufficient presence that would refer only to itself. Essentially and lawfully, every concept is inscribed in a chain or in a system within which it refers to the other, to other concepts, by means of the systematic play of differences. Such a play—difference—is thus no longer simply a concept, but rather the possibility of conceptuality, of a conceptual process and system in general. For the same reason, différance, which is not a concept, is not simply a word, that is, what is generally represented as the calm, present, and self-referential unity of concept and phonic material. (Derrida 1973, 140)

Here we have Derrida's most significant insight, which is that there is no such thing as immediately present and self-evident simple self-identity. While no doubt a stroke of genius, all Derrida had to do was to assert the priority of "difference" over even transcendental, a priori concepts to arrive at the quasi-transcendental conditions of the possibility of all experience, thought, and conception, or what Rodolphe Gasché calls "infrastructures," of "différance," trace, supplement, and such. Simply inserting the "a" silent in French for the "e" in difference provided a powerful critique of the primacy Saussure gave to the presence of speech (the "phonic substance," the phonic signifier) over writing.

Derrida's writings do not limit themselves to merely making a point; they perform and enact it. His texts, by virtue of their singularity and boundless texture, perform the action of opening themselves up to the incalculable, unpredictable, and nonprogrammatic. They exhibit his effort to call out a response by the "Other" for whose arrival they have opened the way. Always on the move, Derrida allows no word, no concept, and no nonconcept to master him or inhibit the play of language. Derrida himself does not think deconstruction "a good word" and concludes, "It deconstructs itself" (Kamuf 1991, 274, 275). Derrida lives in a world without a stable center or circumference. Everyone does; that is one lesson his philosophy teaches. He thus responds to an increased sensitivity in our time to the need for providing spaces for the excluded Other to arrive and express itself. Dewey does not prepare the way for Otherness and difference nearly so well, although his pluralism provides for it.

Derrida develops the notion of différance to deconstruct the pretense to presence found in almost all Western metaphysics. Différance indicates a double meaning in all languages. First, there is "difference"; the sign is different from the signified. Second, there is "deferred presence." For most structuralist thinkers, any system of signs (e.g., a theory, a text, a narrative) eventually terminates either in some master word in the system or in some "transcendental signified," that is, something outside the symbolic system to which all the symbols individually or in grammatical combination refer (see Derrida 1974, 158). These are usually considered either naturalistic elements in experience like "raw data" (or intuitive knowledge) or some abstract ideal meaning like "Rationality." The transcendental signified terminates the play of signs because it is, supposedly, the presence of the indubitable self-identical thing, the referent. Derrida denies the existence of the transcendental signified, and thereby challenges most of Western epistemology and metaphysics. Derrida, though, does understand the desire to escape the anxiety of uncertainty: "The concept of centered structure is in fact the concept of a play based on a fundamental ground, a play constituted on the basis of a fundamental immobility and a reassuring certitude, which itself is beyond the reach of play. And on the basis of the certitude anxiety can be mastered...a history—whose origin may always be reawakened or whose end may always be anticipated in the form of presence" (Derrida 1978, 279).

The promise of certainty is false, but the human need for cognitive security and safety is real.

Derrida's quasi-transcendental stance deprecates the very notion of experience. He finds the very word "empiricism" so offensive that he often swears at it: "[T]he true name of this renunciation of the concept, of the a prioris and transcendental horizons of language, is empiricism. For the latter at bottom, has ever committed but one fault: the fault of presenting itself as philosophy" (Derrida 1978, 151, see also 139 and 288).

Similarly "the value of empiricism," Derrida decides, must "derive all its meaning from its opposition to philosophical responsibility" (Derrida 1973, 135). Or again,

> "Experience" has always designated the relationship with a presence, whether that relationship had the form of consciousness or not. At any rate, we must...exhaust the resources of the concept of experience before attaining and in order to attain, by deconstruction, its ultimate foundation. It is the only way to escape "empiricism" and the "naïve" critiques of experience at the same time. (Derrida 1974, 61)

After all, in his essay "Violence and Metaphysics," Derrida proclaims, "Has not the concept of experience always been determined by the metaphysics of presence?" (ibid., 152).

Meanwhile, as we have seen, Dewey is an empirical naturalist. He rejects traditional Western metaphysics from a completely different stance, which is why he retains the idea of *energeia*, which he thinks we require to account for change and development, including human development, in a pluralistic, constantly evolving, and naturalistic Darwinian universe, although he radically reconstructs it.

Dewey denigrates traditional Western metaphysics as stridently as Derrida, but in another way. Let us approach this rejection through his Darwinian naturalism. In "The Influence of Darwinism on Philosophy," Dewey expresses the significance of an evolutionary theory of nature: "In laying hands upon the sacred ark of absolute permanency, in treating forms [eidos] that have been regarded as types of fixity and perfection as originating and passing away, *The Origin of Species* introduced a mode of thinking that in the end was bound to transform the logic of knowledge, and hence the treatment of morals, politics and religion" (MW 4: 3).

This assessment also includes metaphysics. A species is the ultimate ontological subject of evolutionary theory. Dewey does for all essences (cultural, linguistic, or logical) what Darwin does for biological species (including Homo sapiens).

Dewey turns metaphysical ideas into tools of intelligent, practical, and creative inquiry thereby draining the swamp of Western metaphysics into the basin of logic. The following passage drains off a great deal: "Philosophy forswears inquiry after absolute origins and absolute finalities in order to explore specific values and the specific conditions that generate them" (ibid., 10). Dewey's naturalistic Darwinian world is as bereft of cosmic beginnings or endings as Derrida's deconstructive one. We only comprehend essences, original foundations, and teleology within the context of purposeful inquiry, not metaphysics. Dewey wishes to simply overcome traditional metaphysics by allowing logic (the theory of inquiry) to perform the cognitive functions previously ascribed to it.

Dewey retains two principles of traditional metaphysics in a pragmatically reconstructed form: the notions of the actual and the potential. He notes that we never appeal to the term potential "except where there is change or a process of becoming" (ibid., 11). Dewey, though, bemoans the tendency to appeal to a "latent" potentiality. He observes, "To say that an apple has the potentiality of decay does not mean that it has latent or implicit within it a causal principle which will some time inevitably display itself in producing decay, but that its existing changes (in interaction with its surroundings) will take the form of decay, if they are exposed to certain conditions not now operating" (ibid., 11). Dewey rejects the notion of "latent potential" unfolding to a predetermined perfect telos. It is the same as rejecting such traits of the metaphysics of presence as ultimate foundations and perfect telos. The implications for thinking about education and human development are deep and widespreading.

Derrida and Dewey both reject classical Western metaphysics, but in very divergent ways. While Dewey has empirical, naturalistic motives, Derrida is driven by skepticism toward naive empiricism. It must be said, though, that Derrida in his criticism of empiricism does not directly address pragmatism and Dewey. What he rather has in mind is the tradition of British empiricism as exemplified by proponents like John Locke and David Hume and their modern followers. Nevertheless, his critique can be fruitfully used to deconstruct and reconstruct Deweyan pragmatism today. We can detect possibilities of connecting pragmatism and deconstruction if we look back to some origins of pragmatism before Dewey, namely in Peirce. In *Of Grammatology*, Derrida proclaims, "Peirce goes very far in the direction of what I have called the de-construction of the transcendental signified" (Derrida 1978, 49). He then calls attention to the following passage from Peirce: "*Anything which determines something else (its interpretant) to refer to an object to which it itself refers (its object) in the same way, the interpretant in turn becoming a sign and so on ad infinitum*" (ibid., 50; emphasis in original). Derrida glosses this passage in this fashion: "From the moment that there is meaning there are nothing but signs. We think only in signs" (ibid., 50).

In many important ways, Derrida recognizes that Peirce was a poststructuralist nearly one hundred years earlier. Dewey took a course on semiotics and logic with Peirce while in graduate school and was increasingly influenced by him later in his career. Dewey shared the same semiotics as Peirce, although Dewey does not develop it with much originality. In a paper appearing in 1868, a decade before he published the paper introducing the pragmatic maxim, Peirce writes,

> [M]an can think only by means of words or other external symbols, these might turn around and say: "You mean nothing which we have not taught you, and then only so far as you address some word as the interpretant of your thought." In fact, therefore, men and words reciprocally educate each other...[T]here is no element whatever of man's consciousness which has not something corresponding to it in the word...It is that the word or sign which man uses is the man himself. (Peirce 1992, 54)

Derrida recognizes that in some important ways, Peirce was a post-structuralist as early as 1868, a decade before he published the essay introducing the pragmatic maxim, and a century before the Cultural Revolution in France of 1968 dethroned structuralism while ensconcing poststructuralism.

In his essay, "Remarks on Deconstruction and Pragmatism," Derrida writes, "I think that deconstruction...shares much...with pragmatism...I recall that from the beginning the question concerning the trace was connected with a certain notion of labour, of doing, and that what I called then pragmmatology tried to link grammatology and pragmatism" (Derrida 1996, 78). However, if we apply Derrida's criticism of empiricism to pragmatism, interactive constructivism considers even the pragmatist version of empiricism as problematic, especially when it articulates itself as naturalistic metaphysics. We will discuss, in a later section, Richard Rorty who articulates this criticism of classical Deweyan pragmatism in a more accessible way than Derrida. For the moment, let us briefly discuss what we get out of deconstruction for education. In what sense can a Derridian perspective be profitable to further develop the Deweyan philosophy of education? What practical consequences can educators draw from deconstruction?

The first and foremost issue in this connection is Derrida's attitude against totality. This is a philosophical position that is not alien to pragmatism even though Derrida gives us new ways of arguing against visions of totality like completeness, universality, last words, and so on. He shows that any construction of logical necessities goes hand in hand with manifestation of exclusion. There is always a neglected Other within and against the alleged totality of any system.

Recall that for interactive constructivism, for every self-observer the actual, or in this case, potential distant-observer implies a constant element of strangification, a constant challenge to relativize her/his own observation by trying to grasp the alien view. Deconstruction is wonderfully open to strangers, the marginalized, and excluded. Therefore, we need supplementation or, in the terminology of inter-active constructivism, we need to go on constructing, reconstructing, and deconstructing.

In every comprehensive educational experience, we shall expect to find all three aspects. Although the emphasis may at one point be more on the construction side and at another point more on the reconstruction or deconstruction side, it is always the complex inter-play between all three perspectives that we must keep in mind when talking about constructivist education. Generally speaking, we may say that Dewey is a philosopher of reconstruction, and Derrida is a philosopher of deconstruction, when we look to their respective core interests. Interactive constructivism in combining the three aspects gives us a horizon of interpretation broad enough to integrate both approaches and combine them in mutually supplementary ways.

a. *Education as construction work.* This is the basic perspective for constructivists. They emphasize and support the possibilities of learners to attain their own constructions of reality in active and self-determined learning experiences. Constructivists think that we, as culturally immersed subjects, are the inventors of our own realities. This emphasis on the constructive potentials of learners has its subjectivist implications in that each individual constructs her/his symbolic and imaginative reality in a somewhat unique and personal way that can never be completely and exhaustively commensurate with the realities of others. For interactive con-structivism, though, the recognition of these subjectivist aspects must be qualified by the assumption mentioned above that every observer (as constructor of her/his reality) is at the same time an agent within a cultural context and a participant in an interpre-tive community. Thus, learning is not only a subjective endeavor, but a shared process as well. As an activity, it involves interaction; as a construction, it relies on coconstructions within a commu-nity of learners; and as a self-determined process, it presupposes communication and coordination with others in a social envi-ronment. Such interaction, coconstruction, communication, and coordination would of course be impossible if each individual had to invent her/his reality completely on her/his own. Education as a constructive process always implies the reconstructive use of cultural resources that precede individual disposal and invention. They represent the indispensable means of each individual's constructions of reality.

b. *Education as reconstruction work.* Reconstruction is the way learners come to discover the abundant richness and wide variety of reality constructions that have already been accomplished by others in culture. These reality constructions are now available as symbolic resources and imaginative powers of the lived cultures that the learners inhabit. It is through the reconstructive discovery of cultural resources, values, goods, vocabularies, languages, images, and the various techniques and products of the arts of living (including scientific principles, explanations, and theories) that individuals come to appropriate the symbolic resources and imaginative powers they need to become responsible selves and to attain critical-constructive competencies in dealing with the social and cultural environments they live in. This in turn is a prerequisite for effectively partaking in the practices, symbolic representations, and discourses of a society—including participation in fields like politics, science, arts, economics, and consumption. Especially, the Deweyan use of reconstruction emphasizes the need of participating in culture and finding new constructive ways of solving problems in whatever context of human living they appear.

The importance of this reconstructive side of education and learning processes plays a crucial role with regard to both the contents and relationships of learning in every human society. However, constructivists more decidedly than many other educational theories claim that education should never be reproductive appropriation of cultural resources *for its own sake.* That is to say, they particularly emphasize the possibilities of *construction through reconstruction.* They suggest that the necessarily reproductive elements of learning should—as far as possible—be used as part of and means for the self-determined and active learning experiences of students. Cultural reconstructions are not seen as finalities, but become the starting points for the students' own constructions. Given the diversity and heterogeneity of discourses and symbolic representations in liquid modernity, education as reconstruction work must be highly selective, anyway. Constructivists claim that already the selection of subject matter for reconstructive learning is a task of not only administrators and curriculum experts, but primarily of those actively involved in concrete learning situations—that is, the teachers and students themselves. Constructivist educators must, first of all, take account of the different viabilities of their learners—their specific educational situations, interests, needs, and requirements. Second, they need to select and develop the reconstructive materials most appropriate for coconstructive learning processes with as high a degree as possible of active participation in the processes of selection and development on the part of their learners.

c. *Education as deconstruction work.* This perspective reminds us that, in an open and pluralist universe, our so far achieved cultural constructions and reconstructions are always incomplete versions of world making that of necessity exclude other possible perspectives and interpretations. The deconstructivist—sometimes ironically—suggests that just when we think we have understood something properly and thoroughly, it might be helpful to look at things from a different and hitherto neglected viewpoint. Such deconstructions make the familiar look strange, if only for a moment. They disturb the certainty of our taken-for-granted beliefs, understandings, and prejudices. Interactive constructivists think that at times such disturbances or perturbations are a precondition for the release of new constructive potentials and reconstructive interests on the part of both learners and teachers. Deconstruction in this sense is never an end in itself; it is no "-ism." Constructivist educators should try to cultivate a genuine appreciation not only of the constructive capacities of their learners, but also of their deconstructive ideas and articulations. Again, this applies to both the contents and relationships of learning. Deconstruction oftentimes begins with asking supposedly silly questions. It is very easy to overhear its inchoate articulations or simply dismiss them as irrelevant or annoying. Indeed, the deconstructivist is often a troublemaker in that s/he questions and disturbs beliefs that seem obvious to everybody else. S/he prevents us from being satisfied with an achieved solution; s/he makes things more complicated; and s/he insists on unconsidered and apparently irrelevant implications that no one knows where they will lead to. But in hindsight, we often find that successful new constructions (both in our individual and collective lives) were first prompted by tentative deconstructions of habitual and customary perspectives that held us captive until some unexpected move opened a new horizon of observation and interpretation. Education as deconstruction work reveals and partly unmasks such captivities implied in our symbolic constructions of reality.

Summary

Dewey is a philosopher of reconstruction while Derrida is a philosopher of deconstruction. Both want to overcome traditional Western metaphysics. However, they have very different motives for their rejection. Derrida starts from a quasi-transcendental stance that seeks to deconstruct all absolute symbolic foundations of experience. Dewey rejects transcendentalism and seeks only immanent (naturalistic and empirical) conditions of possibility. However, both agree with Peirce that only a sign can interpret a sign. Also, Derrida is somewhat sympathetic to the construction of a pragrammatology.

From the viewpoint of Deweyan pragmatism, Derrida's perspective seems to be constrained by language, semiotics, and the source of semiotics in quasi-transcendental conditions of the possibility (the "infrastructures" of "différance," trace, supplement, etc.). From Derrida's perspective, Dewey is so concerned with empirical naturalism that he largely ignores semiotics and so cannot recognize the necessity of a transcendental ground for language and thought that prepares in advance the ground for the arrival of the excluded Other.

Questions for Discussion

Dewey prefers empirical naturalism while Derrida seeks transcendental grounds for the possibility of experience. What are the advantages and disadvantages of each?

Pragmmatology would mix Derrida's deconstruction with Dewey reconstruction. Do you think this is possible? If so, what would it mean for education?

Can you name some instances of the excluded Other? Is it important to provide spaces for their arrival and recognition? If so who is more useful, Dewey or Derrida?

Both Dewey and Derrida want to overcome traditional Western metaphysics. What are the educational consequences?

EMANUEL LEVINAS

In "The Trace of the Other," Levinas (1963) independently developed a notion of the trace whose ethical content increasingly influenced Derrida over the years.[35] For Levinas, the problem of the ethical relation to Otherness and difference arouse from the holocaust wherein he lost his father and brothers.[36] His call for an ethical response to radical alterity is a desperate appeal to care for the Other even before the call of justice (rules, laws, judgment, etc.). In terms of interactive constructivism, for those self-observers that answer this call, there is always a duty toward observers potentially so distant that they are and will remain radically incommensurable with all our participant perspectives, all our agent perspectives, and all we know, or believe we know. We are called out into the Other on a journey from whence there is no return.

In *Totality and Infinity*, Levinas argues that there is a pervasive tendency in Western philosophy, and especially Western metaphysics, to reduce all Otherness to "Sameness" by violence if necessary. Levinas rejects the traditional metaphysical claim that the "meaning of individuals (invisible outside of this totality) is derived from the totality" (Levinas 1961/1995, 22). In his opinion, the originary relationship of the individual with the transcendence of an infinite Other is "a relationship with *a surplus always exterior to the totality*," such that "the objective totality did not fill out the true measure of being" (ibid., 23; emphasis in original). Thus, this originary relationship with the a priori transcendent, infinite Other prevents the individual subject or self from being absorbed into the totality of any system. Thus, individual "beings have an identity 'before eternity,' before the accomplishment of history" (ibid.). Such transcendence cannot be "reabsorbed into the unity of the system"; therefore, our relation with the Other can always preserve our subjectivity from "Totality" and reduction to Sameness (ibid., 26).

Levinas relies on Descartes' "Third Meditation," which is Descartes' ontological proof of God's existence, to provide an a priori awareness of the transcendental infinite Other. Levinas notes that "things, mathematical and moral notions are also, according to Descartes, presented to us through their ideas, and are distinct from them. But the idea of infinity is exceptional in that its *ideatum* [the object of knowledge as known by mind] surpasses its idea" (Levinas 1961/1995, 48–49). Levinas identifies this idea of infinity with the Other: "Infinity is characteristic of a transcendent being as transcendent; the infinite is the absolutely other" that is "exterior, because it is infinite" (ibid., 49). Further, he argues, "To think the infinite, the transcendent" is "not to think an object" (ibid., 49).

Levinas's seeks to show that "the Other" is not an ordinary empirical object or person. On this account, the remarkable relation of the distinct individual with the infinite Other breaks the pattern wherein all differences are assimilated within the unity of the "Same," such as we find, for instance, in Heidegger's "Being": "The Cartesian notion of the idea of the Infinite designates a relation with a being that maintains its total exteriority with respect to him who thinks it... The absolute exteriority of the exterior being... 'absolves' itself from the relation in which it presents itself" (ibid., 50).

Without reciprocity, Levinas argues, our relation to the infinite Other is absolutely incommensurable and asymmetric. While it may transform us, we cannot transform it. For interactive constructivists, "the Other" is rather like a symbol of what exceeds all imagination, a reality that flows in upon us that is beyond our control or comprehension, but to which we must respond constructively.

What distinguishes Levinas's ethics from any other is the lack of reciprocity. Levinas's "ought" signifies "an obligation, anachronously prior to any commitment," and this "anteriority is 'older' than the *a priori*" (Levinas 1974/1981, 101). Levinas finds that the "self, a hostage, is already substituted for the others" (ibid., 118). In the primordial relation with the Other, the "self is through and through a hostage, older than the ego, prior to principles" (ibid., 117). The ethical force of this relation is that the self *ought* to substitute for the Other to the point that "the outrage inflicted by the Other" demands "the expiation for his fault by me" (ibid., 118). It extends so far that the "subjectivity of a subject is responsibility or *being in question* in the form of the total exposure to offence in the cheek offered to the smiter" (ibid., 111). We can only expatiate the violence concealed within the Western tendency to reduce Otherness to Sameness through our ethical "sacrifice" to the Other (ibid., 120).

Levinas's neo-Cartesian a priori awareness of the transcendent infinite Other conflicts with Dewey's empirical naturalism as well as with his commitment to interaction and communication. It definitely threatens Dewey's theory of democratic community. Alphonso Lingis, a prominent translator and interpreter of Levinas, argues that the very idea of "community" stresses commonality, including a common language, common self-concept, and common values leading to Levinasian totalization and sameness (see Lingis 1994, ix).

Pluralism and otherness are essential not only to Deweyan democracy but also to his entire philosophy. However, so too is commonality, although not Sameness. Recall his two pluralistic criteria for assessing the quality of a given group, community, or society. The first criterion, "How numerous and varied are the interests which are consciously shared?" (MW 9: 89). This criterion emphasizes internal unity in diversity. Dewey's second criterion asks, "How full and free is the interplay with other forms of association?" (ibid., 89). The second standard emphasizes external Otherness and difference, at least as Dewey understood it. Interactive constructivism suggests we might need a third criterion to better provide for radical alterity (see the discussion of Bourdieu above as well as Reich 2008).

Dewey is greatly influenced by the pluralism of William James. In *A Pluralistic Universe*, James states, "*The treating of a name as excluding from the fact named what the name's definition fails positively to include, is what I call 'vicious intellectualism'*" (James 1909, 32; emphasis in original). For pragmatists, concepts, categories, objects, meanings, essences, and all of ontology are created for finite humane purposes. James writes, "The reality overflows these purposes at every pore" (ibid., 334). There is a significant difference between James's sense of empirical "overflow" and the "relationship with *a surplus always exterior to the totality*" depicted by Levinas (Levinas 1961/1995, 23). For Levinas, the source of the surplus is one special idea—the infinite, a priori transcendent Other. For James and Dewey, reality overflows all ideas, or totalizing systems, of ideas, because no idea can contain the ever-flowing stream of empirical existence. All concepts resemble buckets of water drawn from the stream of reality whose contents we must never confuse with the stream itself.

Levinas sought to evade totalization for ethical reasons. Dewey thought ethical concerns about the reduction of the Other to the Same also stimulated James:

> The animating purpose of James was...primarily moral and artistic. It is expressed, in his phrase, "block universe," employed as a term of adverse criticism. Mechanism and idealism were abhorrent to him because they both hold to a closed universe in which there is no room for novelty and adventure. Both sacrifice individuality and all the values, moral and aesthetic, which hang upon individuality, for according to absolute idealism, as to mechanistic materialism, the individual is simply a part determined by the whole of which he is a part. Only a philosophy of pluralism, of genuine indetermination, and of change which is real and intrinsic gives significance to individuality. It alone justifies struggle in creative activity and gives opportunity for the emergency of the genuinely new. (LW 14: 101)

Artistic creation is important in Dewey and James's pluralistic universe because they thought we must *create* ethical relations, we cannot discoverer them a priori.

In a pragmatically pluralistic universe, there are always other things, persons, and societies with whom we have yet to interact. Indeed, Dewey does not think we have potential for individual freedom and growth unless there are other individuals different from ourselves with whom we are yet to interact. He also believes all interactions are reciprocally transforming. After the interaction, neither interactant can ever return to their previous identities, so complete reduction of the Other to our Sameness is impossible. Of course, Dewey must acknowledge that all interactions are as potentially violent as they are peaceful. He must also acknowledge potential conflict and that conflict commonly leads to the violent reduction of Otherness and difference to the Sameness of those that win the struggle. Dewey thinks we may only ameliorate violence practically and would be skeptical of the practical as well as philosophical value of Levinas's attempt to derive an ethical stance that gives us transcendental grounds for solving the problem.

However, despite this difference we may find considerable value, from the perspective of interactive constructivism, in Levinas' radical understanding of relationships as the encounter of the Other. Levinas reminds us that there is always the danger in lived human relationships to reduce the Other to Sameness in whatever subtle ways. If we think of what has been said in the introduction of this part 4 about the imaginative level of communication we may well recognize that such reduction often takes place in subliminal ways of identity constructions. This has important implications for education, because in the history of education we often observe that institutional systems and personal practices rely on processes of inclusion and exclusion that for the time being are largely taken for granted and often only in hindsight appear as discriminating and unfair. Ours is a time of diversity and inclusion in education, at least in many official statements and programs. With Levinas, we may be reminded to remain self-critical in our encounters with others because we often risk neglecting their real Otherness even in so-called inclusive communities. Levinas would suggest that this self-criticism is the ethical task of responding to the Holocaust as the extreme form of negating Otherness. Of course, the Holocaust stands for violence, which is indeed the specter that haunts in the background of Levinas' discourse. It is good to be reminded of this specter because in pragmatism and its positive account of communication this danger may sometimes be underestimated. This insight partly compensates for the one-sidedness that a Deweyan pragmatist may find in Levinas' accounts of communication. From the perspective of interactive constructivism, again, it seems that there is some value of having it both ways.

Summary

Levinas issues a profound call to care for others that lies even beyond the rigid, totalizing ethics of justice, rules, and regulations. He identifies the tendency in Western thought to reduce all Otherness to Sameness, often by violence. His a priori acknowledgment of a transcendent infinite Other arises out of the pathos of the holocaust and terrible personal loss. Our relation to this Other is entirely asymmetric, nonreciprocal, and involves ethical sacrifice on our part to avoid the violence with the Western tendency to totalization. Dewey pursues an empirical, naturalistic, and interactive pluralism in which all relations, including democratic ethical relations, are reciprocally transforming and from whence we may never completely eliminate violence, although we may seek to ameliorate it.

Questions for Discussion

Can we achieve a priori intuitions of transcendent ethical imperatives or is all ethics a naturalistic, empirical construction? Or is it something completely different from either of these?

Can we eliminate the tendency to violently reduce otherness and difference to the sameness expressed in colonialism, sexism, racism, religious persecution, and so on? If so, should we follow Levinas, Dewey, or someone else?

Are all relations, including ethical relations, reciprocal as Dewey thinks or are some especially important relations (with God or the infinite Other) entirely asymmetric?

RICHARD RORTY

In *Experience and Nature*, one of his most important philosophical books, Dewey uses the phrase "empirical naturalism or naturalistic empiricism" (LW 1: 10) to characterize his approach.[37] He insists that empiricism is a social process and not at all a private work. He believes that science or what he calls inquiry is a process of social construction. But seen from a perspective of our times, his constructivism seems not to be thoroughgoing in all respects. There remains a certain ambiguity about his claim to naturalism because this claim has two sides. On the one hand, nature is understood as the largest conceivable context and precondition of construction. It is the world in which we live, act, participate, and observe. In this sense, naturalism represents a claim to realism that helps to overcome any kind of mere speculative thinking, be it on behalf of supernatural, mystical, or merely intuitive ideas. But on the other hand, Dewey also claims that philosophy can make certain metaphysical observations about nature in the sense of "generic traits of existence" that are "manifested by existences of all kinds without regard to their differentiation into physical and mental" (ibid., 308). Such traits are claimed to be valid for each and every experience independent of context and cultural diversity. For example, Dewey thinks of traits like qualities and relationships, stability and precariousness, eventfulness and connectedness. The tension of these "generic traits" then seems to be simply given by nature, as some of Dewey's formulations seem to imply, and not constructed by specific oberservers, participants, and agents in culture. This is problematic because it suggests that nature as an obvious and given basis of claims that begs for the consent of all who are open-minded. The search for generic traits seems to presuppose an observer position that would be pure and naive in the sense of not being influenced by specific cultural contexts. This presupposition can be considered as a heritage of naturalistic traditions in Western thought. But as developments in twentieth-century thought until now have shown, this easy picture of nature is deceptive because it neglects or conceals the diversity of experiences, interests, and practices (influenced by culture) in which nature is at stake. For instance, if we take the concrete social situation of a scientific inquiry in all the diversity and complexity of social interests that have an impact on the situation we must say that nature as an object of inquiry can never simply be obvious for all. Rather, we should take account of the social powers and interests that have already inscribed themselves into the objects of inquiry. Such inscription, as more recent cultural theories suggest, often happens in subliminal and hidden ways. It implies that the meaning of natural objects is often highly ambitious and even contradictory from the cultural point of view. Think, for example, of the use of nuclear power, the climate catastrophy, the nature of sex, or other relevant debates of human life.

Against this background, the premise of a naive and pure observer implicit even in some parts of Dewey's naturalism seems more doubtful today than it may have in his time. Rather, we always need an explicit observer theory that always specifies cultural contexts before speaking about nature. This gives us more critical perspectives that urge us always to reflect the relation of our observer positions and the ways we transact with nature. In this sense, there is no pure natural science and no pure scientific experiment. If we thoroughly carry through the surrender of dualisms that Dewey already intended, these approaches to nature are interwoven in cultural observations, participations, and actions. This consequence also makes it doubtful today to speak of generic traits of nature in a metaphysical sense. Among other recent philosophers, Richard Rorty (1982, 73ff.) has given powerful arguments that Dewey's approach should be reconstructed in this connection. The net result of what was said in our discussion so far about the transactional relation between culture and nature would indeed be more convincing if we surrender all metaphysical claims. This at least is a conclusion that interactive constructivism draws from its dialogues with Deweyan pragmatism (see Neubert and Reich 2006).

Nevertheless, it is very clear, as we already saw above, that Dewey despite his reflections about naturalism already understood that in human life and conduct, culture is important and one can never explain human behavior on the basis of nature in a narrow sense. To the contrary, he rejected the narrow naturalistic or biologistic ways of thought that were very influential in his time:

> In any case, the idea of culture...points to the conclusion that whatever are the native constituents of human nature, the culture of a period and group is the determining influence in their arrangement; it is that which determines the patterns of behavior that mark out the activities of any group, family, clan, people, sect, faction, class. It is at least as true that the state of culture determines the order and arrangement of native tendencies as that human nature produces any particular set or system of social phenomena so as to obtain satisfaction for itself. The problem is to find out the way in which the elements of a culture interact with each other and the way in which the elements of human nature are caused to interact with one another under conditions set by their interaction with the existing environment. For example, if our American culture is largely a pecuniary culture, it is not because the original or innate structure of human nature tends of itself to obtaining pecuniary profit. It is rather that a certain complex culture stimulates, promotes and consolidates native tendencies so as to produce a certain pattern of desires and purposes. If we take all the communities, peoples, classes, tribes and nations that ever existed, we may be sure that since human nature in its native constitution is the relative constant, it cannot be appealed to, in isolation, to account for the multitude of diversities presented by different forms of association. (LW 13: 75–76)

Here, we have to reflect on the role of transactions. Although today the term transaction is not always explicitly used, for example, in fields like communication theory, the idea behind Dewey's distinction between interaction and transaction has influenced many approaches that in our time go by the label "systemic." One influential contemporary approach, in this connection, is the philosophy of communicative action launched and internationally represented by

Jürgen Habermas in whom we find suggestive uses of the perspective of transaction:

1. For one thing, transactions characterize and delimit systemic conditions of observation, participation, and action, with an understanding that such conditions are always necessary contexts as well as effects in an emergent process that has neither a single cause nor a closed end. For Habermas, this applies among other things to an understanding of scientific practice that involves critical perspectives on the transactions between interests and knowledge. Habermas' approach is well known especially for his postulation of the ideal of a discourse free from domination. This ideal is supposed to clarify the conditions that make possible scientific transactions with sufficient intersubjective control in a democratic process that is regarded as necessary context for scientific practice. This has affinities with Dewey's philosophy of democracy and inquiry although Dewey was more cautious than Habermas with regard to universalistic claims for justifying this ideal and he avoids the tendency to postulate counterfactual ideals like Habermas's ideal discourse. His objection to such procedure would be to refer to experience and to question any attempt to postulate ideals as counterfactual to experience. With Dewey we would always point to discourse as actually experienced in order to find ground for rooting and justifying our ideals.

2. In contrast to Dewey, however, Habermas makes more productive and critical use of the specific form of transactions involved in interpersonal communications in the sense described by George Herbert Mead. Mead was a colleague and friend of Dewey's and there was a strong mutual influence between their philosophical approaches as we showed in part 1. Yet, there is a dimension in Mead's thought, as we saw above, that focuses on the tensional relation between "I" and "Me," "self" and "generalized other," and Dewey never sufficiently picked up this thread of theorizing the intra- and interpersonal process from Mead. Habermas is well known for adapting and further developing this thread and its potential implications for critical theory. His positions, though, have not remained uncontested. One of his most prominent critics is Richard Rorty who shows that the postulate discourse free from domination is not the only possible interpretation of the pragmatist tradition in communication. Two main directions of interpretations have developed about this problem:
    • Habermas's position implies that the tensional relation between "I" and "Me" is constitutive of communicative encounters of all

kinds, but on behalf of the ideal of freedom from domination it has to be determined and qualified by specific conditions. Most important here is the limitation of individual interests and power claims. If the ideal is to be realized, the partakers in discourse have to subject their interests and claims to mutual discursive commitments on the basis of free and rational insight. Habermas provides a sophisticated and original perspective on the conditions of ideal-typical discourse in his theory of communicative action (see Habermas 1984, 1987a).

- Against Habermas, however, critics like Rorty insist that the very process of idealization of discursive norms is problematic insofar as it postulates a position whose actual realization in experience is pragmatically impossible. A more modest pragmatism therefore should be more cautious in taking the unavoidable ambivalence between ideal and experience into account. This articulates with regard to discourse the fundamental relation of the precarious and stable dimensions of experience that we have discussed above in Dewey. It does not surrender our social hopes and critical capacities with regard to issues of power and domination.

The second position is clearly more in accord with pragmatist thought in the wake of Dewey although the ideal developed in the first position can be instructive—though not constitutive—for a pragmatist or constructivist ethics of discourse and inquiry in democracy. Both perspectives of transaction and interaction are highly relevant in this connection.

Dewey's pragmatism rejects the dualism between theory and practice, for example, between rational idealism and disillusioned practice. His pragmatic turn of the critique of knowledge takes into consideration that it is always experience and action in experience that we live and that, then, returns to our theories as experienced.[38] For him, in this sense, there are no final values for the democratic process given to the community from without. Democracy means lived community whose standards and viabilities are developed from within. There is no transcendental justification of democracy. As experience, democracy is always an experimental affair.[39] But this does not mean arbitrariness. Democratic communities must do justice to the conditions of possibility of an acceptable way of life for all. This implies to find the necessary values, norms, and standards by experimenting with democratic possibilities as well as the readiness to change those values, norms, and standards according to the viability of contexts. But community, to be sure, depends on a common good.

Seen in a larger perspective debates about this common good have taken considerable different forms. We will sum up three controversial lines:

1. From the perspective of democratic experimentalism and liberal education as a main force to realize democracy, the participation of all members of a society seems inevitable in order to obtain a sufficiently liberal basis for democracy.[40] This is the call for deep democracy in many variations. For Jack Crittenden (2002), it represents the deeply participatory approach as followed by Thomas Jefferson. In this approach, we need a permanent critical awareness for democratic theories *and* practices.[41] Democratic experimentalism requires a liberal education of all people for creating an appropriate basis for active and critical participation.[42] However, as critical research has shown, it is precisely the educational sector where the claims for liberal equality and equity have failed most heavily.[43]

2. As the practice cannot live up to the ideal, democratic theories based on technocratic or knowledge elites have been promoted. For Crittenden, this is the representative branch propagated by James Madison. Proponents of this approach often argue that the masses are too irrational and they tend to overestimate the dangers of mass manipulation.[44] They want to restrict the direct influence of the public by insisting on representative structures of democracy.[45] To their mind, the ideal of participatory democracy builds on the unrealistic ideal that humans can avoid self-interest on behalf of rational judgments concerning public affairs. Therefore, the masses should not be allowed to have direct political influence.[46] It is quite clear that these assumptions mirror the failures of democratic education and draw a negative conclusion. However, the practical consequence is that the masses often feel misunderstood by politics in representative government. The increase of political disinterestedness in Western societies today is sufficient proof that this model of representation over participation has largely become the standard.

3. Overall, a succession and juxtaposition of different democratic theories has developed that not only lead to confusion and constantly further distinctions in detail but also result in uncertainty with regard to the essential criteria of democracy. In practice, too, democracy has undergone many different and contradictory

movements. The concept democracy thus shows an increasing opening and expansion with the spectrum reaching from direct participation on the one hand to elitist representation and neglect of the interests of the many on the other hand.

These three lines of discourse are playing an important role today. There are proponents of each line contesting each other and maintaining their claims without having last reasons or final success. Richard Rorty has been an influential philosopher who has given point to this controversy. In his reconstruction of pragmatism,[47] Rorty concludes from a perspective of different versions of realities as viewed in the Western cultures nowadays, that there can be no solution, in the long run, as to which explanation of desirable realities is more justified or effective than others. There are no final reasons for choosing between different versions of common good. No metanarrative, no theory of human nature, no metaphysics, or even theology can establish an unambiguous foundation for the just community. All such establishments are open to interpretation. They are constructs, versions of reality made up by observers. And the performance of observing and constructing does not necessarily imply a general, universal, and correct criterion for all claims of validity. Warranty is found in the performances themselves in the context of the cultural and always ethnocentric interpretations of the ways we live.[48] All we need is that these interpretive communities make majority decisions. The viability of interpretations and, thus, the acceptance or refusal of all constructions beyond mere subjective opinions, that is, decisions made in a community are more important than fundamental reasons. There is no necessary rational a priori of democracy. However, Rorty does not deny the importance of democratic structures, because lived democracy, for him, is a practical condition for a free community. Therefore, his approach does not exclude the possibility of deep democracy if we could really show how to live it. This more contextual understanding of democratic communities is one result of our turning away from metaphysical conceptions of the world and final explanations.

There are many other theories that follow this turn today. We find a kind of relativism not only in pragmatism the way Rorty sees it, but also in many other approaches in the cultural sciences and humanities. This relativism expresses social changes and developments in the last decades.[49] In opposition, however, we find others who warn us against putting at risk core values of social progressivism as a heritage of the enlightenment. For them, Dewey is a main reference.

Dewey has developed a clear and critical perspective on the social conditions and movements of his time. In modernity, natural rights theories have been transformed into contractarian models (Hobbes, Locke, and Rousseau). They are still important until today. They articulate the quest and requirement to secure social justice and democratic order. Therefore, we need to stipulate norms, values, and laws. Most important for enlightenment thought is the enforcement of human rights. If we follow this line of discourse with and beyond Dewey, we encounter many sophisticated articulations of such claims, for example, in Rawls (1971), Dworkin (1978), Ackerman (1980), or Habermas (1984, 1987a, 1987b). Their many differences notwithstanding, these approaches all emphasize that social justice needs a foundation more solid than majority decisions. Majorities may vary. But the grounds on which democracy builds must be more stable. The necessary norms, values, and laws must be at least founded and warranted by discourse. Thus, these theories argue for rational ideals critically developed out of the enlightenment movement and articulated in new theoretical shapes. They concede that existing practices, routines, and institutions do not come up with the democratic ideal. Therefore, it can only be articulated counterfactually. But this articulation and theoretical foundation is still indispensable if we do not want to surrender democracy altogether.

The problem with these positions, to our mind, is that they tend to lose contact with conditions of living too easily by taking refuge in idealized rational discourses. They avoid taking sufficient account of the social and cultural ambivalences of democracy. For example, they construct a rational and coherent logical account where, in reality, we rather find particular interests, one-sidedness, contradictions, and ambivalences. On the one hand, this renders them blind to the actual conditions of life. On the other hand, they stand for indispensable claims and democratic hopes to overcome the very particular interests, one-sidedness, and contradictions that threaten democracy.

Even if these positions often take reference to Dewey, they articulate only parts of his pragmatism. We see Dewey in a middle position between them and Rorty. In what follows, we want to clarify this judgment:

1. Dewey's starting point is *experience*. Language is a necessary and generative medium of experience. But for Dewey, language is always realized in actions. Language games cannot do away with experience. This is the very point where Rorty does not want to follow Dewey. Here, he gives pragmatism a different turn. To our mind,

he aptly criticizes pragmatism's naturalism and its hidden consequences in the way of giving preference to natural sciences and technologies. The dominance of instrumentalism does not do justice to the diverse facets of culture as expressed, for example, in literature, art, and social sciences. Even if Dewey's broad understanding of experience comprises these diverse facets, Rorty's objection stresses that they cannot today be adequately articulated by referring to nature. Even the natural sciences succeed or fail in the context of language games. In the case of many technologies, we must admit that these games are warranted by repeated experiments. Normally, we do not doubt their viability. But their reliability concerns only a narrow field of practice (experience). Beyond this narrow field, they often produce unforeseen effects that return to experience as the precarious side of life (risk society). Instrumentalism tends to block critical perspectives on such consequences. The point is not that instrumentalism as such is a wrong perspective but that it is often too one-sidedly connected with natural sciences and technologies. For Rorty, philosophy as critical discourse must be more comprehensive. Philosophical reflections have to deal with linguistic complexities, and they should do so in a most edifying and diverse way. Here, instrumentalism and feasibility are not of primary import. What counts are vocabularies and discourses in which we reflect and find new articulations of diverse cultures. In this move, Rorty, however, misses to pay sufficient attention to the relevance of experience and action as contexts of all language games in culture. Thus, the relativism of vocabularies and language games may easily turn out as arbitrariness. Here, we think, there are more and richer resources in Dewey's pragmatic tradition than have so far been reconstructed by all those who follow Rorty.

2. Rorty radically contests the effectiveness of philosophical discourses. In the wake of the linguistic turn, philosophers have done much work in analyzing the linguistic conditions of modern thought and discourses. We have to admit, though, that philosophy upon the whole has not been very effective in solving concrete social, political, and economic problems in modernity. Therefore, Rorty suggests that we be more modest in our expectations. His "pragmatism shares the Deweyan refusal to empower by appeal to ontological essences and natural rights, but it abandons the idea that philosophy can compensate by proposing effective means for social empowerment" (Shusterman 1997, 81). Rorty more decidedly than Dewey points to the incommensurability and radical plurality of communities.

3. Dewey stands for a more positive liberalism than Rorty. He prefers to focus on democracy as lived in actual, local, and participatory communities. The warranted assertability of democracy as a way of life depends on the experience of local communities as the model of democratic interaction. Rorty prefers a negative liberalism that doubts the possibility to derive warranted assertibilities from the way we live. For him, democratic values are always part of narrations, different vocabularies, and contingencies in language games.[50] From the skeptical perspective on narrations, all criteria of a good democratic life seem to have a weak status. Especially, we miss the political conditions and forces that would enable us to use such criteria as powerful cultural instruments. Rather, democratic practice shows that all "good criteria" are most often called upon when democratic rights and liberties are under attack. They are then used as weapons of defense rather than tools of construction. Against this sober skepticism, Dewey has spoken of democracy as a struggle for active and free participation for all. This implies the responsibility to take care of sufficient democratic conditions and structures as something we have to create and reconstruct ourselves. In this connection, he did not hesitate to demand radical reforms of culture including the economical system. By comparison, pragmatists like Rorty are today much more cautious in their criticism. This weakens the case of political emancipation, because democratic freedom is understood as standing for tolerance rather than active reconstruction (see Shusterman 1997, 72).

4. For Dewey the creation of social responsibility depends on a positive development of individuality in interaction within a community. Rorty here, too, sounds a more negative tone. Not only his idea of liberty but also his understanding of solidarity is defined in defensive categories. Where Dewey still holds on to the modern idea of the coherent subject as the necessary agent for achieving the common good, Rorty points to the postmodern experience of decentralized subjectivity and accentuates the necessity to avoid cruelty and suffering as remaining liberal strategy. This is a minimum requirement of solidarity that Rorty insists on. Where Dewey looks for commonalities of values and a unity in diversity, Rorty rejects this as illusionary. The unity looked for, after all, has always been more wishful than actual. On principle, the contingency of individual life-forms and identities has increased considerably in the transition from modernity to postmodernity. Chance more and more becomes a crucial factor in the conduct of life. Against this background, Rorty expands the perspectives

on democratic liberties especially in direction of an *"aesthetic life"* that furthers *self-enlargement, self-enrichment,* and *self-creation.* Where Dewey emphasizes the social tie that binds the different members of a society together, Rorty questions the unambiguousness of this tie and points to contradictions. For him, a social tie and frame is still necessary, but we have lost secure grounds to argue for its legitimation. In these different accounts, we partly can recognize the different ages in which Dewey and Rorty live (see Shusterman 1997, 73ff.).[51]

5. Rorty is especially critical against any preconception on the side of philosophers as to how people should live together. Such predecisions have shown their futility too many times to be convincing anymore. Philosophers should keep their hands off people's affairs and leave them alone (see Rorty 1991, 194); they should care about tolerance rather than emancipation (ibid., 213). In privacy, one can cultivate irony that is necessary for critical reflection. On the one hand, the aim of irony, for Rorty, is not arrogance but modesty. But on the other hand, such irony is not appropriate for public matters like government and constitution, for laws and justice, for liberties in political life. Liberals must protect the existing political conditions to secure the possibility of ironical self-reflection and the diversity of aesthetic lives. For Rorty, the point is to organize private and public life in ways that support diversity and pluralism as concrete choice of people with democratic orientations. Rorty is right in warning us against the overestimation of the impact of critical thinking in our society. But the weak point of this position, to our mind, lies in the unclear distinction between public conditions and private affairs. This implies that it remains unclear in Rorty what are the concrete conditions for establishing a liberal community. Here, Dewey's classical pragmatism has more resources than Rorty draws on.

If we consider more closely the differences between Dewey and Rorty as far as we have discussed them, we find some interesting shifts. Taken on the surface, it may seem that the development of capitalist societies corresponds to the tendencies already expressed in Dewey's works. We have had an increase of diversity, pluralism, and differences in communities and an increase of interrelations between communities. Thus, they still seem to be appropriate today. But if we look more closely, we have to reconstruct them in order to employ them as critical perspectives today. With Bauman, we have been reminded of the subtle and complex forms of ambivalence in solid and liquid modernity. With Foucault, as we have discussed, we may recognize and analyze the power ties and power structures involved in these developments. With Bourdieu, we have to acknowledge the effects of different interests articulated in different forms of capital and unequal expectations implied in the process. With Derrida, we have seen the necessity of providing space for the arrival of the excluded Other, and with Levinas, we have discussed the ethical challenge of preventing the reduction of Otherness to Sameness. With Rorty, we can say that these processes and structures take their themes in various language games. But with Foucault and Bourdieu, we can emphasize that linguistic actions are important here. Even if the professionals of discourses act mainly in language games this does not mean that language games are disconnected from interests and power relations. And there exists a world beyond language games, even if this world may only be articulated in such games. Especially, economic differences have grown much more in the last decades compared to the progress made in educational systems and other symbolic forms of equity. The new economic inequality has built up new concentrations of capital and power. This effects the reconstruction of Dewey's approach. Dewey's vision of meliorism and his concept of democracy as a frame of global democratic orientation on the basis of relative equality of society members is put to the test through the increase of differences between the rich and the poor, between the propertyless and the propertied classes, and between the uneducated and educated. This test is critical for the development of democracy. It will show whether democracy will destroy itself in the ecstasy of the differences between individuals, groups, or classes or whether it will succeed in a diversity of real chances for all. Dewey was quite aware of this contradiction: "We are educating more citizens than ever before for participation in democratic processes of control, but there are influential forces ready to abandon even political democracy in order to prevent the extension of democracy into industry and finance" (LW 11: 536).

Dewey's philosophy offers a possible and reasonable frame to reflect this contradiction and possible solutions. Even if they cannot lead to a complete analysis, they are an entrance into the crucial reflection of democratic conditions that are at stake if we consider democracy not only as a given structure but also as a contradictory process.

Rorty implicitly uses a lot of Dewey's arguments. He especially emphasizes solidarity as a necessary frame for a life of increasing liberties. At this point, Rorty is more pragmatist than many of his critics think. However, Dewey would argue that solidarity needs community life and cannot be restricted to mere language games. Already in his "Early Works," he says,

> It is community life, participation in the organized and continuous resources of civilization, which alone enables the individual to realize the high capacities which are latent in him. As mere individual, man cannot ascend above savagery. As an individual, he is an insignificant affair, as social whole he constitutes a living miracle. It is through social relations that the individual emerges from his animal and natural state and becomes really a spiritual being. (EW 5: 378)

Later, he emphasizes that in such communities participation is a main aim in education and school: "Apart from participation in social life, the school has no moral end nor aim. As long as we confine ourselves to the school as an isolated institution, we have no directing principles, because we have no object" (MW 4: 271). Or in regard to society, "A society which makes provision for participation in its good of all its members on equal terms and which secures flexible readjustment of its institutions through interaction of the different forms of associated life is in so far democratic" (MW 9: 106).

This democratic society is not yet achieved. We still have to fight for it. And there is no final orientation as well as no ultimate principle for this struggle. "Freedom is a growth, an attainment, not an original possession, and it is attained by idealization of institutions and law and the active participation of individuals in their loyal maintenance, not by their abolition or reduction in the interests of personal judgments and wants" (LW 3: 103).

Dewey is hopeful to help society on its better way. But Rorty does not want to intervene from a philosophical standpoint in the societal development because he sees no chances for success. He bets his hope and confidence on the prosperity of diversity and, in face of his negative approach, he proposes to avoid attempts to delimit and regulate the increase of differences and the pluralism of language games. Thereby, however, he tends to neglect the increase of unequal chances and to play down the damages to democratic communities generated by insufficient solidarity. In his view on America, he seems to trust that democracy as a whole still seems to be functioning. At the same time, he doubts that the current society is sufficiently social and democratic. Like Dewey in his time, Rorty criticizes the unsocial and unfair conditions, the self-adulation, and greed of many that endanger both—the chances of individuals and the democratic life in society. But Rorty also doubts that a critical theory can change much at that. Do we not have to admit that our criticism of cultural practices, routines, and institutions has achieved only very little? What grounds do we have to believe that it will change more in the future? For Rorty, this consideration forces us to admit that we should achieve the common good in our private and individual lives. What we hoped for in general can only be gained in particular. With this turn to the private, Rorty disposes of the explanatory model of discourse on behalf of a therapeutic model. But from this position, our struggle for democracy can give but a very general orientation. Especially, it does not seem necessary to determine the concrete ways of realizing liberties and to specify the concrete forms of solidarity. Dewey is more concrete here. For him what counts are not only the growth of societies in direction of an increase of pluralism, diversity, and individual chances, but also the building of communities in local and more global contexts. In postmodern discourses, as elaborated, for example, by Rorty, we may see the consequences of pluralist growth as well as the problems of establishing communities. A new struggle appears: More than before we need a culture of tolerance in order to be able to live the new liberties. However, we cannot do without a culture of solidarity, lest the increase of liberties creates an increase of unequal chances that will in the long run subvert the grounds of tolerance.

For education, Rorty's famous philosophical female figure of the liberal ironist can provide an instructive model. She can help educators to gain critical distance for deconstructing their own involvements in claims and expectations that allegedly secure comprehensive orientation, stable knowledge, and safe practices. To be an ironist means to live dangerously. It does not mean to behave arrogantly from a superior deconstructivist position. Understood this way the ironist attitude is a self-critical attitude. It goes hand in hand with a sensitivity and readiness to accept diversity and ambivalence as necessary qualities in contemporary life. The Rortyan emphasis on the importance of the ironist is a clearly new tone in pragmatism compared to the classical philosophers like Dewey. It articulates what we could call a general atmosphere of our time and our perception of the challenges of diversity and change in an increasingly globalized world. For the individual educator, being an ironist in the Rortyan sense helps to avoid getting trapped in unproductive illusions of modernity, its dreams of perfection in living together as well as in educational practices and outcomes. It also helps them to delimit their own egocentric, ethnocentric, gendercentric, or otherwise culturally pervaded views even if the ironic position denies the possibility of ever overcoming once and for all such limitation. Furthermore, being an ironic supports us against exaggerated and unrealistic claims of being perfect educators ourselves. On the one hand, this can have the positive effect that the ironic educator allows herself to be more calm to herself and more generous to others. On the other hand, it can have the negative effect of being too distanced to get involved in struggling for more equity, social justice, and democracy in society. Basically, Rorty leaves us with this ambivalence, because we in democratic living together must find our answers and solutions in the tension between irony and solidarity.

If we close by considering some further implications from Rorty for education today, we may start with a reminder that theories of communication are of particular importance. Rorty's philosophy provides an abundance of insights regarding communication. For instance, his ideas about final vocabularies and the narrative and poetic dimensions of discourses help to overcome naive and everyday assumptions about communication as purely information proceeding processes. Especially in education, it is important to understand that there is no one-dimensional control of discourses. Practically this means, in the terminology of interactive constructivism, that there is always more than one observer perspective for different participants and agents. Rorty's figure of the ironists seems, against this background, as a valuable metaphor to indicate a necessary role change in teaching and learning (see Reich 2006). If we understand irony as a self-critical relation of observers, participants, and agents toward their own life-experience, we may say that to a certain extent our time of liquid modernity is a time of irony in response to the ambivalence as portrayed by Bauman.

Interactive constructivism tries to capture this necessary awareness of ambivalence and irony in its specific account of the interplay of contents and lived relationships in communication and education. One crucial thesis is that the level of relationships has a stronger influence on the level of contents than vice versa. Some authors use the so-called "iceberg metaphor" as an illustration, according to which the level of contents relates to the level of relationships like the one-tenth of the iceberg above the surface relates to the nine-tenth below.[52]

For interactive constructivism, the emphasis on relationships in learning and education constitutes an important challenge for educational practice and research today. Much too often in the past educational theories and practices focused too exclusively on the level of contents—the symbolic orders and arrangements of learning—while being much too oblivious to the level of relationships. As communication theory shows, however, learning always takes place in the context of lived relationships. It is crucial for constructivist educators to understand that they do not only construct—together with their students—the symbolic orders of learning, but also the communicative relationships in which learning takes place. Constructivists think that it is an important precondition for constructive and effective learning processes that educators develop and cultivate a sense for the art of creating pedagogical relationships that allow for mutual respect and appreciation for the Otherness of the Other and that provide an atmosphere of mutual self-esteem, openness, self-determination, and responsibility for both teachers and students (see Reich 2010, 51–70). To prepare teachers for this difficult yet crucial task requires, among other things, to introduce new ways and methods of self-experience, self-perception, and self-reflection as an integral part of teacher education classes. With Rorty, we may say that part of the role of teachers and learners in our time is to become "strong poets," who are able to invent new vocabularies to overcome the finalities of limited discourses and go on in the games of conversation. This is part of the necessary constructive solutions, but we may observe critically toward Rorty and other neopragmatists that experience is more than language and conversation. Learning from experience in a Deweyan sense means openness to the real in the terminology of interactive constructivism. With Rorty, it implies being self-critical toward the vocabularies that we culturally (or even scientifically) inhabited because these vocabularies tend to appear as final versions of the world. In instruction at school, they are often presented that way. The Deweyan educator will insist on the primacy of experience to overcome such limitedness. Interactive constructivism would suggest that it is precisely the tension between the symbolic, the imaginative, and the real what is at stake here and that a productive way of dealing with that tension is to combine processes of construction, reconstruction, and deconstruction. The comprehensive frame for educational practice that combine and realizes the constructivist perspectives introduced here—namely the roles of observer, participant, and agent; the registers of symbolic, imaginative, and real; the processes of construction, reconstruction, and deconstruction—is the context of democratic communications and practice, routines, and institutions that actualizes Dewey's criteria of democratic living together and Rorty's claims to solidarity.

Summary

Rorty insists on contextualism and relativism in their import for critical thought in our time and culture. He focuses more on the hopes of increasing liberties than on a critical investigation of concrete social conditions. With Rorty, we are warned not to overestimate our theoretical ideas and expectations. But Dewey would not have been satisfied with a position that favors the private more than the public, because in the private the dangers of social forgetfulness are too big. Even if Rorty is right that intellectuals cannot change the world in a more or less utopian way right now, the acceptance of this statement leads to the risk of becoming a mere observer. We can only delimit this risk through our roles as participants and agents in the struggles for democratic progress.

Questions for Discussion

With Rorty, we may say that all language games are built on contingency and imply a certain amount of arbitrariness. Can you find concrete examples for this observation in the language games or speech situations in which you participate?

Can you give examples of situations where democracy fails?

What practices, routines, and institutions of democratic living could be helpful against such failure?

Do you think that we need idealizations of such practices, routines, and institutions in our democratic struggles today? Do you agree that without giving concrete answers to this question, we run the risk of losing our orientation in struggles for freedom and solidarity?

Do you believe that the ironic position makes us more sober with regard to educational practices, routines, and institutions? Or are you afraid that the ironist puts us in a too detached position and leads to disengagement?

What active forms of participation can we achieve in our local and global communities? Do you agree that if we do not organize partaking well, we will increase the risks of a split of interests with new classes and future class struggles?

What concrete forms of support can you develop for more equity in education and life opportunities?

What do you think the following claim?

The rich and prosperous will be measured by how they promote the poor and less advantaged. The rich will be questioned by the poor, who lead "wasted lives" (see Bauman 2004), in how far solidarity has come to an end. A continuously negative answer could be the end of the democratic project.

NOTES

INTRODUCTION

1. For the program and perspectives of interactive constructivism see Reich (1998, 2006, 2010), Neubert (1998, 2003), and online Neubert and Reich: http://www.uni-koeln.de/hf/konstrukt/reich_works/index .html (August 8, 2011).
2. See, for example, Reich (2007, 2008, 2009, 2012), Neubert (2008, 2009a), Neubert and Reich (2002, 2006, 2008, 2012), and online Neubert and Reich: http://www.uni-koeln.de/hf/konstrukt/reich_works/index.html (August 8, 2011).
3. See the broad collection at http://www.pragmatism.org/.

1 EDUCATION AND CULTURE— THE CULTURAL TURN

1. Sidney Hook wrote in the introduction to *Experience and Nature,* "Discussion today of Dewey's metaphysics in Experience and Nature must take note of the well-known fact that Dewey regarded the use of the terms 'metaphysics' and 'experience' as unfortunate. He was prepared to jettison both terms at the end of his long philosophical career in order to avoid misunderstanding. For 'experience' he would have substituted 'culture' in the anthropological sense … He vowed on the eve of his 90th year 'never to use the words [metaphysics and metaphysical] again in connection with any aspect of my own position' because, he complained, his use of the terms had been assimilated to the sense they bear 'in the classic tradition based on Aristotle.'"
2. This section draws largely on Neubert (2009b).
3. There are, however, already in Dewey's *Middle Works* a number of minor writings in which his mature concept of experience is already prefigured and progressively worked out. Compare, for example, the writings indicated by the key words "experience" and "immediate empiricism" in the index of MW 3 (1903–1906), the essay "The Subject-Matter of Metaphysical Inquiry" (1915; MW 8: 3–13), the eleventh chapter of *Democracy and Education* (1916; MW 9: 146–158), and chapter four in *Reconstruction in Philosophy* (1920; MW 12: 124–138).

4. In addition to *Experience and Nature* compare especially his two books *Reconstruction in Philosophy* (1920; MW 12: 77–201) and *The Quest for Certainty: A Study of the Relation of Knowledge and Action* (1929; LW 4).
5. Dewey's own contributions to the *Studies* of 1903 can be found in MW (2). His *Essays* that were collectively published in 1916 are scattered about several volumes of the *Middle Works* in the critical edition. It is easy to find them with the help of the edition's Index.

3   EDUCATION, COMMUNICATION, AND DEMOCRACY—THE COMMUNICATIVE TURN

1. Donald Finkel (2000) develops suggestive consequences from this thought for what he calls "teaching with your mouth shut."
2. Later on, Dewey's term "occupation" was largely displaced by the term "project," which became popular largely through the work of Dewey's student and colleague Kilpatrick.
3. This passage is taken from a stenographic report of an address that Dewey gave to the Teachers Union in 1933.
4. Although he warns us that "what is called 'modern' is as yet unformed" and "inchoate" (MW 12: 273), this development, in his view, has greatly been advanced by the "scientific," the "industrial," and the "political revolution" of modernity (ibid., 257).
5. This quote is from the second version of *Ethics* (1932), a textbook coauthored by Dewey and James Hayden Tufts.
6. This section draws largely on Neubert (2009b).
7. See also the essay "Three Independent Factors in Morals" (1930/1966; LW 5: 279–288) as well as Dewey's extraordinarily subtle discussion of the relation of means and ends—for example, in his *Theory of Evaluation* (1939; LW 13: 189–251, especially 226ff.: "The Continuum of Ends-Means")—which completely refutes the still existing misunderstanding of his pragmatism as a narrow utilitarianism.
8. See also examples given in Dewey's *Art as Experience* (e.g., LW 10: 49–50).
9. This means no rejection of representative structures, but rather the combination of forms and methods of direct and representative democracy.
10. Dewey's Chicago school experiment, afterward often labeled as "Dewey-School," existed until 1904 when he moved to Columbia University in New York City.

4 CRITICISM AND CONCERNS—RECONSTRUCTING DEWEY FOR OUR TIMES

1. Interactive constructivism has developed a theory of discourses that distinguishes and combines four perspectives that should be taken into

account in contemporary analyses of discourses—namely, "power," "knowledge," "lived relationships," and "the unconscious."

2. The three registers are common in (post)modern French philosophy, especially in those (post)structuralist approaches that draw on the work of Jacques Lacan. Interactive constructivism has transformed these theoretical perspectives in a decidedly constructivist way that, for example, rejects the ontological implications of Lacanian psychoanalysis (see Reich 1998, vol. 1).

3. For a more detailed discussion see Reich (2010, Ch. 4).

4. Human relationships as imaginative encounters always have their unconscious phases that delimit intentional direction and control (see Reich 1998, vol. 2; Neubert and Reich 2002). However, the possibilities of consciously reflecting on the imaginative aspects of pedagogical relationships are of crucial importance for constructivist educators.

5. Dewey himself clearly anticipated this insight, for example, in "Context and Thought" (LW 6: 3–21).

6. This section partly relies on Neubert and Reich (2011).

7. This section draws extensively on Reich (2011).

8. In view of a more extensive interpretation, Kersten Reich discusses Foucault in a more differentiated way in Reich (1998).

9. See, for example, Foucault (1979, 1980, 1988).

10. See as introductory works especially Foucault (1980) and Rabinow (1985).

11. As classic metatheories hereof see, for example, Foucault (1970, 1972, 1981).

12. In "The History of Sexuality," Foucault investigates such orders and patterns of interpretation in a subtly differentiated way. See Foucault (1978, 1985, 1986).

13. This was one essential observation of Foucault's late works. See Martin (1988).

14. In this direction points a deconstructed Marxist analysis too. See, for example, Laclau (1990), Mouffe (1994, 1996, 2000), and Laclau and Mouffe (2001).

15. See, for example, Foucault (1988).

16. On this, see, in particular, Habermas (1984, 1987a, 1987b).

17. Many interesting ideas can be found, for example, in Auxier (2002) and Stuhr (2002).

18. As one of many examples: "We are educating more citizens than ever before for participation in democratic processes of control, but there are influential forces ready to abandon even political democracy in order to prevent the extension of democracy into industry and finance. Americans, when they look at some of the totalitarian states, prize highly the greater freedom of this country, but in spite of this violations of civil liberties and assaults upon educational freedom seem to be increasing" (LW 11: 536).

19. See Hewitt (2007) for some more aspects on Dewey and power.

20. See Reich (2008).

21. This section draws extensively on Reich (2011). See also for a more detailed discussion of forms of capital and their implications for democracy and education Reich (2013).

22. At this point, only a few aspects of Bourdieu's work can be taken into consideration very briefly. On the relation between his theory and theories of democracy see, as an introduction, especially Wacquant (2005).

23. As an introduction to this see, in particular, Bourdieu (1986).

24. Bourdieu in URL: http://www.viet-studies.org/Bourdieu_capital.htm.

25. See especially Bourdieu (1984).

26. See, in particular, Bourdieu (1990, 1991, 1993).

27. See, as an introduction, Bourdieu (1994).

28. With regard to the French school and university system, see Bourdieu (1988). For Bourdieu, equality of chances by educational means is shown as an illusion, see Bourdieu and Passeron (1977). To the actual discussion about equality and equity in school systems see Hutmacher, Cochrane, and Bottani (2001).

29. For an account of the connection between habitus and the practical field, see Bourdieu and Wacquant (1992).

30. See also the essay "Democracy and Education after Dewey—Pragmatist Implications for Constructivist Pedagogy," Reich (2008).

31. See Bauman (1997) and Mouffe (2000).

32. In the German tripartite school system especially early selection and the rigid separation between different tracks of qualification stand against more democracy in education, see Reich (2008). The nations worldwide differ in their aims and resources for diversity and inclusive education very much. See "Education at a Glance 2010: OECD Indicators," URL: http://www.oecd.org/document/52/0,3746,en_2649_39263238 _45897844_1_1_1_1,00.html (August 8, 2011).

33. http://www.tdsb.on.ca/_site/viewitem.asp?siteid=15&menuid=682& pageid=546 (September 16, 2011).

34. This section draws extensively on Garrison (1999, 2002).

35. This section draws partly on Garrison (2008, 2011).

36. See also, Bernasconi (1988), "The Trace of Levinas in Derrida."

37. This part draws extensively on Reich (2011).

38. The combination of experience and cultural instrumentalism in Dewey's theory is, for example, discussed in Eldridge (1998).

39. See, for example, Stuhr (1997).

40. Pragmatism is a main force in this struggle for democracy. Dewey had developed a complex cultural theory in this line. See as introduction in the broad approach especially Hickman (1998). The revival of pragmatism today is discussed, for example, in Dickstein (1998).

41. In John Dewey, this stands in the context of his diagnosis of time. More general and within the range of leftist theories are the argumentations of, for example, MacPherson (1966, 1975, 1977), Barber (1984), and Green (1999). Contrary to these approaches, Talisse (2005) gives a

minimalist account of deliberative liberalism that tends to overestimate the side of procedures and to neglect experience.

42. A good introduction in the educational theory in this sense is given by Garrison (1998). I try to reflect on Dewey's democratic criteria for education in Reich (2008).

43. On the lacking transposition of equity in the school systems of democratic countries see, in particular, Bourdieu and Passeron (1977) and Hutmacher, Cochrane, and Bottani (2001).

44. Westbrook, for example, writes, "unlike Dewey, who believed that 'the world has suffered more from leaders and authorities than from the masses,' realists continued to fear most the threat they believed an ignorant and irrational public posed" (Westbrook 1991, 546).

45. Or they claim in a more democratic way, like Rawls in an egalitarian philosophy, utopian norms, values, and rules of how we could live in equality and justice without sufficiently caring about the real experiences.

46. A classic theory thereof is offered by Schumpeter (1942); see also Hollinger (1996, xiii).

47. See Rorty (1979, 1989, 1991, 1998). See as introductions in controversies about Rorty in pragmatism, for example, Bernstein (1992, 1998), Kuipers (1997), Langsdorf and Smith (1995), Shusterman (1997), Margolis (2002), and Pettegrew (2000).

48. See Rorty (2000).

49. See, for example, Bauman (1993, 1997, 2000, 2004).

50. This negative liberalism concerns all truth claims that are founded on consensus. But for Rorty there are also truth claims based on scientific principles in hard sciences and technologies that are warranted as empirical findings. Even if they, too, are part of the cultural language games, they somehow seem to have a higher validity for Rorty.

51. Shusterman observes, "Rorty's view of the self as a random composite of incompatible quasi selves constantly seeking new possibilities and multiple changing vocabularies seems the ideal self for postmodern consumer society: a fragmented, confused self, hungrily enjoying as many new commodities as it can, but lacking the firm integrity to challenge either its habits of consumption or the system that manipulates and profits of them" (1997, 77). But Rorty's description does not simply mirror contemporary life conditions. His skepticism as to the power of philosophers to change our ways of life does not mean that he would be saying we should embrace capitalistic consumerism.

52. The distinction of contents and relationships goes back to Gregory Bateson. It was used by Watzlawick, Beavin, and Jackson (1967).

BIBLIOGRAPHY

Citations of the works of John Dewey are to the critical edition published by Southern Illinois University Press. Volume and page numbers follows the initials of the series. Abbreviations for the critical edition are:

Dewey, John: *Collected Works*. Edited by Jo Ann Boydston:

The Early Works (EW 1–5): 1882–1898. Carbondale and Edwardsville: Southern Illinois University Press; London and Amsterdam: Feffer & Simons.

The Middle Works (MW 1–15): 1899–1924. Carbondale and Edwardsville: Southern Illinois University Press.

The Later Works (LW 1–17): 1925–1953. Carbondale and Edwardsville: Southern Illinois University Press.

As far as possible, all references to Peirce are to *The Essential Peirce* (EP), 2 vols. (Indiana University Press, 1992, 1998). The volume and page number, separated by a colon, follow EP references. All other references are to the *Collected Papers of Charles S. Peirce* (CP), 8 vols. (Harvard University Press, 1931–1958). The volume and paragraph number, separated by a colon, follows CP references.

Ackerman, B. (1980): *Social Justice in the Liberal State*. New Haven, CT: Yale University Press.

Alexander, T. (1987): *John Dewey's Theory of Art, Experience, and Nature: The Horizons of Feeling*. Albany: State of University of New York Press.

Auxier, Randall E. (2002): "Foucault, Dewey, and the History of the Present." *Journal of Speculative Philosophy* Vol. 16, No. 2, 75–102.

Barber, B. (1984): *Strong Democracy*. Berkeley, CA: University of California Press.

Bauman, Z. (1989): *Modernity and The Holocaust*. Ithaca, NY: Cornell University Press.

Bauman, Z. (1993a): *Modernity and Ambivalence*. Cambridge, UK: Polity Press.

Bauman, Z. (1993b): *Postmodern Ethics*. Oxford, UK: Basil Blackwell.

Bauman, Z. (1997): *Postmodernity and Its Discontents*. New York: New York University Press.

Bauman, Z. (1998): *Globalization: The Human Consequences*. New York: Columbia University Press.

Bauman, Z. (2000): *Liquid Modernity*. Cambridge, UK: Polity Press.

Bauman, Z. (2003): *Liquid Love: On the Fragilty of Human Bonds*. Cambridge, UK: Polity Press.

Bauman, Z. (2004): *Wasted Lives. Modernity and Its Outcasts.* Cambridge, UK: Polity Press.

Bauman, Z. (2005): *Liquid Life.* Cambridge, UK: Polity Press.

Bauman, Z. (2006): *Liquid Fear.* Cambridge, UK: Polity Press.

Bauman, Z. (2007a): *Liquid Times: Living in an Age of Uncertainty.* Cambridge, UK: Polity Press.

Bauman, Z. (2007b): *Consuming Life.* Cambridge, UK: Polity Press.

Bauman, Z., and M. Yakimova (2002): " 'A Postmodern Grid of the Worldmap?' Interview with Zygmunt Bauman." *Eurozine* http://www.eurozine.com/pdf/2002–11–08-bauman-en.pdf.

Bernasconi, R. (1988): "The Trace of Levinas in Derrida." In D. Wood and R. Bernasconi (eds.), *Derrida and Différence.* Chicago, IL: Northwestern University Press, 13–29.

Bernstein, R. J. (1983): *Beyond Objectivism and Relativism.* Philadelphia, PA: University of Pennsylvannia Press.

Bernstein, R. J. (1992): *The New Constellation. The Ethical-Political Horizons of Modernity/Postmodernity.* Cambridge, MA: MIT Press.

Bernstein, R. J. (1998): "Community in the Pragmatic Tradition." In M. Dickstein (ed.), *The Revival of Pragmatism.* Durham, NC; London: Duke University Press, 141–156.

Boisvert, R. D. (1998): "Dewey's Metaphysics: Ground-Map of the Proto-typically Real." In L. A. Hickman (ed.), *Reading Dewey. Interpretations for a Postmodern Generation.* Bloomington, IN; Indianapolis, IN: Indiana University Press, 149–165.

Bourdieu, P. (1984): *Distinction: A Social Critique of the Judgement of Taste.* Trans. Richard Nice. London: Routledge.

Bourdieu, P. (1986): "Forms of Capital." In John G. Richardson (ed.), *Handbook of Theory and Research for the Sociology of Education.* New York: Greenwood Press.

Bourdieu, P. (1988): *Homo Academicus.* Cambridge, UK: Polity Press.

Bourdieu, P. (1990): *The Logic of Practice.* Cambridge, UK: Polity Press.

Bourdieu, P. (1991): *Language and Symbolic Power.* Cambridge, MA: Harvard University Press.

Bourdieu, P. (1993): *The Field of Cultural Production.* Cambridge, UK: Polity Press.

Bourdieu, P. (1994): "Rethinking the State: On the Genesis and Structure of the Bureaucratic Field." *Sociological Theory* Vol. 12, No. 1 (March 1994): 1–19.

Bourdieu, P., and C. Passeron (1977): *Reproduction in Education, Society and Culture.* Trans. Richard Nice. London: Sage Publications.

Bourdieu, P., and L. J. D. Wacquant (1992): *An Invitation to Reflexive Sociology.* Chicago, IL: University of Chicago Press.

Campbell, J. (1992): *The Community Reconstructs. The Meaning of Pragmatic Social Thought.* Urbana, IL; Chicago, IL: University of Illinois Press.

Caspary, W. R. (2000): *Dewey on Democracy.* Ithaca, NY; London: Cornell University Press.

Crittenden, J. (2002): *Democracy's Midwife: An Education in Deliberation*. Lanham, MD: Lexington Books.

Derrida, J. (1973): *Speech and Phenomena*. Evanston, IL: Northwestern University Press.

Derrida, J. (1974): *Of Grammatology*. Trans. Gayatri Chakravorty Spivak. Baltimore, MD: Johns Hopkins Press.

Derrida, J. (1978): *Writing And Difference*. Trans. Alan Bass. Chicago, IL: The University of Chicago Press.

Derrida, J. (1984): "Deconstruction and the Other: An interview with Jacques Derrida." In R. Kearney (ed.), *Dialogues with Contemporary Continental Thinker*. Manchester: Manchester University Press.

Derrida, J. (1996): "Remarks on Deconstruction and Pragmatism." In C. Mouffe (ed.), *Deconstruction and Pragmatism*. London: Routledge, 77–88.

Dickstein, M., ed. (1998): *The Revival of Pragmatism. New Essays on Social Thought, Law, and Culture*. Durham, NC; London: Duke University Press.

Dworkin, R. (1978): *Taking Rights Seriously*. Cambridge, MA: Harvard University Press.

Eldridge, M. (1998): *Transforming Experience. John Dewey's Cultural Instrumentalism*. Nashville, TN: Vanderbilt University Press.

Festenstein, M. (1997): *Pragmatism and Political Theory*. Oxford, UK: Polity Press and Blackwell.

Finkel, D. L. (2000): *Teaching With Your Mouth Shut*. Portsmouth, NH: Boynton/Cook Publishers.

Foucault, M. (1970): *The Order of Things: An Archeology of the Human Sciences*. London: Tavistock.

Foucault, M. (1972): *The Archeology of Knowledge*. Trans. A. M. Sheridan-Smith. London: Tavistock.

Foucault, M. (1978): *The History of Sexuality, Vol. I: An Introduction*. Trans. Robert Hurley. New York: Pantheon.

Foucault, M. (1979): *Discipline and Punish: The Birth of the Prison*. Trans. Alan Sheridan. New York: Vintage.

Foucault, M. (1980): *Power/Knowledge: Selected Interviews and Other Writings: 1972–1977*. Trans. Kate Sopor. New York: Pantheon.

Foucault, M. (1981): "The Order of Discourse." Trans. R. Young. In R. Young (ed.), *Untying the Text: A Poststructuralist Reader*. London: Routledge.

Foucault, M. (1985): *The Use of Pleasure: The History of Sexuality*, Vol. II. Trans. Robert Hurley. New York: Pantheon.

Foucault, M. (1986): *The Care of the Self: The History of Sexuality*, Vol. III. Trans. Robert Hurley. New York: Pantheon.

Foucault, M. (1988): *Politics, Philosophy, and Culture: Interviews and Other Writings, 1977–1984*. M. Morris and P. Patton (eds.). New York: Routledge.

Fraser, N. (1994): "Rethinking the Public Sphere: A Contribution to the Critique of Actually Existing Democracy." In H. A. Giroux and

P. McLaren (eds.), *Between Borders. Pedagogy and the Politics of Cultural Studies*. New York; London: Routledge, 74–100.

Fraser, N. (1998): "Another Pragmatism: Alain Locke, Critical 'Race' Theory, and the Politics of Culture." In M. Dickstein (ed.), *The Revival of Pragmatism. New Essays on Social Thought, Law, and Culture*. Durham, NC; London: Duke University Press, 157–175.

Garrison, J. (1997): *Dewey and Eros: Wisdom and Desire in the Art of Teaching*. New York: Teachers College Press.

Garrison, J. (1998): "John Dewey's Philosophy as Education." In L. A. Hickman (ed.), *Reading Dewey—Interpretations for a Postmodern Generation*. Bloomington, IN: Indiana University Press, 63–81.

Garrison, J. (1999): "John Dewey, Jacques Derrida, and the Metaphysics of Presence." *Transactions of the Charles S. Peirce Society* Vol. XXXV, No. 2, 346–372.

Garrison, J. (2002): "Dewey, Derrida, and 'the Double Bind.' " In P. P. Trifonas and M. A. Peters (eds.), *Derrida, Deconstruction and Education*. Oxford, UK: Blackwell, 95–108.

Garrison, J., ed. (2008): *Reconstructing Democracy, Recontextualizing Dewey: Pragmatism and Interactive Constructivism in the Twenty-First Century*. Albany, NY: State University of New York Press.

Garrison, J. (2011): "Dewey and Levinas on Pluralism, the Other, and Democracy." In Judith M. Green, Stefan Neubert, and Kersten Reich (eds.), *The Other, and Democracy: Pragmatism and Diversity. Dewey in the Context of Late Twentieth Century Debates*. New York: Palgrave Macmillan, 99–126.

Garrison, J., and S. Neubert (2005): "Bausteine für eine Theorie des kreativen Zuhörens." In R. Voß (ed.), *LernLust und EigenSinn. Systemisch-konstruktivistische Lernwelten*. Heidelberg: Carl Auer, 109–120.

Gasché, R. (1994): *Inventions of Difference*. Cambridge, MA: Harvard University Press.

Good, J. (2005): *A Search for Unity in Diversity: The "Permanent Hegelian Deposit" in the Philosophy of John Dewey*. Lanham, MD: Lexington Books.

Green, J. (1999): *Deep Democracy*. Lanham, MD: Rowman and Littlefield.

Green, J., S. Neubert, and K. Reich, eds. (2011): *Pragmatism and Diversity. Dewey in the Context of Late 20th Century Debates*. New York: Palgrave Macmillan.

Gutmann, A., and D. Thompson (2004): *Why Deliberative Democracy?* Princeton, NY: Princeton University Press.

Habermas, J. (1984): *The Theory of Communicative Action*. Vol. 1. Boston: Beacon Press.

Habermas, J. (1987a): *The Theory of Communicative Action*. Vol. 2. Boston: Beacon Press.

Habermas, J. (1987ba): *The Philosophic Discourse of Modernity*. Oxford, UK: Polity Press.

Hall, S. (1992): "The West and the Rest: Discourse and Power." In S. Hall and B. Gieben (eds.), *Formations of Modernity*. Cambridge, UK: Polity Press, 275–332.

Hall, S. (1997): "The Work of Representation." In S. Hall (ed.), *Representation. Cultural Representations and Signifying Practices.* London; Thousand Oaks, CA: Sage, 13–74.

Haskins, C., and D. I. Seiple, eds. (1999): *Dewey Reconfigured.* Albany, NY: State University of New York Press.

Hewitt, R. (2007): *Dewey and Power. Renewing the Democratic Faith.* Rotterdam; Taipei: Sense.

Hickman, L., ed. (1998): *Reading Dewey—Interpretations for a Postmodern Generation.* Bloomington, IN: Indiana University Press.

Hickman, L., S. Neubert, and K. Reich, eds. (2009): *John Dewey—between Pragmatism and Constructivism.* New York: Fordham.

Hollinger, R. (1996): *The Dark Side of Liberalism.* Westport, CT: Praeger.

Huntington, S. P. (1996): *The Clash of Civilizations and the Remaking of World Order.* New York: Simon & Schuster.

Hutmacher, W., D. Cochrane, and N. Bottani, eds. (2001): *In Pursuit of Equity in Education.* Dordrecht; Boston; London: Kluwer.

James, W. (1909/1977): *A Pluralistic Universe.* Cambridge MA: Harvard University Press.

Kamuf, P., ed. (1991): *Letter to a Japanese Friend. A Derrida Reader.* New York: Columbia University Press.

Kearney, R., ed. (1984): *Deconstruction and the Other. In Dialogues with Contemporary Continental Thinkers.* Manchester, UK: Manchester University Press.

Kestenbaum, V. (1977): *The Phenomenological Sense of John Dewey—Habit and Meaning.* Atlantic Highlands, NJ: Humanities Press.

Kuipers, R. A. (1997): *Solidarity and the Stranger. Themes in the Social Philosophy of Richard Rorty.* Oxford, MS: University Press of America.

Laclau, E. (1990): *New Reflections on the Revolution of Our Time.* London; New York: Verso.

Laclau, E., and C. Mouffe (2001): *Hegemony and Socialist Strategy. Towards a Radical Democratic Politics,* Second edition. London; New York: Verso.

Langsdorf, L., and A. R. Smith, eds. (1995): *Recovering Pragmatism's Voice. The Classical Tradition, Rorty, and the Philosophy of Communication.* Albany, NY: State University of New York Press.

Levinas, E. (1961/1995): *Totality and Infinity.* Trans. Alphonso Lingis. Pittsburgh, PA: Duquesne University Press.

Levinas, E. (1963/1986): "The Trace of the Other." In M. C. Taylor (ed.), *Deconstruction in Context: Literature and Philosophy.* Chicago, IL: University of Chicago Press, 345–359.

Levinas, E. (1974/1981): *Otherwise than Being or Beyond Essence.* The Hague: Martinus Nijhoff.

Lingis, A. (1994): *The Community of Those Who Have Nothing in Common.* Bloomington, IN: Indiana University Press.

Lyotard, J. F. (1984): *The Postmodern Condition. A Report on Knowledge.* Minneapolis, MN: University of Minnesota Press.

MacPherson, C. B. (1966): *The Real World of Democracy.* New York: Oxford University Press.

MacPherson, C. B. (1975): *Democratic Theory: Essays in Retrieval.* New York: Oxford University Press.

MacPherson, C. B. (1977): *The Life and Times of Liberal Democracy.* New York: Oxford University Press.

Margolis, J. (2002): *Reinventing Pragmatism.* Ithaca, NY; London: Cornell University Press.

Martin, L. H. et al. (1988): *Technologies of the Self: A Seminar with Michel Foucault.* London: Tavistock.

Mead, G. H. (1903/1964): "The Definition of the Psychical." In Andrew J. Reck (ed.), *Selected Writings: George Herbert Mead.* Chicago, IL: The University Of Chicago Press, 25–59.

Mead, G. H. (1907/1964): "Concerning Animal Perception." In Andrew J. Reck (ed.), *Selected Writings: George Herbert Mead.* Chicago, IL: The University Of Chicago Press, 73–81.

Mead, G. H. (1910/1964): "Social Consciousness and the Consciousness of Meaning." In Andrew J. Reck (ed.), *Selected Writings: George Herbert Mead.* Chicago, IL: The University Of Chicago Press, 123–133.

Mead, G. H. (1912/1964): "The Mechanism of Social Consciousness." In Andrew J. Reck (ed.), *Selected Writings: George Herbert Mead.* Chicago, IL: The University Of Chicago Press, 134–141.

Mead, G. H. (1913/1964): "The Social Self." In Andrew J. Reck (ed.), *Selected Writings: George Herbert Mead.* Chicago, IL: The University Of Chicago Press, 142–149.

Mead, G. H. (1922/1964): "A Behavioristic Account of the Significant Symbol." In Andrew J. Reck (ed.), *Selected Writings: George Herbert Mead.* Chicago, IL: The University Of Chicago Press, 240–247.

Mead, G. H. (1932/1959): *The Philosophy of the Present.* LaSalle, IL: The Open Court Publishing Company.

Mead, G. H. (1934/1967): *Mind, Self, and Society: From the Standpoint of a Social Behaviorist.* Charles W. Morris (ed.). Chicago, IL: The University of Chicago Press.

Mead, G. H. (1935): "The Philosophy of John Dewey." *International Journal of Ethics* Vol. 46, No. 1, 64–81.

Mouffe, C. (1994): *The Return of the Political.* London: Verso.

Mouffe, C., ed. (1996): *Deconstruction and Pragmatism.* London; New York: Routledge.

Mouffe, C. (2000): *The Democratic Paradox.* London; New York: Verso.

Neubert, S. (1998): *Erkenntnis, Verhalten und Kommunikation. John Deweys Philosophie des Experience in interaktionistisch-konstruktivistischer Interpretation.* Münster u.a.: Waxmann.

Neubert, S. (2002): "Konstruktivismus, Demokratie und Multikultur." In S. Neubert, H. J. Roth, and E. Yildiz (eds.), *Multikulturalität in der Diskussion*. Opladen: Leske, Budrich, 63–98.

Neubert, S. (2003): "Some Perspectives of Interactive Constructivism on the Theory of Education." University of Cologne: http://konstruktivismus .uni-koeln.de (see "Texte": "Introduction").

Neubert, S. (2008): "Dewey's Pluralism Reconsidered—Pragmatist and Constructivist Perspectives on Diversity and Difference." In Jim Garrison (ed.), *Reconstructing Democracy, Recontextualizing Dewey: Pragmatism and Interactive Constructivism in the Twenty-First Century*. Albany, NY: State University of New York Press, 89–117.

Neubert, S. (2009a): "Pragmatism, Constructivism, and the Theory of Culture." In L. Hickman, S. Neubert, and K. Reich (eds.), *John Dewey Between Pragmatism and Constructivism*. New York: Fordham, 162–184.

Neubert, S. (2009b): "Pragmatism—Diversity of Subjects in Dewey's Philosophy and the Present Dewey Scholarship." In L. Hickman, S. Neubert, and K. Reich (eds.), *John Dewey Between Pragmatism and Constructivism*. New York: Fordham, 19–38.

Neubert, S. (2009c): "Reconstructing Deweyan Pragmatism—A Review Essay." *Educational Theory* Vol. 59, No. 3, 353–369.

Neubert, S. (2010): "Democracy and Education in the 21st Century— Deweyan Pragmatism and the Question of Racism." *Educational Theory* Vol. 60, No. 4, 487–502.

Neubert, S., and K. Reich (2001): "The Ethnocentric View: Constructivism and the Practice of Intercultural Discourse." In Bill Cope and Mary Kalantzis (eds.), *Learning for the Future. Proceedings of the Learning Conference 2001*. Australia: Common Ground Publishing, 1–25.

Neubert, S., and K. Reich (2002): *Toward a Constructivist Theory of Discourse: Rethinking the Boundaries of Discourse Philosophy*. University of Cologne 2002, http://www.uni-koeln.de/hf/konstrukt/neubert_works /aufsaetze/index.html.

Neubert, S., and K. Reich (2006): "The Challenge of Pragmatism for Constructivism – Some Perspectives in the Programme of Cologne Constructivism." *Journal of Speculative Philosophy* Vol. 20, No. 3, 165–191.

Neubert, S., and K. Reich (2008): *Perspectives of Pragmatism—The Cologne Video Project and the Dialogue between Pragmatism and Constructivism*. http://www.hf.uni-koeln.de/dewey/31679.

Neubert, S., and K. Reich (2011): "Reconstruction of Philosophy and Inquiry into Human Affairs–Deweyan Pragmatism in Dialogue with the Postmodern Sociology of Zygmunt Bauman." In J. Green, S. Neubert, and K. Reich (eds.), *Pragmatism and Diversity*. New York: Palgrave Macmillan, 127–164.

Noddings, N. (1995): *Philosophy of Education*. Boulder, CO: Westview Press.

Norris, C. (1988): *Derrida*. Cambridge, MA: Harvard University Press.

Parker, S. P., ed. (1992). *McGraw-Hill Encyclopedia of Science & Technology*, Vol. 6, Seventh edition. New York: McGraw-Hill, 570–572).

Peirce, C. S. (1868): *The Collected Papers of Charles S. Peirce*, Vol. 2. Cambridge, MA: Harvard University Press (1931–1958).

Peirce, C. S. (1992): "Some Consequences of Four Incapacities." In *The Essential Peirce*, Vol. 1. Bloomington: Indiana University Press.

Pettegrew, J., ed. (2000): *A Pragmatist Progress? Richard Rorty and American Intellectual History*. Lanham, MD; Boulder, CO; New York; Rowman & Littlefield.

Popkewitz, T. S., B. M. Franklin, and M. A. Pereyra, eds. (2001): *Cultural History and Education. Critical Essays on Knowledge and Schooling*. New York, London: RoutledgeFalmer.

Rabinow, P., ed. (1985): *The Foucault Reader*. New York: Pantheon.

Rawls, J. (1971): *A Theory of Justice*. Cambridge, MA: Harvard University Press.

Reich, K. (1998): *Die Ordnung der Blicke*. Vol. 1: *Beobachtung und die Unschärfen der Erkenntnis*. Vol. 2: *Beziehungen und Lebenswelt*. Neuwied u.a.: Luchterhand.

Reich, K. (2006): *Konstruktivistische Didaktik*, Third edition. Weinheim: Beltz.

Reich, K. (2007): "Interactive Constructivism in Education." *Education & Culture* Vol. 23, No. 1, 7–26.

Reich, K. (2008): "Democracy and Education after Dewey—Pragmatist Implications for Constructivist Pedagogy." In J. Garrison (ed.), *Reconstructing Democracy, Recontextualizing Dewey: Pragmatism and Interactive Constructivism in the Twenty-First Century*. New York: Suny, 55–88.

Reich, K. (2009): "Observers, Participants, and Agents in Discourses—A Consideration of Pragmatist and Constructivist Theories of the Observer." In L. Hickman, S. Neubert, and K. Reich (eds.), *John Dewey between Pragmatism and Constructivism*. New York: Fordham, 106–142.

Reich, K. (2010): *Systemisch-konstruktivistische Pädagogik*, Sixth edition. Weinheim: Beltz.

Reich, K. (2011): "Diverse Communities—Dewey's Theory of Democracy as a Challenge for Foucault, Bourdieu, and Rorty." In J. Green, S. Neubert, and K. Reich (eds.), *Pragmatism and Diversity*. New York: Palgrave Macmillan, 165–194.

Reich, K. (2013): *Chancengerechtigkeit und Kapitalformen* (Equity and Forms of Capital). Forthcoming.

Rorty, R. (1979): *Philosophy and the Mirror of Nature*. Princeton, NJ: Princeton University Press.

Rorty, R. (1982): *Consequences of Pragmatism*. Minneapolis, MN: University of Minnesota Press.

Rorty, R. (1984): "Dewey between Hegel and Darwin." In D. Ross (ed.), *Modernism and the Human Sciences*. Baltimore, MD: John Hopkins University Press.

Rorty, R. (1989): *Contingency, Irony, and Solidarity*. Cambridge, UK; New York: Cambridge University Press.

Rorty, R. (1991): *Objectivity, Relativism, and Truth*. Cambridge, MA: Cambridge University Press.

Rorty, R. (1998): *Truth and Progress*. Cambridge, MA: Cambridge University Press.

Rorty, R. (2000): *Philosophy and Social Hope*. New York: Penguin.

Ryan, A. (1995): *John Dewey and the High Tide of American Liberalism*. New York; London: W. W. Norton & Company.

Saussure, F. (1959): *Course in General Linguistics*. Trans. Wade Baskin. New York: Philosophical Library.

Schumpeter, J. A. (1942): *Capitalism, Socialism, and Democracy*. New York: Harper and Brothers.

Seigfried, C. H. (2002): "John Dewey's Pragmatist Feminism." In C. H. Seigfried (ed.), *Feminist Interpretations of John Dewey*. University Park, PA: Pennsylvania State University Press, 47–77.

Shusterman, R. (1997): *Practicing Philosophy. Pragmatism and the Philosophical Life*. New York; London: Routledge.

Shusterman, R. (1999): "Dewey on Experience: Foundation or Reconstruction?" In C. Haskins and D. I. Seiple (eds.), *Dewey Reconfigured*. Albany, NY: State University of New York Press, 193–220.

Slavin, R. E. (2006): *Educational Psychology, Theory and Practice*, Eighth edition. Boston u.a.: Pearson.

Stuhr, J. (1997): *Genealogical Pragmatism. Philosophy, Experience, and Community*. Albany, NY: State University of New York Press.

Stuhr, J. (2002): "Power/Inquiry: The Logic of Pragmatism." In F. D. Burke, D. M. Hester, and R. B. Talisse (eds.), *Dewey's Logical Theory*. Nashville, TN: Vanderbilt University Press, 275–286.

Talisse, R. B. (2005): *Democracy after Liberalism: Pragmatism and Deliberative Politics*. New York: Routledge.

Thompson, J. B. (1991): "Introduction." In P. Bourdieu, *Language and Symbolic Power*. Cambridge, MA: Harvard University Press, 1–32.

Tomasello, M. (1999): *The Cultural Origins of Human Cognition*. Cambridge, MA: Harvard University Press.

Tomasello, M. (2008): "Cooperation and Communication in the 2nd Year of Life." *Child Development Perspectives* Vol. 1, No. 1, 8–12.

Wacquant, L. (2005): *Pierre Bourdieu and Democratic Politics*. Cambridge, UK: Polity Press.

Watzlawick, P., J. Beavin, and D. Jackson (1967): *Pragmatics of Human Communication—A Study of Interactional Patterns, Pathologies and Paradoxes*. New York: Norton.

Westbrook, R. (1991): *John Dewey and American Democracy*. Ithaca, NY: Cornell University Press.

AUTHOR INDEX

SUBJECT INDEX

absolute(s), 46, 112, 149–50, 153, 159, 161–2
absolutist-transcendentalist approaches, 103
action
  intelligent, 63
  motives of, 52, 54
  plan of, 67
activism, 12
activities
  hermeneutic circles of, 50
  joint, 81–2
  learner's ongoing, 42
actor, 9
aesthetic lives, 174
Africa, 91
agent(s), 18, 27–33, 35, 37, 48–9, 110–13, 115, 129, 131, 134, 136, 141, 156, 160, 165, 173, 178–80
ambiguity, ambiguities, 15, 20, 104, 115, 117–18, 122, 124, 131, 164
ambivalence(s), 22, 32–4, 37, 95, 104, 123–5, 127, 129, 132, 134–6, 140, 168, 171, 174, 177–8
American life, 127
ancient Greeks, 47, 69, 71
antagonism(s), 4, 83, 114, 131
anthropology, 40
antidemocratic, 87, 105, 133, 135
approach, educational and psychological, 19
approaches
  discovery-learning, 65
  pragmatic and constructivist, 110

a priori(s), 41, 103, 134, 150–2, 160–2, 164, 170
arbitrariness, 20, 168, 172, 180
art, 3, 27, 37, 39, 61, 65, 68–9, 74, 89, 97, 101–2, 117, 125, 172, 179, 182
articulations, antagonistic, 113
artistic creation, 162
Asia, 91
assimilation, 14, 23
authority, 32, 83–4, 140, 146
autonomy, 119, 131, 141

banking model, 62
benefits, cultural, 145
Big Brother, 128
binary code, 124
biological, 5–7, 30, 42–4, 46–7, 56, 58, 153
bureaucracy, 128

capital, 133–4, 142–5, 147–8, 175, 184
capitalism, 88, 90–1, 132–5, 139, 142
  antidemocratic effects of, 133
  global, 139
  liquid, 134
Cartesian, 160–1
Chicago School of functionalism and instrumentalism, 39
civic councils, 92
civilization, 2, 9, 127, 139, 176
  American, 127
civil society, 86